Philosophy and Human Geography

For Rita

Philosophy and Human Geography

An Introduction to Contemporary Approaches

Second Edition

R. J. Johnston

Professor of Geography, University of Sheffield

Edward Arnold

©R. J. Johnston 1983, 1986

First published in Great Britain 1983 by Edward Arnold (Publishers) Ltd, 41 Bedford Square, London WC1B 3DQ

Edward Arnold (Australia) Pty Ltd, 80 Waverley Road, Caulfield East, Victoria 3145, Australia

Edward Arnold, 3 East Read Street, Baltimore, Maryland 21202, U.S.A.
Reprinted 1984
Second edition 1986

British Library Cataloguing in Publication Data

Johnston, R.J.
   Philosophy and human geography: an
   introduction to contemporary approaches.—
   2nd ed.
   1. Anthropo-geography — Philosophy
   I. Title
   304.2'01   GF21

   ISBN 0-7131-6490-5

Text set in 11/12pt Bembo (Compugraphic)
by Colset Private Limited, Singapore.
Printed and bound by Richard Clay plc,
Bungay, Suffolk.

Contents

Acknowledgement

The publishers would like to thank John Wiley & Sons Ltd for their permission to reproduce a figure from D T Herbert and R J Johnston: *Geography and the Urban Environment* Volume 5.

Preface

Human geography is currently characterized by a great deal of lively debate which focuses not so much on its subject matter as on its philosophy: its orientation to its subject matter. Much more than was so in previous decades, human geographers are being exposed to debates within philosophy as they refer to the natural and, in particular, the social sciences. The foundations of geographical study are being excavated with questions such as 'What are the goals of human geographical research?', 'How can these be achieved?', 'What does pursuit of these goals imply with regard to the nature of evidence?' and so on. No longer can human geographers sit aside from such questions by offering themselves as the presenters of 'mere facts' – such things do not exist, the critics argue.

The present book has been designed as a companion to an earlier volume which traced the debates within human geography since 1945 over philosophical and methodological issues. In *Geography and geographers: Anglo-American human geography since 1945* (Johnston, 1979 and 1983a), I showed how those debates covered the replacement of an empiricist philosophy by one that was positivist and how, in turn, the latter perspective was challenged by individuals of humanistic and of structuralist persuasions. The aim there was to examine the contemporary pluralism within the discipline rather than to explicate the details of the various philosophies. Here, the task is the complementary one of introducing the nature of the various philosophies with little reference to the debates over the relevance and validity of each.

The preface to that earlier book on the 'contemporary history' of human geography argued that students of the discipline need an understanding of why the content of their discipline is as it is and require a framework within which their own perspective can be developed. A similar case is made for the present book. In a discipline characterized by competition between a variety of philosophies, students need an introduction to those philosophies, a statement of their fundamentals and of their relevance to human geography. Such an introduction can be provided in a variety of ways. That chosen here is perhaps the simplest. The introductory chapter suggests that three competing philosophies (termed approaches here because each embraces a variety of related viewpoints) dominate contemporary human geography.

Each of the next three chapters takes one of these approaches and outlines its basic characteristics and use in human geography. Finally, the last chapter looks at attempts to link those approaches.

As an outline of the philosophy of social science, this book is very much a primer, a first statement. It does not pursue any topic in depth, and certainly does not offer a detailed explanation of any philosophies from which a reader could go away feeling schooled in the relevant approaches. The literature on these philosophies is extremely large: much of it, including some written specifically for geographers, is difficult, especially to the uninitiated. All that is attempted here is an introduction to the nature of the philosophies which human geographers are now exploring; any student wishing to join that quest will need to read a great deal more. Here, much of the discussion relies on secondary sources, so that the presentation has passed through several lenses before reaching the present pages, with all the potential for distortion that this implies. The main justification for this approach is that the secondary sources themselves isolate the main elements, whereas the primary works are in general too detailed – and often difficult. For a primer, succinctness and clarity are desirable; for later work in a philosophy, depth, detail and internal argument must also be explored.

As a primer directed at human geographers, this book does not seek to cover all philosophies. Nor are those included given the same amount of treatment. The general criterion determining the amount of coverage – within each of the three main chapters (2 to 4) – is the amount of use of the individual philosophy within human geography at the present time. Thus within the chapter on humanistic approaches, for example, existentialism is given less coverage than either idealism or phenomenology because it does not represent as substantial a part of the geographical literature. Such selectivity undoubtedly reflects some personal bias. It is not intended, however, to be prescriptive and to outline which are the better philosophies for geographers, or the better parts of particular philosophies (although some of the discussion in Chapter 5 refers to my attempts to integrate the various approaches). It is hoped that enough detail has been provided to indicate both the nature of each approach and its relevance to human geography – enough, that is, to stimulate the interested reader to investigate the topic further.

Like its companion, this book is in part based on the material presented in a final-year undergraduate course on the history and philosophy of contemporary human geography. As such, it assumes some knowledge of the substantive content of the discipline, some familiarity with its literature, and some experience of working (perhaps implicitly) within some of the approaches outlined here. For readers, it seeks to explicate the major features of the three sets of approaches, providing a foundation for understanding current philosophical debates in human geography, a basis for further exploration, and material on which they might base their own decisions about the proper approach to the discipline.

In producing this book, I am grateful to a number of people. The publishers prompted me to write it – leading me to read much more and to think many things through more fully than I had done previously; I, at least, have benefited from the project. Of my colleagues, Alan Hay has been a consistent focus of useful discussion and debate and I am extremely grateful to him for his continued intellectual companionship. Malcolm Lewis read through a complete draft, and made many useful suggestions which were very much appreciated; the usual disclaimer applies. My wife Rita also read a full draft and told me of the many places where I had not made things clear; I hope I have been able to improve them. Finally, I am once again in debt to Joan Dunn for her efficiency in translating handwritten manuscript into a final text.

Preface to the second edition

When it was suggested in early 1985 that a further reprint of this book would be needed in 1986. I decided to take the opportunity to prepare a new edition. There were three reasons for this. First, a number of misrepresentations and infelicitous statements had been identified in the first edition, which needed correction. Secondly, I was unhappy with one part of the book – Chapter 5 – and wished to rewrite it. Thirdly, in the four years since the book was written (i.e. 1982–85 inclusive) a substantial volume of work had been produced clarifying the arguments by human geographers for the adoption of the approaches outlined here and extending the debates on their relative merits. A book to be published in 1986 needed to take this work into account. The present edition was completed in November 1985.

Some people have argued to me that the polarization of views represented by the central three chapters of this book is obsolescent: most geographers, it is claimed, have accepted the force of the humanistic and structuralist critiques of the excesses of positivism and have modified their working practices accordingly. There is consensus rather than dissensus, I am told, with the majority of human geographers occupying a middle position which accepts the existence of structural mechanisms, which realizes the importance of human agency, and which involves rigorously analysing how human agents have created a world in the context of those mechanisms. I remain to be fully convinced. Nevertheless, even if the claim were correct, it is necessary to understand the origins of that middle ground, in separate approaches the debate over which led to the consensus. Hence a brief introduction to the various approaches, to illustrate how we got to where we are.

In preparing this new edition, I am grateful to the reviewers of the first, and the many others who have written or talked to me about it, for their useful, constructive comments. The University of Sheffield granted me a term's study leave, which released me from teaching and administrative duties in the Department of Geography; it then decided that I should continue to play a role in the central University planning mechanism ('planning' being a misnomer for 'preparing for cuts') and so half of the term was hardly 'study leave' – nevertheless, I found the needed time for reading and reflection. John Wallace was as ever encouraging and tolerant of the whims of an author whose campanological interests seemed to take precedence. Joan Dunn was always tolerant of my handwriting and efficient in its transformation. Rita Johnston was more tolerant than ever, and the dedication of this book is too small a tribute of my gratitude for that.

1

Human geography

Within the academic community disciplines are almost invariably defined by their subject matter, by what it is that they study rather than how they study it. The boundaries between disciplines are rarely clearly delimited, however, because the reality that is being studied comprises an interrelated whole rather than a series of discrete parts. The division of knowledge into disciplines is therefore both artificial and, to a certain degree, arbitrary; the aim is to isolate certain topics that can be sensibly investigated separate from, though not independent of, others, although this ideal is not easily achieved. The boundaries are relatively porous, to allow for inter-disciplinary contact, which increases as the volume of knowledge expands, and more specialized – yet at the same time less independent – disciplines are established to study particular topics.

From the above description, it could be deduced that the division of knowledge into academic disciplines is the result of logical decision-making and reflects the consensus of opinion of all those involved. This is far from the case. The academic division of labour at any one time is the result of earlier decisions that are difficult to overturn. Once established, a discipline not only marks out an intellectual territory but it becomes self-perpetuating; in particular it instructs students, who are socialized into that particular view of the world of learning and who propagate it. Attempts to change the division of labour, to create a new disciplinary structure, must therefore challenge the established orthodoxy, with all the potential dangers to personal status which such a conflict may generate (see Taylor, 1976). Some challenges succeed, but not necessarily everywhere, so that in different countries, and sometimes in the same country, the allocation of topics to disciplines may vary; in some cases, the successful challenges reflect the efforts of particular individuals who are able to establish new academic centres around themselves, perhaps to the detriment of one or more existing disciplines.

A discipline is brought into existence because those propagating it are able to show to potential sponsors that its topical content is worthy of study and that its means of study are valid (Taylor, 1985b). In the broadest sense, therefore, a discipline has to demonstrate its utility. Once established, to some extent its utility will be self-generating. The discipline will need a continuing supply of researchers to provide new knowledge, for example, and a stream of trained teachers, to induct the next generations of students. Failure to maintain the support of sponsors may lead to disciplinary decline – perhaps at the expense of an expanding 'invader'. This too may be self-generating, for fewer students need fewer teachers and doubts about the discipline's utility may mean a falling demand for its research. Thus the established members of a discipline find it necessary to promote it. Such promotional activity is especially strong when resources are scarce and the potential for decline considerable (Johnston, 1985a).

Although to a considerable extent a discipline sells itself according to what it studies, it must also develop a philosophy regarding the orientation: how should it study its particular subject matter, and why? In some disciplines it may be argued that this is an irrelevant question, that there is only one possible philosophy. But in others this is not so, and there may be considerable debate on philosophical issues. To some extent this too revolves around questions of utility: which philosophy is best suited to the demands of the sponsors? (Not all academics subscribe to the view that they must orient their disciplines towards sponsors, who increasingly are governments. Some claim that they have a more correct interpretation of what is valuable and what is not, and interpret their function as convincing either the sponsors or society as a whole of the rightness of this interpretation.) It may well be, therefore, that within a discipline there is considerable debate about its conduct, which may focus not only on what should be done but on who the discipline should serve.

The preceding paragraphs suggest that the academic world comprises a set of disciplines, each occupying a niche within the structure of knowledge (but allowing a certain amount of light to filter in from adjacent niches). The nature of that niche has been created, and is continually being recreated, around a particular focus – the disciplinary subject matter. Within it, there may be considerable debate about how that subject matter should be studied, and to what ends. Human geography occupies one such niche, and it is currently experiencing major philosophical discussions. The aim of the present book is to provide a brief introduction to the foundations of those discussions by outlining the nature of the competing philosophies, the claims for them as valid approaches to human geography, and their contribution to the development of the discipline as a store of knowledge.

The topical content of human geography

Ever since its promulgation as a separate discipline in the nineteenth century, geography has had a twin focus on space and place. (For an outline history, see James and Martin, 1981.) At any location on the earth's surface (most geographers have concentrated on the land surface) there are both vertical and horizontal relationships: the vertical relationships link different elements in the same location, whereas the horizontal relationships link elements in separate locations. The relative importance of these two sets of relationships has varied over time, with human geographers becoming increasingly concerned in recent decades with the horizontal (Cox, 1976). Many geographers stress that it is the twin focus, however, and even more so the integration of the two sets of relationships, that provides the discipline with its identity and integrity (see Haggett, 1980).

Within this academic niche, human geographers study only some of the relationships, leaving others to physical geographers. On the vertical theme, they investigate interrelationships between people and their environment (natural and created – some argue that the two cannot be separated). On the horizontal theme, they study inter-place inter-relationships, emphasizing the flows of people and of human creations across the earth's surface. The integrating, or synthesizing, theme seeks to bring these two together, emphasizing the totality of interrelationships that makes up a particular location. (The size, or scale, of the location influences the nature of that totality. At some scales certain relationships are vertical, whereas at others they are horizontal; what is intra-regional trade – a vertical relationship – at one scale may be inter-regional trade – a horizontal relationship – at another.)

The history of geography as an academic discipline is such that in many places there is a long and continuing tradition of combining the study of physical and of human geography. Each may be treated separately under both vertical and horizontal themes, but some geographers claim that the integrity of the discipline can only be maintained by seeking to integrate the two. The strength of this tradition is greater in some countries – notably the United Kingdom and its former colonies – than in others; in Sweden and the Netherlands, for example, the two are almost totally divorced. Other countries lie between these two positions; in the United States of America, in particular, the links have been relatively weak in the past, but there is movement towards greater integration at present. The position taken in this book favours the separatist viewpoint, and so the focus is on approaches to human geography alone. This does not deny the many valuable contributions to human geography, especially methodological and technical, that have resulted from close contact between human and physical geographers; they have shared interests in methods of data capture, analysis and display, for example. Nor does it deny the valuable role played by geography as an educational discipline (especially in schools) by promoting the study of both human and physical aspects. But only one of the approaches discussed here (positivist) is relevant to both (as I stress in Johnston, 1986a), and in its application there is a very little evidence of conjoint study of the human and the physical. Of course, as Cooke (1985a) has stressed and illustrated (1985b), there has been much study by physical geographers of the impact of human activities on earth surface processes and landforms (see Gregory, 1985, for a full review), and similarly human geographers have focused on the physical environment as a resource which is used, and abused, by people and societies (as in Rees, 1985). But there is no evidence that either body of work *integrates* human and physical geography (Johnston, 1983d). Indeed, the claims of the integrationists appear to be based on differences in semantics. The word geography has two major definitions: one is vernacular, and refers to the environment; the other is academic, and refers to the study of the environment. Thus physical geography means either the physical environment or the study of the physical environment. Those who claim that it should be integrated with human geography appear to argue either (a) that human geographers should study the physical environment or (b) that physical geographers should incorporate the human environment in their research agenda. Neither is unacceptable to me, since neither implies a merging of the two academic geographies – a task which I see as philosophically infeasible (Johnston, 1986b).

Human geography is presented here as a social science, therefore, one which studies particular aspects of society relating to space and place (including the physical environment). No attempt is made to justify this definition, or to discuss the interrrelationships among the social sciences and their debate over the academic division of labour (or even whether such should exist). Human geography exists. The focus here is on what it does, and how it does it. Thus the main concern is with the philosophy of the social sciences and its interpretation for and by human geographers.

Elements of a philosophy of human geography

Any practitioner of an academic discipline undertakes research within a framework provided by a philosophy of that discipline. Such a philosophy may be explicit, in that the researcher has established certain guidelines prior to commencing work, or it may be implicit – there are guidelines but these are not overtly recognized; instead they form part of the researcher's taken-for-granted, everyday world. In the case of an explicit philosophy, this is almost certainly shared with other researchers. With implicit philosophies, however, a greater degree of idiosyncracy is possible, especially in the social sciences.

Philosophy – derived from the Greek and meaning 'love of wisdom' – is a term which is not readily defined, even by philosophers. It is a reflective discipline, involving the consideration of methods of reasoning and argument. The philosophy of a discipline, or group of disciplines, involves the study of the ways in which work is conducted within the disciplinary boundaries (that are, as indicated above, usually defined by subject-matter). The central element in such a philosophy is its *epistemology*, or its theory of knowledge; it provides answers to fundamental questions such as 'What can we know?' and 'How can we know it?'. Four aspects of knowledge are covered by epistemology: its nature – what it is that one believes; its type – such as knowledge by acquaintance and knowledge by description (i.e. firsthand and secondhand knowledge); its objects – the subject matter of knowledge; and its origins. Associated with epistemology in the philosophical framework is *ontology*, which is the theory of existence, or of what can be known. In metaphysics – which is argument about the nature of the world that goes beyond factual issues – the theory of ontology defines what can exist (as, for example, in religions). In the philosophy of academic disciplines, however, it relates to what are accepted as 'facts'.

Every disciplinary philosophy, therefore, contains both an epistemology and an ontology – a framework which defines what we can know and how we can come to know about it. Together these are used to define a *methodology*, a set of rules and procedures which indicates how research and argument are to be conducted within the discipline. Use of the methodology allows the accumulation of a disciplinary store of knowledge, the results of work aimed at comprehending a particular topic and which are accepted as valid because they were collected within the criteria of epistemology and ontology that are part of the relevant philosophy.

A number of philosophies has been suggested over the centuries. Many are little more than variations on others, and so can be grouped together into categories. For human geography, four such categories are relevant:

1 **Empiricist approaches** whose epistemology is that we know through experience and whose ontology is that the things we experience are the things that exist – the methodology simply requires a presentation of the experienced facts.

2 **Positivist approaches** whose epistemology is also that knowledge is gained through experience, but which requires that this experience be firmly established as verifiable evidence on which all will agree. Their ontology is thus one of agreed evidence and the methodology is one of verifying factual statements.

3 **Humanistic approaches** whose epistemology is that knowledge is obtained subjectively in a world of meanings created by individuals and whose ontology is that what exists is that which people perceive to exist. Their methodology involves the objective investigation of these individual worlds and, in opposition to the positivist approaches, emphasizes individuality and subjectivity rather than replicability and truth.

4 **Structuralist approaches** whose epistemology is that the world of appearances (that which is apprehended) does not necessarily reveal the world of mechanisms (that which causes the world of appearances). To

investigate the latter it is necessary to have an ontology which states that what really exists (i.e. the forces creating the world, or the structures) cannot be observed directly but only through thought, and the associated methodology involves the construction of theories which can account for what is observed but which cannot be tested for their veracity because direct evidence of their existence is not available.

Here, the first two approaches are considered together in the one chapter (on positivist approaches), since positivism is built on a foundation of empiricism. Following a vigorous promotion campaign, which originated in North America (Johnston, 1983a), positivist approaches dominated the Anglo-American research practice of human geography in the 1960s. Since then, humanistic and structuralist approaches have been introduced initially very much as critiques of the positivist but increasingly as separate research schools making their own distinctive contributions to knowledge. Thus the three approaches provide the subject matter for the central three chapters of the book. That on positivist approaches includes some discussion of empiricism, however, in particular to clarify some intra-disciplinary debates regarding the equation of quantitative methods with positivism.

In much debate over these three approaches, positivism is conventionally associated with *science*, so that its methodology is know as *the scientific method*. By implication, the other two approaches are non-scientific. Such a distinction is not adopted here. Science is the pursuit of systematic and formulated knowledge, and as such is not confined to any particular epistemology; humanistic and structuralist approaches are just as systematic (and rigorous) as positivist, but using different methodologies because of their separate epistemologies. Even so, most of what is known as 'the scientific method' by many – i.e. the rigorous collection and evaluation of data – is not exclusive to positivist approaches (Johnston, 1986b). Hence the presentation here is of three sciences of human geography, not of one science and two non-sciences/antisciences. First, however, a brief outline of the development of human geography is provided, as context for the later discussion.

The development of human geography

Most disciplines have originated with empiricist practices, not surprisingly since disciplines are defined by what they study and most focus on particular topics which relate to empirical facts. (Though, of course, the definition of 'facts' implied a prior epistemology, however implicit and vague.) Human geography was no exception to this, and much of its development in the late nineteenth and early twentieth centuries was based on its collection and organization of material about places, which was deemed extremely useful, especially in the growth of the capitalist world-economy and the colonial expansion of the period. Not surprisingly, geography developed rapidly in the service of the major colonial powers which required information for mercantile activity. It was strongly linked with expeditions for the gathering of new material, and with the encyclopaedic presentation of such material – in some cases in volumes known as commercial geographies. Associated with this collection of facts was the campaign to propagate them through the educational system, in a school and university discipline designed to widen the horizons and extend the factual knowledge of the average citizen (Freeman 1961, 1980).

Initially, therefore, much of human geography (as part of a general discipline rather than in a full sense separate from physical geography) was concerned with filling in the detail on empty maps and, indeed, in the drawing of the maps themselves. It was strictly empiricist, collecting information and presenting it as fact: its particular methodology involved the cartographic presentation of material.

Out of this collection of facts, relating to both the physical environment and to human activities on the earth's surface, sprang two separate schools within the discipline. The first – known widely as *environmental determinism* – involved the correlation (using a very general, always verbal, method) of the two sets of information in order to show that the one (the natural environment) was the cause of the other (the spatial distribution and nature of human activities): places vary in their natural conditions and these variations determine what people do there. This philosophy had an epistemology akin to the positivist, but it had no firm criteria for verifying its statements and no explicit methodology: it was speculation without rigorous assessment of its hypotheses and was rapidly discredited.

The other approach – that of *regionalism* – sprang also from contemplation of the material collected in the empiricist tradition, and was to some extent also a reaction to the excesses of environmental determinism. Map comparison showed that certain distributions of phenomena overlapped, creating areas of the earth's surface – regions – with particular combinations of characteristics and producing a unique identity for each area. To some, most notably the French geographers inspired by the work of Paul Vidal de la Blache, each area had its own personality, which could be experienced and identified in the field. The methodology involved the collection of field and other data and their presentation to show the unique personality and characteristics of each area. The task of the geographer was to identify the separate areas – the regions – and to define their boundaries (Johnston, 1984a). This, too, was essentially an empiricist approach, with the collected facts providing the evidence of differences between places – a theme which became widely known as areal differentiation (Hartshorne, 1939). As practised, much work in this regionalism frame-work had a strong vein of environmental determinism running through it. Almost invariably, regional geographers presented facts about the physical environment first and of human activity second, implying a strong causal link between the two. To some, the region could be compared with an organism – something in which the whole is greater than the sum of its parts – and the organic analogy was also used in systematic studies, such as Ratzel's political geography (see Stoddart, 1966).

Development of the regionalism approach required more and more information, and to provide this geography was divided into two main approaches: systematic and regional. The former involved the investigation of particular topics only: it was divided into physical and human, with each being subdivided (the former into geomorphology, climatology, biogeography etc., and the latter into economic geography, social geography, etc.). Such specialized systematic approaches were considered necessary for the collation of relevant information, and most geographers were expected to concentrate on one such specialism. But systematic studies were to be subsidiary to regional geography, to the synthesis of material from all specialisms into a regional 'whole', and as well as being a topical specialist each geographer was expected to develop expertise about a particular part of the world.

According to this view of geography, which prevailed into the 1950s, systematic studies were subservient to regional synthesis, thus maintaining the goal of integration as the central point of geography's integrity. To this end, geographers were not encouraged to develop their systematic investigations to such an extent that the regionalism goal was lost sight of. In the United States of America, for example, the study of geomorphology was discouraged, as being properly a part of geology, and only study of 'the geography of landforms' was considered necessary as an input to regional geography.

Despite these constraints suggested by the leaders of the discipline, the study of systematic topics increased in relative importance and was more and more considered a worthwhile end in itself (Johnston and Gregory, 1984). Regional geography was correspondingly discredited (Freeman, 1980; Gould, 1979).

The expansion of systematic studies led unsurprisingly to closer contacts between geographers and scholars in related disciplines. The geographers retained their perspective on space and place, and many continued to work on particular areas only, without aiming towards the regional synthesis. But these contacts led geographers to appreciate the philosophies of other disciplines and many sought to introduce them – or elements of them – to their own subject. It has been in this way that the split between human and physical geography has become more pronounced in recent decades and that the positivist, humanistic, and structuralist approaches (especially the last two) have been introduced to human geography alone.

The subdivisions of human geography

It is not the aim of the present book to trace the introduction, reception and development of particular approaches to human geography nor to examine international differences in these processes (the former is undertaken in Johnston, 1983a, and the latter in Johnston and Claval, 1984). The emphases on systematic studies – albeit within the context of space and place – and on the horizontal rather than the vertical interrelationships in contemporary human geography are taken for granted. The focus here is on the philosophies that have been proposed for human geographical study and adopted by some researchers. In seeking to show how these philosophies have been used within the discipline, however, it is necessary to provide a brief outline of its substantive interest.

For this purpose, human geography is divided into four main categories into which most pieces of work fit relatively easy. The first two are by far the largest, and are subdivided into several separate subcategories. *Economic geography* covers the production and distribution of goods and services. Its traditional subcategories are industrial geography, agricultural geography and transport geography, whose titles clearly indicate the substantive topics covered: the spatial distributions of different industries and agricultural practices were to be described and accounted for, for example. *Social geography* refers more to the consumption of goods and services and to the nature of social life apart from the world of work. Its subcategories include cultural geography, a dominantly North American subject dealing with the interrelationships between cultural groups and environments and with the spread of cultural traits, population geography, urban geography and rural geography. *Political geography*, the third division, is clearly defined by its title. It, and its subdivision electoral geography, have been relatively weak until recent years. Finally, *historical geography* is another division whose title readily identifies the substantive interests of practitioners: they focus on either or both of the economic/social/political geography of past periods and changing geographies over time; some of this work has been at least implicitly influenced by Darwinian ideas regarding evolution (Stoddart, 1966).

Although, as claimed above, most pieces of work can readily be allocated to one of these divisions and subdivisions, there are areas of overlap and indecision; Sayer (1984) suggests that many of the subdivisions are 'chaotic conceptions' rather than 'rational abstractions'. Within urban geography, for example, the study of residential patterns – of who lives where – is clearly social geography, but the study of central places – of shopping centres within urban areas and the pattern of shopping opportunities and their use over a set of urban places – incorporates the perspectives of both economic and social geographers. Most human geographers associate themselves with one of these divisions, however, if not with one of the subdivisions, but the boundaries are relatively porous and there is much interconnection.

As with the larger world of academic disciplines, so within human geography there are attempts to remove the existing subdivisions. Some of these seek closer integration of the various topical research areas, arguing, for example, that economic and social issues cannot be separated from their political and historical contexts. Thus, for example, there have been arguments for a welfare geography (Smith, 1977) and for a greater emphasis on development studies, both of which seek integration of the whole of human geography around a particular focus rather than its subdivision into what are seen as arbitrary categories the existence of which can be a hindrance to understanding. As will be made clear in Chapter 4, the strongest arguments against these divisions are made by adherents to the structuralist approaches, whose case for a holistic human geography is allied to one for a holistic approach to social science.

In summary

Contemporary human geography is characterized by its division into topical categories and subcategories, each of which analyses the space and place interrelationships of particular substantive elements of society, such as agriculture, industry and housing. These systematic interests overlie the remains of an earlier geographical focus on regional integration, but whereas many geographers confine their research interests to particular areas of the earth's surface, very few now seek to provide comprehensive surveys and analyses of those areas. Human geography is, then, something of a divided discipline although the divisions, because they are concerned with separate topics, are not necessarily in conflict one with another (except for scarce resources to support research and related activity).

The study of human geography has only recently emerged from its empiricist origins, whose epistemology, ontology and methodology were based on the collection, collation, and presentation of 'facts'. In the last few decades, several other philosophies of human geography have been suggested. Three main sets of approaches have been identified here. All are practised at the present time, so that human geography is divided not only in terms of the substance of the work carried out but also in terms of the philosophy of the work. The latter division has generated much more conflict than the former. The next three chapters outline the characteristics of these three approaches, presenting introductory discussions of their epistemologies, ontologies and methodologies and indicating how they have contributed to the literature of human geography. The final chapter looks at various attempts to link the three.

2

Positivist approaches

Positivist approaches are involved with the making of empirical generalizations, statements of a law-like character which relate to phenomena that are empirically recognized. As such, these approaches are basic to the methodology and philosophy of the natural sciences. Their application in human geography reflects a belief that similar aims are realizable in what is essentially a social science.

The origins of positivism are traced by many to the French nineteenth century social philosopher Auguste Comte (Lacey, 1976, p. 165). He, according to Andreski (1974, p. 9), 'believed in the supremacy of science' as the only method of investigation, although his developments of positivist ideas were sometimes unusual. To him, the study of science led to the understanding of natural laws, and this understanding allowed society, guided by scientists, to modify nature. Thus:

> Our natural means of acting on the bodies surrounding us are extremely feeble, and quite disproportionate to our needs. Every time we produce a big effect upon nature, it is because the knowledge of natural laws has enabled us to introduce modifying elements . . . so as in certain cases to modify in our interest the final result of a complex of causes. In short: science = foresight, foresight = action (Andreski, 1974, p. 44).

And since Comte believed that scientific methods could be applied to the study of social phenomena, this implies that: first, natural laws can be developed in social sciences; second, these natural laws provide the basis for foresight – i.e. the basis for predictions; and third, the realization of these predictions can be modified by manipulating the causal variables, to change the nature of society.

According to Lacey (1976, 1. 165), Comte used positivism 'to convey six features of things: being real, useful, certain, precise, organic, relative'; Gregory (1978, p. 26, following Habermas, 1972) lists only five: *le réel, la certitude, le précis, l'utile and le relative'* (organic is omitted). According to these features, science is the study of real, empirically observable phenomena and the relationships between phenomena, and certainty means that there is a common method of observation, so that experiments are replicable in that all scientists proceed in the same way. This common method of working – *le précis* – establishes a unity of scientific method, so that individual sciences are identified by *what* they study rather than *how*. *Le relative* indicates that science proceeds step by step, incorporating new, scientifically obtained knowledge into established theories and thereby extending its understanding of the world. (The organic feature enters here, in that Comte recognized that 'the more phenomena are general, simple and abstract, the less they depend on other phenomena, the more exact will be the knowledge relating to them, and the more complete will be the co-ordination of that knowledge' (Andreski, 1974, p. 59). Finally, the utility feature implies a central role for scientific knowledge in social engineering: knowledge of the natural laws regarding social phenomena enables society to improve its self-regulation.

Comte's works were published in the period 1830–54, and influenced the conduct of social science inquiry from then on. But the major developments of positivist thinking, to which most contemporary work refers, were undertaken by a group of philosophers (most of them with a natural science rather than a social scientific background) working at the University of Vienna in the 1920s and early 1930s (Kraft, 1953; Hanfling, 1981). Their debates and statements are central to what is known as logical positivism (or logical empiricism).

The logical positivists very largely accepted Comte's outline scheme of a positive science. They codified it with regard to current practice and focused most of their attention on how scientific enquiry might be conducted so as to lead to firmly established generalizations. Theirs was very largely a concern with verification and meaning. Thus:

> the verification of an ordinary statement was to consist of two stages, corresponding to the words 'Logical Empiricism'. The statement would be analysed by a logical process into 'elementary' statements, and then would come the crucial contact with experience, as required by empiricism (Hanfling, 1981, p. 77).

Thus any statement – a proposition – is first analysed and rewritten in ways which allow it to be verified. Such testable statements – hypotheses – are then compared with reality, to establish their veracity.

The fundamentals of positivist science and of logical positivism

Logical positivism is a philosophy concerned with the development of knowledge in the form of general statements, obtained by accepted procedures, about observable phenomena; such statements can then be used in the manipulation of the phenomena. This incorporates what is widely known as scientific method or what Keat (1981, p. 17) calls 'the positivist conception of science'; as stressed above, however, it is not the sole scientific method. But the philosophy involves much more, for Keat (p. 15ff.) identifies three other 'doctrines, each of which may not unreasonably be termed "positivist" ' and adherence to which is central to logical positivism. These are:

1 **Scientism** which is the claim that the positivist method is the only true method of obtaining knowledge, and that non-positivist methods produce meaningless material. Unless one works according to the positivist scientific method what one has to say is irrelevant and of no value, because it is not verified knowledge.
2 **Scientific politics** which is the argument that positivism provides the method for finding rational solutions to all problems, so that it offers the basis for social engineering.
3 **Value-freedom** – the doctrine that scientific judgements are objective, with decisions on the veracity of propositions being made on the basis of criteria that are independent of 'particular moral or political commitments' (p. 18).

All three of these involve making claims that positivist science is relevant in all walks of life and forms of enquiry, and they are represented in some geographical uses of positivism. Critiques of positivist approaches (in geography and elsewhere) in part focus on one or more of these three doctrines as well as on the validity of the scientific method associated with a 'positivist conception of science'. The nature of such critiques must be recognized. For the current discussion, however, the focus is upon *the positivist conception of science*, and on whether the philosophy and methodology of the physical sciences can be validly employed in human geography.

The literature on positivism is large, much of it concerned with issues that are irrelevant to a general treatment as conceived here. With regard to human geography, four elements of the positivist programme have been isolated (the first refers to logical positivism; the other three to the positivist conception of science): first, the elimination of metaphysics; second, the centrality of the verification principle; third, the aims of positivist science; and fourth, the structure of positivist science. The four are related, as indicated below, but are treated separately.

The elimination of metaphysics Metaphysics (literally 'after physics') has been defined as the study of questions that 'arise out of, but go beyond, factual or scientific questions about the world' (Lacey, 1976, p. 128). A metaphysician, then, may be defined as someone claiming 'knowledge of a reality which transcended the phenomenal world' (Ayer, 1964, p. 33).

The study of metaphysics is the study of people's experiences and beliefs and of the meanings that they give to things; such experiences, beliefs and meanings cannot be subjected to positivist analysis. As stated by Ayer (1964, p. 41):

> a metaphysical sentence [is] . . . a sentence which purports to express a genuine proposition, but does, in fact, express neither a tautology nor an empirical hypothesis.

(A tautology is a statement which is true in itself, because it says the same thing in two or more ways; most mathematical statements are tautologies. A hypothesis is a statement not yet accepted as true, but whose truth or falsity can be established by recourse to evidence.) The positivist conception of science ignores such metaphysics and is concerned solely with empirical hypotheses having a factual content:

> every empirical hypothesis must be relevant to some actual, or possible, experience, so that a statement which is not relevant to any experience is not an empirical hypothesis, and accordingly has no factual content (Ayer, 1964, p. 41).

The elimination of metaphysics establishes positivist science as the study of the empirically knowable, and argues that all knowledge must be obtained according to agreed procedures. This can be extended into scientism, into statements such as:

> as tautologies and empirical hypotheses form the entire class of significant propositions, we are justified in concluding that all metaphysical assertions are nonsensical (Ayer, 1964, p. 41).

(Note that this was Ayer's position when he published the first edition of *Language, Truth and Logic*, in 1936.) But it is not necessary to proceed this far; metaphysics may be eliminated from certain aspects of human existence, but not all (see Hay, 1979).

The verification principle Having established that the positivist conception of science is built around empirical hypotheses – propositions with factual content – a central feature of that science must be the testing of hypotheses: the verification principle. All statements within the science must be genuine:

> a sentence is factually significant to any given person, if, and only if, he knows how to verify the proposition which it purports to express – that is, if he knows what observations would lead him, under certain conditions, to accept the proposition as being true, or reject it as being false (Ayer, 1964, p. 35).

A genuine statement, therefore, must be capable of verification (it is correct) or falsification (it is wrong). Only if a statement is verified is it meaningful for scientific study (i.e. it provides useful knowledge).

The question of verification was central to the work of the Vienna school of logical positivists (Hanfling, 1981). To say that an empirical hypothesis is acceptable only if it can be either verified or not falsified would seem to be relatively straightforward, but the problems of verification are many. Can one achieve 'complete verification', for example, with regard to statements referring to an infinite series of events? ('All men are mortal' is commonly used as an example of such a proposition: Hanfling, 1981, p. 61.) In this case, it seems, one can speak only of incomplete verification: the proposition has yet to be falsified. In other cases, complete verification is possible, since the proposition does not imply an infinite number of occurrences. ('Some men are yetis', for example, would require the observation of only two yetis to be verified. Complete verification would depend, of course, on prior agreement on the definitions for both men and yetis.)

Conclusive verifiability may be impossible with certain classes of propositions, therefore. Thus Ayer, in the introduction to the second edition of *Language, Truth and Logic*, distinguished between what he termed weak and strong verification:

> a proposition is said to be verification in the strong sense of the term, if and only if its truth could be conclusively established in experience, but that it is verifiable in the weak sense, if it is possible for experience to render it probable (Ayer, 1964, p. 9)

According to this view, much of positivist science is composed of weakly verified statements, of propositions which appear to be true, but which remain as 'hypotheses which are continually subject to the test of further experience' (Ayer, 1964, p. 9). Thus while one can identify propositions that can 'be verified conclusively' (p. 10), such *basic propositions* are invariably related 'to the content of a single experience'. However:

> the vast majority of the propositions that people actually express are neither themselves basic statements, nor deducible from any finite set of basic statements (Ayer, 1964, p. 11).

Although one might be certain in one's explanation of a particular event (rainfall at place x being caused by the passage of a cyclone overhead), therefore, one might not be able to reach a strongly verified conclusion with regard to all such examples of the proposition (that the overhead passage of a cyclone at place x always produces rainfall). With regard to the latter, the positivist scientist has a weakly verified proposition expressed in terms of probabilities: the likelihood of the outcome. The aim is to strengthen the verification, by increasing the number of verified propositions with regard to the behaviour of the phenomena under consideration.

Thus the positivist conception of science involves the development of verified statements. It is realized, however, that complete verification may not be achievable and that strong verification is not always immediately possible, because of the limits of empirical knowledge (Ayer admits also that 'most empirical propositions are in some degree vague'; p. 12). Thus positivist science is cumulative. Hay (1979, p. 9) expresses it in slightly different terms:

> the question to be asked of a geographic theory is not 'does this theory *totally* explain the observed variation?' but the more modest question, 'does this theory contribute an explanation of a part of the observed variation which would otherwise remain obscure?'

(In the terms of the present discussion, for 'theory' substitute 'proposition' or 'empirical hypothesis'.)

Positivist science proceeds by the verification of propositions, according to the common view. However, one philosopher associated with, though never a member of, the Vienna school has argued against the use of the verification principle as the central focus of positivist methodology and has replaced it by the falsification principle. Popper had observed that a theory, or series of propositions, could continue to be accepted if some evidence favoured it:

> no theory could ever be relied on to be the final truth. The most we can ever say is that it is supported by every observation so far, and yields more, and more precise, predictions than any known alternative. It is still replaceable by a better theory (Magee, 1973, p. 29).

But why and how to produce that better theory, if the existing one is being verified? Popper's solution rests in the problem of complete verification: although a proposition may not be conclusively verifiable it can be (indeed must be) conclusively falsifiable. In this way, Popper claims one can separate science from pseudo-science by the following:

> If somebody proposed a scientific theory he should answer, as Einstein did, the question: 'Under what conditions would I admit that my theory is untenable?'. In other words, what conceivable facts would I accept as refutations, or falsifications, of my theory? (Popper, 1976, p. 41).

Falsification would add to knowledge, since it would show where the theory (proposition) failed, a piece of information more valuable than another piece of verification because it indicates the lacunae in knowledge and the areas for further work. Thus Popper's scientific method (sometimes termed critical rationalism) proceeds by the conduct of critical experiments designed to refute propositions: if a proposition is not falsified, the experiment has corroborated it, but not confirmed its validity. (See Hay 1985a; Marshall 1985.)

The aims of positivist science Whether one proceeds by the verification or the falsification route, positivist science according to this discussion seeks to establish the veracity of propositions (empirical hypotheses) about the phenomena under discussion. As indicated in the outline of the verification principle, this veracity may be established with regard to particular circumstances, and produce a basic proposition, or it may be phrased more widely, producing a general proposition whose application is not specific to a particular set of circumstances. (The former are restricted propositions and the latter are unrestricted propositions.) The aim of positivist science is to achieve the latter, which will encapsulate the former; if we can provide general explanations, then clearly we can explain particular realizations of the phenomena under investigation.

This aim is usually expressed as the search for scientific laws. Thus:

> The function of a science . . . is to establish general laws covering the behaviour of the empirical events or objects with which the science in question is concerned, and thereby to enable us to connect together our knowledge of the separately known events, and to make reliable predictions of events as yet unknown (Braithwaite, 1953, p. 1).

A law, according to Braithwaite (1953, p. 12), is:

> equivalent to [a] generalization of unrestricted range in space and time of greater or lesser degrees of complexity of generality.

It is a statement whose only qualification concerns the subject matter to which it relates and 'the fundamental aim of a science is the establishment of such laws' (p. 2). With them, it is then possibe to tackle the explanation of particular events (although, of course, it may well be the existence of such events that stimulates the search for a law: see below). The methodology for achieving the aim of producing laws is the subject of a later section of this chapter (pp. 19–27).

The structure of positivist science Positivist science, according to this outline, is a means of attaining objective knowledge about the world, knowledge which is independent of the scientists. To achieve this, science must not only have certain aims, as described above, but also agreed procedures. Thus Mulkay (1975) suggests that scientists must conform to the following norms:

1 *Originality* – their aim is to advance knowledge, by the discovery of new material.
2 *Communality* – all knowledge is shared, with its provenance fully recognized.
3 *Disinterestedness* – scientists are interested in knowledge for its own sake, and their only reward is the satisfaction that they have advanced understanding.
4 *Universalism* – judgements are on academic grounds only, and

incorporate no reflections on the individuals concerned.
5 *Organized scepticism* – knowledge is advanced by constructive criticism.

If these norms are met, positivist science is conducted in a neutral fashion, without partiality, self-seeking, secrecy or intellectual prejudice; objective criteria are applied in all assessments, and scientists are humble individuals.

This leads to what Mulkay (1979, pp. 19–20) calls the 'standard view of science':

> the natural world is to be regarded as real and objective. Its characteristics cannot be determined by the preferences or intentions of its observers. These characteristics can, however, be more or less faithfully represented. Science is that intellectual enterprise concerned with providing an accurate account of the objects, processes and relationships occurring in the world of natural phenomena . . . . Although the natural world is, in a certain sense, undergoing continuous change and movement, there exist underlying and unchanging uniformities. These basic empirical regularities can be expressed as universal and permanent laws of nature, which tell us what is always and everywhere the case. Unbiased, detached observation furnishes the evidence on which these laws are built.

Research is conducted within this framework. Further, the concept of a social science that can be subject to the same positivist method, and which according to some includes human geography, implies the belief that all that has been outlined here applies to the so-called 'human world' as well as to the 'natural world'. The remainder of this chapter is concerned with the working-out of that contention and the search for 'universal and permanent laws' in the social science of human geography. (This, of course, avoids the contention by some that human geography is not a social science.)

At this point, the differences between positivism, as it will be used here, and logical positivism should be stressed. Positivism is interpreted as what Keat calls the positivist conception of science; it involves rigorous enquiry and the search for generalizations. It is a part of, but only a part of, logical positivism. This latter not only advances a particular mode of inquiry but also claims that this is the sole valid route to knowledge. Anything else is metaphysical, and thus non-scientific (and nonsense). Thus logical positivism embraces scientism, scientific politics and value-freedom as well as the positivist conception of science. It is an ideology as well as a philosophy and methodology. Whereas positivism is the search for generalizations via a rigorous procedure, logical positivism is the argument that this is the only path to knowledge.

Positivism is a much-abused word in the social sciences (not least by those who wish to abuse others for being positivists!). According to Giddens (1974) the 'positivistic attitude' in sociology combines the following three suppositions:

1 The methodological procedures of the natural sciences can be applied to

the social sciences – reality can be observed (whether the subject matter is
phenomena, events or aspects of human subjectivity);
2 The outcome of those procedures can be stated in the same way in the
social as in the natural sciences – the goal is the formulation of laws, or law-
like generalizations; and
3 The knowledge so produced is technical in character, and can be used in
the pursuit of practical policy.
(A similar list of five propositions is provided by Platt, 1981.)

Note, however, Giddens's important qualification that

> Obviously, acceptance of any one of these three suppositions does not necessarily
> entail adoption of the other two (p. 4)

Thus, if one argues that 'all social science need not use the same procedures
as natural science', that 'law-seeking is not necessarily the goal of social
science', or that 'social science knowledge cannot be used in policy' then
one is not fully committed to the positivistic attitude. The qualification is
crucial to debates over positivism in geography (see below, p. 38ff).

The methodology of positivism

Positivist science is built on the verification principle. To know that
something is true is to know, and to accept, the method of substantiating its
truth. (If someone says something is true, that statement is accepted because
the method by which it was reached – i.e. how the proposition was
verified – is accepted.) Thus verification implies a methodology. This is
indicated in a passage (quoting Waismann) by Hanfling (1981, p. 24)
which indicates the link between methodology and epistemology:

> To understand a proposition means to know what is the case if the proposition is
> true. One can understand it without knowing *whether* it is true.
> To become aware of the sense of a proposition one has to get clear about the
> procedure for establishing its truth. If one does not know this procedure, then
> one cannot understand the proposition either.
> *The sense of a proposition is the method of its verification.* (His italics)

One accepts that a statement is true only because one accepts that the
method of establishing its veracity is valid. Thus the positivist conception of
science must incorporate an accepted methodology.

This methodology goes under a large variety of titles including, simply,
'the scientific method' and also the hypothetico-deductive method. Its aim,
as outlined above, is the production of laws, but not simply laws as isolated
statements. To be truly meaningful in a scientific sense, laws should be
embedded within a theory, which sets them in context, links them with
other laws, and provides a unity for the particular science. Thus the aim of

producing laws is part of a more general aim, that of producing theories.

A scientific theory, according to the positivist view, comprises a particular deductive system, which is composed of two elements: a set of initial propositions (or assumptions) and a set of deduced, or empirical, propositions (hypotheses) which follow from them, because of the operation of the laws (themselves part of the initial propositions) within the system. The development of the theory involves the deduction of new propositions. The logical sequence from assumption to deduced proposition, to another deduced proposition, and so on, through a continuous chain, is likened by most philosophers of science to a calculus (Braithwaite, 1953).

In an abstract science, such as mathematics, the deduced propositions of the scientific theory are not given any external meaning. The theory is self-contained, and any hypotheses derived can be verified within it because of the tautologous characteristic of mathematics. This is not so with empirical sciences, however, in which the hypotheses relate to some (pre-defined) phenomena. In order for the theory to be extended, by the incorporation of the deduced propositions into the initial propositions, the validity of the deduced propositions must be verified by an accepted methodology. This is the methodology of hypothesis-testing.

An hypothesis is an empirical proposition, a statement of what should be, given certain conditions; it is deduced from what is already known (or assumed) and is an attempted *explanation*. If it is true, then it is a scientific law, within the prescribed domain of that law (i.e. the range of phenomena, conditions, etc. to which it applies), which *explains* the phenomenon under investigation. Thus:

> a scientific hypothesis is a general proposition about all the things of a certain
> sort. It is an empirical proposition in the sense that it is testable by experience;
> experience is relevant to the question as to whether or not the hypothesis is true,
> i.e. as to whether or not it is a scientific law (Braithwaite, 1953, p. 2).

This raises three main issues for an empirical science: the classification of phenomena; the derivation of hypotheses; and the testing procedure.

The classification of phenomena

Classification is the basic first step of an empirical positivist science, as it defines the concepts to be studied. Since the goal of positivist science is to establish generalizations, then clearly it assumes that there are classs of phenomena about which generalizations can be made; if everything is singular, then no generalizations are possible since there are no two examples of any concept. (There is an important difference to note between uniqueness and singularity in this context. The concept of uniqueness implies a single empirical example, but not a single causal mechanism producing that example. Outside the closed environment of a laboratory, where all other influences can be removed, mechanisms work not in isolation but in a great range of interactions. It may well be that a particular set of interactions – two or more laws operating together – occurs only once, producing a unique outcome, one that is not replicated. But that set of interactions could recur, and would result in the same outcome, so that the latter is not singular; it is the result of general laws interacting in a particular way. The concept of singularity, on the other hand, denies the possibility of a recurrence; the laws are not general therefore. The positivist conception of science accepts the empirical possibility of unique events, but not of singular events.)

Most scientific laws are presented as *functional laws*, in many cases statements of the inter-relationships among two or more classes of phenomena. Prior to the search for those functional laws, however, it is necessary to define the *membership laws*, which allocate phenomena to their relevant classes (such as the allocation of plants to genera and to species). In abstract, this would appear to be a straightforward task. Empirically it is more difficult, and there may be much debate over the classification of a phenomenon or event. (When does drizzle become rain or youth become adulthood?) Errors in drawing up the membership laws can lead to failures in the search for functional laws, because the classes are not internally homogeneous; the membership laws must then be reconsidered in order to allow scientific progress. (Some membership laws may be built on functional laws – a class of phenomena is defined according to responses to certain external stimuli.)

Positivist science is built on membership laws, therefore, so that classification is a crucial initial stage in its operations. Other sciences are similarly built on classifications – as Chouinard, Fincher and Webber (1984) make clear in their comparison of empirical research in positivist and realist social science.

The derivation of hypotheses

In an abstract science such as mathematics, hypotheses are derived by processes of logical reasoning from prior assumptions, which should be accepted laws. Such logical reasoning is usually of the form 'Given x, then y follows', and the veracity of that claim can be established through accepted mathematical procedures of reasoning. (It results in the acronym QED – *quod erat demonstrandum*.) In an empirical science, the process is that a set of givens (the known laws) is taken. From them a potential new functional law is deduced, and presented as a hypothesis. The veracity of this hypothesis can then be tested by experiment (or refuted by a critical experiment designed to falsify it).

But what of an empirical science with few established functional laws, especially if the laws are irrelevant to the particular subject matter being considered? In this case, the deductive procedure is likely to be relatively barren, and to produce few testable empirical hypotheses. Instead, the scientist is forced to speculate on less certain ground, to produce hypotheses with less substantial bases, perhaps using analogies or metaphors to advance potential understanding of a particular topic (Harrison and Livingstone, 1982).

Two major sources for the empirical scientist in this situation are personal experiences (plus, perhaps, the reports of those of others) and a reading of the results of other scientific experiments. With regard to the former, sense experiences are perhaps the major stimulus to work in certain sciences. The scientist observes certain phenomena, in the course either of work or everyday life, and is led (by natural curiosity if nothing else) to speculate about these phenomena. The scientist is seeking laws to account for their existence, and will accumulate evidence to back up those speculations.

This process of law-making by the accumulation of evidence is criticized by positivist scientists. Rather than proceeding from the general to the specific – from the proposition to the test – and thence, if valid, back to the general (the law), it proceeds from the specific to the general without any intervening critical test. This is the problem of *induction* (or inductive reasoning), in which the premisses are presented as logical consequences of their conclusion, rather than the other way round (Braithwaite, 1953, p. 258). Induction, according to Lacey (1976, p. 94), is:

> any rational process where from premisses about some things of a certain kind a conclusion is drawn about some or all of the remaining things of that kind.

This is invalid as form of reasoning, because the 'sample' of things actually observed may be very biased (as Lacey puts it, 'the smaller n is, the weaker the argument will be', p. 94), and because the observation that certain consequences are associated with certain antecedent conditions cannot incorporate situations where such conditions are not associated with those consequences. (Critical rationalism – p. 16 – is presented as a way of avoiding this problem of induction: Marshall, 1985.)

Induction can be the source of hypotheses, therefore, but not of generalizations and laws. (Because of the problem of incomplete verification, however – see p. 15 – much positivist science includes an inductive component. Because the populations of many phenomena are finitely large, if not infinite, verification of hypotheses is conducted on samples only, which may be biased: if those samples are empirical, in the context of uncontrolled for other laws, rather than in closed laboratory experiments, the generalizations drawn are correspondingly weak.) For generalizations to be made, the hypothesis must be properly tested according to accepted procedures. There is no doubt, however, that induction can be extremely stimulating to scientific advance, especially if it involves the scientist placing observations in the context of accepted theories.

All work in empirical sciences begins with images of the world. These images may be derived entirely from existing theory, or they may be derived from some combination of (relatively unstructured, i.e. not in the context of the test of a hypothesis) empirical observation, consideration of the findings of other sciences, and accepted theory. From them, if the scientist is to develop laws and extend the available theory, hypotheses must be deduced and stated as testable propositions.

A commonly–used device for the development of hypotheses is the *model*, which provides a formal structuring of the images. The term model has been used in a variety of ways by scientists (not least by geographers: Chorley and Haggett, 1967, Chapter 1). In the sense implied here, however, it is a representation of a segment of the world, as the scientist believes it to be structured. This representation involves not a series of relatively unordered observations but a formal 'picture', one from which a hypothesis may be derived. It is thus an aid to hypothesis-derivation. It may be a formal ordering of observations, or it may be a representation of part of a theory. Whatever its provenance, its purpose is to further the presentation and testing of hypotheses.

Hypothesis-testing

Perhaps the most critical stage in the methodology of positivist science is the testing of hypotheses. In this, the propositions are to be set against empirical data.

Empirical hypotheses may take a number of forms, including:

1 If A, then B – if event A occurs, then event B will follow.
2 B = f(A) – the magnitude of event B, at a place, is a function of the magnitude of event A there.
3 If no A, then no B – if event A does not occur, then event B will not occur.
4 If A, then no B – if event A occurs, then event B will not occur.

These can clearly be tested against empirical evidence. With regard to hypothesis 1, for example, occurrences of event A could be investigated to see whether event B followed; if not, the hypothesis is falsified. The procedure seems very straightforward, but two major problems arise.

The first problem relates to the issue of complete verification discussed earlier. If the context of the hypothesis is not finite then it can never be firmly established if it is valid, only whether it is confirmed by available data. This problem of the (potential) infinity of tests relates to the universal content of (many) hypotheses, though not exclusively so. It has been extended in much work to the related problem not of the infinite number of potential tests but to the very large number. Should every possible test be conducted, or is it possible to make a generalization regarding the veracity of the hypothesis from a sample of tests, and if so, how should that sample be selected?

The answer to this second problem has been sought in the development of the (abstract) science of statistics, particularly that branch known as inferential statistics which is based on probability theory. The basis of this theory is that it allows statements to be made of the form 'given that I have an unbiased sample of x observations, taken from a known population y, I can conclude that the result I have observed relating to that sample also holds for the population from which the sample was drawn, at a given level of probability' (i.e. I can express my degree of certainty about this statement, ranging from 0.0 – complete uncertainty – to 1.0 – complete certainty). To be able to make such a statement implies that I know the population from which the sample has been drawn, and that the sample has been taken in such a way that no member of the population has a greater or lesser chance of being studied than does any other.

There is also a problem relating to the use of the verification principle rather than that of falsification. It asks 'how well do the empirical data have to fit in order for me to accept the hypothesis as valid?'. (For the falsification principle, the answer would be 'perfectly'; one failure and the hypothesis would be confounded. Using sample data, however, this would not avoid the problem of how one could be sure that there were no confounding cases in the population at large.) Thus with regard to hypothesis 4 above, what proportion of events in which both B and A occurred would lead me to decide that the hypothesis is invalid?

The solution to this problem is again usually found in probability theory. To return to hypothesis 4, it may be that 20 occurrences have been studied: in 10, event A has been observed but not event B; in 8, event B has been observed but not event A; and in 2, both events A and B have been observed. Probability theory is then asked, 'Given that 12 occurrences of event A take place, and 10 of event B, what is the likelihood that as few as 2 of those events will occur simultaneously?'. In other words, in a population with a similar proportion of events A and B, what is the likelihood that the two events will occur together by chance? The smaller this probability, the more certain the scientist is that the hypothesis is valid; the confounding cases occur very rarely (in relative terms) and can be associated either with chance (some random process that is not identified in the hypothesis) or with another mechanism not identified as yet in the theory/model. In terms of the quotation from Hay (see above, p. 16), the test has provided evidence that the hypothesis – and the model from which it is drawn – is contributing to the development of an explanation of the subject-matter.

Hypothesis-testing, then, involves the collection of empirical evidence with which to assess the veracity of the hypothesis. Because hypotheses, as preludes to scientific laws, are assumed to have universal properties across a pre-defined empirical domain, conclusive tests are often impossible, and in many cases all possible events cannot be studied. Thus the scientists must devise tests (experiments, collection of data) according to strictly defined procedures regarding populations and samples, so that it is possible to make statements regarding the former from the latter (see Hay, 1985b). Further, in many empirical sciences the investigator accepts that all speculations are incomplete and cannot incorporate every eventuality (i.e. they study open systems: Sayer 1984, 1985). It may be, therefore, that hypothesis 4 should be 'If A and C, then no B', but the theory and model did not include C. Thus the scientist is interested in the likelihood that the existence of A means that B will not be present. If the conclusion is only a likelihood, the conclusion may be that A is a necessary but an insufficient condition for the non-existence of B; study of the deviant cases may lead to formulation of a new hypothesis 'If A and C, then no B', which must be tested in a new experiment, independent of the previous one, otherwise it faces the problem of induction. (Note that 'If A and C, no B' is not symmetrical with 'If no B, then A and C'. This is a separate hypothesis, implying a different theory.)

Included in this discussion of hypothesis-testing are the notions of randomness and chance events. In a complete scientific explanation, these should not occur, unless there are elements of the phenomena being studied whose behaviour is entirely random. A belief that this is so is contrary to a basic assumption of positivist science that everything can be explained, that all events have a determinate cause. Randomness may be allowed to enter, however, if:

1 The study is being conducted at an aggregate level, of how a mass of individuals behaves rather than each individual, in which case the aggregation process may involved averaging, around which the individual variation can be treated as random.

2 The study is only partial in that its hypotheses specify only part of the relationship (i.e. 'If A and C then B' is the complete hypothesis but only 'If A then B' is being studied) and it can be assumed that the effect of the other variables is the same as random.

3 If measurement error, which is unbiased and therefore random, has taken place. (This last assumes that the elements in the hypothesis being tested – A, B and C or whatever – can be both isolated and measured in the 'real world'.)

In such situations, the investigator may be prepared to accept some randomness in the relationship being studied, and asks whether the result that has been observed is very likely to have occurred simply by the random allocation of the observations (see Hay, 1985b, on this second type of use of inferential statistics). If probability theory indicates that the likelihood of a random occurrence of such a relationship is very small, the analyst concludes that the result obtained is 'real' and indicative of the operation of the postulated law.

Theories, models, hypotheses, and laws
Positivist science is a cumulative process, therefore, whereby knowledge is acquired in a structured manner so that every additional piece contributes to scientists' comprehension of the world. It beings with theories, and ends with them. The aim is to extend existing theories, by incorporating within them the findings from the latest round of speculation, the newly established laws.

As such a science develops, so does it body of theory(ies). Initially, it will be in a state of weak theoretical development, probably lacking any established laws. The first rounds of model-building and hypothesis-generation will not be atheoretical, however, since this implies that the process of thinking takes place in some sort of vacuum. All thought is theoretically guided, although often by a weak, if not inaccurate, theory. (It is for this reason that pure empiricism is impossible. Any work, however unstructured, is guided by notions of what is worth thinking about. In human geography, any data collection is influenced by theories of what is worth measuring – and mapping.) Scientists are socialized into the processes of scientific research and into the substance of disciplines, and the bodies of knowledge and research methodologies that they learn structure the ways in which they identify and tackle new problems (see Kuhn, 1962; Barnes, 1982). When faced with a new situation, they will react to it in the context of what they already know, seeking to incorporate it within their existing theoretical framework and to develop laws about it using their established methodology. Thus positivist science is a conservative process, with knowledge accumulating along predetermined lines. (Allowing some scope, of course, for the individual whims of the scientists; however, scientists are considerably constrained in that, in many cases, certain problems must remain insoluble until others have been solved. Some phenomenologists – e.g. Pickles, 1985 – argue that the contents of science are pre-given categories independent of human individuals). Occasionally, it is necessary to break this conservatism, to bring fresh light onto problems, not by starting *de novo* but by tackling the problems in the context of a different theoretical structure, a different set of initial propositions leading to new deductions which may demand development of a new methodology, before they can be tested.

All positivist scientists are presented in their education with a method of thinking about research problems – a theoretical structure – and a procedure for testing hypotheses – a research methodology. Their tasks involve using the theoretical structure plus their observations of the world (including, perhaps, the results from work in other theoretical structures) to identify as-yet unsolved research problems. This may involve the derivation of a new model or the creation of a new concept, but in many cases problems will be identified within existing models. Hypotheses are generated; experiments are designed to test them; data are gathered; and the test is concluded. The result (hopefully) is positive, and a further law – a scientific generalization – is added to the theoretical structure.

Most scientists are involved in all aspects of this procedure to a greater or lesser extent. Some are happier to work in the theoretical structure, to manipulate the known information in the search for new questions. Others may prefer to work at the modelling stage, representing ideas in a formal manner. And still others may prefer to be experimenters, collecting data and testing hypotheses generated by others. Such a division of labour is for convenience only. Science is a continuous, integrated process of structuring, speculating and experimenting.

Not all scientific effort is successful. If it fails – the hypothesis is not verified, or the critical experiment leads to a falsification of the hypothesis – this could be for one or more of several reasons. The failure may have been in the structuring: the theory and the model were wrongly assembled. Or the speculations were in error: the hypothesis was applied to irrelevant situations, perhaps indicating that existing theory applies to a more restricted empirical domain than was originally believed. Or the testing was invalid: the experiment was improperly conducted perhaps. Such negative findings are valuable in pointing future work in more fruitful directions – the failures usually indicate the fallibility of scientists rather than the fallibility of science!

Positivist social science

The above description of positivist science outlines the basis of a unified structure which is applicable, according to Comte and the many who have followed him, to the social sciences as much as to the natural sciences. As a structure it has been developed almost entirely by and for natural scientists, however, and has then been adapted for the social sciences. As such, the application of positivism in the social sciences (i.e. to the study of individuals and society) is based on the premise of *naturalism*, the 'doctrine that there can be a natural scientific study of society' (Thomas, 1979). This in turn is founded on certain assumptions, which can be enumerated as follows:

1 That events which occur within a society, or which involve human decision-making, have a determinate cause, that is identifiable and

verifiable. This is the assumption of *causation* (i.e. that A, B and C in the hypothesis – p. 23 – can be isolated and linked in a particular way).

2 That decision-making is the result of the operation of a set of laws, to which individuals conform. This can be called the assumption of *behaviourism*, that a given stimulus produces a particular response under predefined circumstances.

3 That there is an objective world, comprising individual behaviour and the results of that behaviour, which can be observed and recorded in an objective manner, on universally agreed criteria. This is the assumption of (direct or naïve) *realism*. Without it, use of the positivist procedure would be impossible since this is based on the acceptance of evidence – 'the sense of a proposition is the method of its verification' – and so, if the nature of the evidence is not acceptable to all, the application of the procedures is impossible. (Note that this form of realism differs from transcendental realism, discussed in Chapter 4.)

4 That scientists are disinterested observers, able to stand outside their subject matter (even though in another segment of their life they may be a part of it). They can observe and record its features in a neutral way, without in any aspect changing those features by their procedures, and can reach dispassionate conclusions about it, which can be verified by other observers. This is the assumption of the *disinterested observer*.

5 That, as in the study of inanimate matter, there is a structure to human society (an organic whole) which changes in determinate ways, according to the observable laws. This can be called the *functionalism* assumption, that the various elements of society occupy a particular location within it.

6 That the application of the laws and theories of positivist social science can be used to alter societies, again in determinate ways, either by changing the laws which operate in particular circumstances or by changing the circumstances in which the laws will operate. This can be called the *social engineering* assumption.

The existence of these assumptions, whose underpinning of all positivist social science may go unrecognized by many practitioners, does not imply a crude, mechanistic model of society involving simple laws of cause and effect (if A, then B), although many such have been proposed. Human societies are complex, perhaps more complex than the subject matter of natural sciences, but complexity should not, according to Thomas (1979), be presented as a reason for not seeking to unravel society positivistically. It means that there are many rather than few laws operating, a large proportion under very restricted circumstances and interacting with many others. This leads some to argue that each event, each item of human decision-making, is unique. The response to this is that its uniqueness represents a particular combination of circumstances, and thus operation of the relevant laws, rather than a singular situation which is incomparable with any other. Thus:

> Wide differences in the manifest characteristics and behaviour of a group of phenomena do not exclude there being a common set of variables that underlie and can be used to explain all the phenomena; to think otherwise is to make the cardinal confusion of generalizations with initial conditions (Thomas, 1979, p. 18).

Because the laws are likely to be many, and the circumstances in which they operate very much more numerous in type, the process of uncovering them is likely to be slow. Comprehension is extended with each round of successful research, providing an empirical generalization which, while lacking the universality required of a law, furthers knowledge of the phenomena being studied.

A major issue for social scientists is clearly the identification of their membership laws, which allocate individual people and events to classes. As noted above, such classification is the foundation of positivist science. The classes should be logically defined, according to the relevant theory, otherwise the concepts involved in the formulation and testing of hypotheses are what Sayer (1984) terms 'chaotic conceptions' – concepts that are internally heterogeneous and so not capable of yielding valid functional laws. (In social science, for example, the nature of the concept of social class is the focus of much attention on how the membership laws should be defined, as Dunleavy and Husbands, 1985, argue.) In the absence of much valid theory on which to base the definition of membership laws, social scientists may resort to inductive procedures, seeking to identify homogeneous classes from empirical data – as in much behavioural geography: p. 39 – as a prelude to more formal developments.

For social science, the definition of membership laws is crucial for two reasons. The first refers to the identification of *individual functional laws*, which state that individuals in a particular category behave in a certain way as a response to certain stimuli. The second refers to *group functional laws*, which refer to the responses of population aggregates rather than those of individuals. (In some social theories, it is social classes that act, not individuals, for example.) These are the perspectives of individualism and holism respectively. They are not characteristics of the social sciences alone, as Simmons and Cox (1985) make clear, but they are central to it; if theories imply that it is not just similar individuals who act similarly but also that groups act as if they were individuals, then correct identification of the membership laws is crucial.

The argument, therefore, is that the positivist model of science can be applied within social science. It is built on the assumptions outlined above, which can be reduced to one sentence: human behaviour is subject to the operation of laws of cause and effect, and the nature of these laws can be identified by the process of hypothesis-testing against empirical evidence. By looking at society in a particular way, it will tell us how it works. Note that some would argue that the laws are never deterministic – they never provide complete verification – because people have 'free will'. There are two basic responses to this. The first is to claim that the individual's freedom to choose is limited and that all behaviour and beliefs are ultimately determined; the problem is the inability of social science to identify the causal chains. This is the logical positivist argument associated with the elimination of metaphysics. (The failure may be accommodated in the short-run – until the development of better theories – by the incorporation of random error in the preferred explanation to encompass what is presented as free will but is, in fact, as-yet-unexplained variation.) The second response is to accept that the positivist conception of science does not apply to all aspects of social science. In this case, the assumptions listed above are qualified in the single-sentence statement so that: some aspects of human behaviour are subject to the operation of laws of cause and effect and can be studied according to the positivist conception of science. Others cannot, so that positivism relates to a limited domain. In logical positivism, as applied to the social sciences, there is no such limitation.

Positivism and human geography

Human geography was one of the last of the social sciences to adopt positivist approaches on a wide scale. In part this was because of its relatively weak links with the other social sciences until relatively recently; in part because its main links to the natural sciences, through physical geography, were with geology, in which positivism was not dominant (empiricism was, and so were the evolutionary ideas introduced by Darwin and widely adopted in the earth and life sciences; see Stoddart, 1966); and in part because its firm base in the humanities (alongside a non-social scientific history) and the exceptionalist philosophy, the promotion of the unique (interpreted by some, wrongly, as the singular: Hartshorne, 1984) as codified by Hartshorne (1939). No precise date for the introduction of positivist approaches to the discipline can be identified, for there were elements of them in isolated papers. But it was in the mid- and late- 1950s in the United States of America that widespread introduction occurred, at a number of institutions (Johnston, 1983a). From these it spread rapidly, dominating the discipline throughout North America and much of the rest of the English-speaking world by the end of the 1960s.

Reasons for the adoption of positivist approaches were varied and are not readily uncovered. In general, they seem to be related to disgruntlement with existing approaches (see Gould, 1979) and the attractions of a 'scientific' social science, as being practised in economics, sociology, psychology and politics. (There were also links, via physical geographers, to geologists introducing positivist procedures, such as Krumbein, Schumm and Strahler.) Science was academically and socially respectable, and so was *social science*; it was useful, and geographers perceived that they, by becoming more scientific, could become more useful too, so advancing disciplinary and personal esteem.

Whatever the general attraction of the positivist approaches, it is clear that in most cases these were not fully assimilated into geographical training. There was little evidence of courses in philosophy of science or even in positivistic scientific method, nor of any study of these subjects by the proponents of the positivist conception of science (see, however, Golledge, 1983). The major terms – law, model, theory and hypothesis – were all widely used, but the main impression is one of only partial appreciation of the details of the positivist arguments. Some advanced the three other arguments noted by Keat – scientism, scientific politics, and value-freedom – without a great deal of careful analysis (or so it appears in hindsight).

But the bandwagon rolled on. To many, it seemed, the major attraction of the positivist approaches was quantification: the expression of research results in mathematical or statistical form, in a way which implied precision, replicability, and certainty (*la certitude* of Comte). Thus a number of the proponents of the new approaches called themselves 'statistical or quantitative geographers'. Indeed, their arguments were widely known as the 'quantitative revolution', as indicated in a widely referenced paper by Burton (1963), which heralded the success of that revolution and the likely ensuing:

> mathematization of much of our discipline, with an attendant emphasis on the construction and testing of theoretical models (Burton, 1963, p. 151).

Most revolutions are taken to excess by some of the proponents, and there is little doubt that some of the early work was relatively trivial, led by the availability of data, and involving the testing of hypotheses that were weakly linked, at best, to any well articulated theory or model. (The term hypothesis, for example, was much abused at the time; Newman, 1973.) Nevertheless, to suggest that positivist approaches were being widely misused and abused is to overstate the case. There was considerable debate over certain fundamental aspects of the relevance of the positivist conception to geographical work, with reference to the literature of the philosophy of science. Chorley (1964), for example, published a classic paper on the role of models in geographical work, with the term 'model' being defined in a very catholic way, to incorporate theory; this paper was the precursor to a widely acclaimed large volume on the theme of models in geography (Chorley and Haggett, 1967). The relevance of laws was discussed too, with an important short paper by Lewis (1965, p. 27) concluding that:

> It was agreed that, logically everything is unique. But similarities can be found among unique things and general statements can be made from these similarities. These statements are then expressed as formal laws. These laws do not imply that one event A is always followed by another event B, but they state a functional relationship between given determinants. Finally, it was seen that determinism in this sense involves no conflict with introspective free will.

Golledge and Amedeo (1968) also tackled the important issue of laws in and for geography, arguing from the premise that 'the ultimate existence of laws is predicated on accepting the principle of rationality or non-randomness in a universe' to the conclusion that 'Presenting research results in a rigorous manner and examining the possibility that a form of lawfulness may have been discovered is as good a way as any to start developing a meaningful and sound philosophical base in the discipline' (p. 774). Finally, several authors (including Grigg, 1965) examined the relationships between the traditional geographical interest in regionalization (the division of the earth's surface into types) and the more general scientific procedure of classification (the identification of individuals with common features and thus presumably subject to the same functional laws).

A full statement of, and argument for, a positivist approach in human geography was not published until 1969. Drawing on the writings of various members of the Vienna school and its followers, Harvey's (1969) *Explanation in geography* emphasized methodological rather than philosophical issues. He acepted the assumptions of the positivist conception of a (social) science and devoted virtually all of his attention to its *modus operandi* in a geographical context. Thus at the outset of the book he argued for the centrality of explanation as the focus of geographical work and for the positivist scientific method as the set of rules which govern the acceptance/non-acceptance of a proposed explanation. He then discussed the issues involved in applying these rules in the social sciences – noting that in their application most 'have not been particularly rigorous' and that 'Each discipline tends to be autonomous with respect to the criteria it employs in deciding whether or not statements are justified' (pp. 60–1) – and examined the history of attitudes to theory in geography. He concluded, with Ballabon (1957, p. 218), that geography is 'short on theory and long on facts' and argued that:

> the development of theory appears vital both to satisfactory explanation and to the identification of geography as an independent field of study (p. 78).

This led to his conclusion to the book, that geographers should:

create theoretical structures which, in turn, will give our discipline the identity and direction it so badly needs at the present time. Without theory we cannot hope for controlled, consistent and rational explanation of events. Without theory we can scarcely claim to know our own identity (p. 486).

Given this end, Harvey contended that there is much misunderstanding about the means of a positivist conception of science and about the roles of its central elements: theories, laws, models and hypotheses. Thus these are given extended treatment, as are the roles of mathematics ('the language of science') and probability ('the language of chance'). What Harvey provided, therefore, was a series of insights into the major elements of the positivist conception of science, set within a framework of belief that the development of a body of theory (scientifically obtained) is necessary for a scientific discipline to obtain independent status.

It is interesting to note that, although Harvey drew considerably on the writings of the logical positivists, he did not argue for scientism. He noted with regard to temporal studies, for example (pp. 80–1), that one should not impute an historical determinism to unfolding landscapes; and he argued that 'It is not the role of the methodologist . . . to curb speculation, to decry metaphysics, to chain the imagination' (p. 481) and that, in the context of the scientist as decision-maker, 'Decisions cannot be made in a moral or ethical vacuum' (p. 40). He presented a methodology. Clearly he believed it to be of considerable and widespread value to geographers, for he continues on p. 481 from the quote above that:

> at some stage we have to pin down our speculations, separate fact from fancy, science from science fiction. It is the task of the methodologist to point to the tools which can be used to accomplish this, to assess their efficiency and worth.

This comes close to arguing for scientism, and it leads on to the already quoted statement that:

> Without theory we cannot hope for controlled, consistent and rational, explanation of events (p. 486).

But, as he admits in that book and elsewhere (Harvey, 1973), philosophical issues were very largely avoided (neither epistemology nor ontology is in the index). Thus *Explanation in geography* was basically a presentation of a particular scientific methodology and as such was positivist. Any suggestion of logical positivism was very much implicit.

The content of positivist human geography

Positivists, as indicated earlier, believe in the unity of their scientific method. It is not how their particular research is conducted which distinguishes between disciplines according to this view, therefore, but what they study, since all use the same methodology. Thus the development of a positivist human geography required the development of a particular focus, which bestowed upon the discipline a separate identity within the social sciences. It was to be positivist scientific method applied to a particular, geographical, subject matter.

The chosen focus, building on the earlier traditions within the discipline, was 'place and space'. As Harvey (1969, p. 191) expressed it:

> The whole practice and philosophy of geography depends upon the development of a conceptual framework for handling the distribution of objects and events in space.

Geographers had long been interested in 'What is where?', which can be broken down into two related questions: 'What complex of phenomena characterizes a particular place?' and 'What distribution pattern characterizes a particular phenomenon?'. The two are clearly linked. What is in a particular place reflects the distributions of various phenomena, whereas those distributions may be influenced by the attractions of particular places (becauses of what is already present) for certain phenomena.

Within this focus, certain aspects of space were emphasized, notably its role as an impedance factor. To cross space involves time, various costs, and other factors. These costs are to be avoided as far as possible, and so the organization of society is spatially structured to keep down, if not to minimize, the so-called 'frictions of distance'. Thus to many, human geography became the study of 'spatial science' (or spatial social science), and attempts were made to develop theories reflecting this position (e.g. Nystuen, 1963.) Alongside this, attempts were made to justify such a situation and focus within the social sciences (e.g. Cox, 1976).

This theme of a spatial focus for human geography evolved out of its previous concerns with the characteristics of places (i.e. regionalism) and was a positivist approach to the topic of areal differentiation. If unique events (in geography, places) result from particular combinations of general laws (in geography, those of spatial distributions), then the characteristics of those events (places) can only be explained by an articulation of the relevant laws. These laws have status conferred on them in terms of their theoretical location: the theories are located in systematic rather than regional geography, hence the latter must be secondary to the former. Spatial science required theories, therefore, from which models and hypotheses could be derived and tested. Initially, a few main topics were developed in this way. In each case, the theoretical basis was drawn from outside human geography, mainly other social sciences. In those, they were relatively minor foci, but in geography they were elevated to a central importance (see Pooler, 1977). (The only competition was from regional science, a new discipline – based in economics – with a similar focus. This has never attracted many member academics, however, and teaches relatively few students because it has failed to establish an institutional base in more than a few universities. In recent decades, geography alone has emphasized spatial aspects within the social sciences.)

Central place theory This is a theory (really, a family of theories) of the size, functions and spatial distributions of settlements which provide services for the populations of hinterlands. Its twin origins lay in the work of two German economist-geographers, Walter Christaller and August Losch, although several other authors had noted some of the empirical regularities whose existence the theories generalized.

Central place theory, in its simplest form, is based on the following initial propositions: that entrepreneurs locate service establishments to maximize turnover, which involves them being as close to their customers as possible; that customers purchase goods and services from the nearest available outlet, to minimize their acquisition costs; that different types of establishment require different levels of turnover, and thus different sizes of customer populations, to support their existence; and that there are no impediments to movement, the costs of which are linearly related to the distance travelled. From these it was deduced that establishments – and thus settlements – should be uniformly distributed in areas of uniform population density, and that the clustering of establishments with similar turnover levels should (according to Christaller's theory but not Losch's) create a hierarchical structure of settlements.

Central place theory is based, therefore, on certain assumed laws of behaviour. From it was developed a model of a settlement pattern. This provided a number of testable hypotheses related to the size, spacing and functional composition of settlements, and also of shopping centres within urban areas. It stimulated a large volume of empirical work. As well as investigations of the deduced regularities, numerous researchers also used the initial propositions as the bases for hypotheses, particularly that with regard to consumers shopping at the nearest available outlet. Few of the studies found the theory provided a full explanation of observed distributions, but most found some conformity between hypothesis and evidence and concluded that the experiment (test) had at least partially verified the theory and the assumptions on which it is based. (See Beavon, 1976.)

Land-use theory This developed a theory of the organization of agricultural land-uses about a market, formalized by a German economist, J.H.von Thunen, in the early nineteenth century on the basis of observations of his own Prussian estate. Set, like central place theory, in the context of neo-classical economics, whereby individual producers cannot affect the price of their commodities, it argued that the use of any piece of land would be a function of its productivity and the costs (borne by the producer) of transporting its output to the market. Assuming that land was equally suitable for all commodities, the argument was that the greater the cost of transporting a particular product (because of its bulk and/or perishability) then, at a given price, the greater the benefit to the farmer of producing it close to the market. The economic rent yielded was then greatest at the market, and declined with distance from that point.

Two models were deduced from this theory: one, that there would be a zonal spatial organization of agricultural activities around a market; and the other, that the intensity of agricultural activity would decline (over all zones and also within each zone) with distance from the market. Again, such models provided a number of hypotheses which were amenable to testing.

Thunen's theory was also used as an analogy, as the model for the development of a theoretical structure regarding the organization of land-uses within an urban area. The work of Alonso, Muth, Wingo and others was based on this and, on the assumption of a monocentric urban area, produced the following testable hypotheses (*inter alia*): there is a zonal organization of land-uses around the centre of an urban area; land values decline with distance from the urban centre; and population densities decrease with distance from the city centre. All have been at least partially verified. (See Chisholm, 1979; Berry and Horton, 1970.)

Industrial location theory First expressed in the work of economists such as the German, Alfred Weber, and the American, Edgar Hoover, this theoretical structure was based on the initial assumption that all owners of manufacturing industries seek to locate their plants so as to minimize costs of production and of distribution to the market. Among these costs are those of transport, and so among the initial propositions was one that the location of manufacturing industry is undertaken so as to minimize transport costs. From such propositions, models of the distribution of industry could be developed, and hypotheses about particular locations could be derived. The body of theory was applied in a variety of contexts, increasingly emphasizing the importance of linkages between industries in the flow of goods, services and information, and the desire to maximize these links as a major influence on location. (See Lloyd and Dicken, 1978; Smith, 1981.)

Urban social areas Whereas the first three topics are concerned largely with economic geography, and derived their stimuli from work in economics and regional science, in the fourth the context was social and the main stimuli came from sociology, especially in the United States of America (where, in their turn, the sociologists were stimulated by an analogy between person/person and plant/plant – plant/environment interrelationships; through this analogy they developed the study of human ecology). The basic propositions were that society, especially advanced urban society, is divided into economic status groups (often termed classes), ethnic groups and various interest groups and that members of these groups, for a variety of social and economic reasons, wish to live in separate parts of the urban area and to minimize inter-class and inter-group contacts. Distance was presented as a social rather than an economic barrier, therefore, although the two are obviously linked, and the groups compete for positions in urban space (just, according to the analogy, as plants do in any ecological situation). The spatial organization of urban residential areas reflects this use of distance as a social mechanism.

The model derived from this ecological theory had two components. The first was one of spatial congregation and segregation: like people tend to live together in the same areas, whereas unlike people live in separate areas. The second related to the morphology of this congregation and segregation: there is a particular spatial organization of cities with various social area types occupying particular type areas (inner city, outer suburb, etc.). Again, hypotheses could readily be derived from such models. (See Timms, 1971; Johnston, 1984b.)

Spatial interaction theory This final theoretical structure encompassed aspects of the other four, but was frequently treated separately. It focused on one aspect of the spatial organisation of society – movement. Its basic initial proposition was that in any activity that involves movement, people seek to minimize the costs involved. Thus, the whole of the spatial organization of society involves an exercise in movement-minimization.

This thesis has a long history in the social sciences (Tocalis, 1978). Its development has been bolstered by an analogy with Newton's law of gravity, which relates interaction between two bodies with the product of their masses, and (inversely) with the distance separating them. Many hypotheses have been formulated and tested based on this 'gravity model': simply stated, they have claimed that the greater the distance between two places, the less the interaction between them. (See Wilson, 1980, and Gould, 1985.)

Initially, this body of work focused largely on economic flows, of commodities and of people migrating between settlements, for example. But, as already indicated, the gravity-model thesis underlies most spatial science, and so it has been applied, in a catholic way, to movements of goods, people, capital, ideas, etc. Associated with it has been the development of a body of theory regarding *spatial diffusion*, which argues that any innovation, including information and ideas, is spatially biased in its spread by the friction of distance. Thus the general hypothesis was developed that the further a person is from the source of a piece of information, the less likely he or she is to know of it, or the later that it reaches him or her; this has been applied in a variety of contexts (Cliff *et al.*, 1981).

These five bodies of theory by no means encapsulate all of the work initially undertaken as part of the development of a positivist human geography. But the initial propositions outlined here were typical of much of the work. They illustrate how human geographers took certain basic ideas, mostly from other disciplines, and used them to develop models and hypotheses regarding patterns on the earth's surface (of settlements, as in central place theory, and of land-use types, as in agricultural location theory and the study of urban social areas) and regarding movements across that surface. (A classic early synthesis of the material was Haggett, 1965.) Testing of those hypotheses involved the collection of data and the use of statistical procedures as verification methods (some of the modelling involved the use of mathematics). A large research literature has ensued. In addition, texts have been provided. Three types can be identified. The first (e.g. Haggett, 1965) seeks to structure the content of human geography as a spatial science, emphasizing the relevant bodies of theory. The second (e.g. Abler, Adams and Gould 1971; Amedeo and Golledge, 1975) puts greater emphasis on the positivist conception of science, as a means of doing geography within a contextual framework. And the third (e.g. Ebdon, 1985; Bennett, 1979b) emphasizes the techniques necessary for positivist work.

Problems of the positivist approach
In adopting the positivist conception of science, and applying it to human geography defined as spatial science, geographers encountered a number of problems, and also avoided tackling certain issues. Some of these problems and issues were general ones related to the relevance of a naturalistic, positivist methodology in social science, and thus the validity of the search for laws and theories. These major points were raised in critiques of the positivist approaches and presentations of alternative philosophies of the social sciences (these are discussed in the remaining chapters of the book). Similarly, there were discussions of what has been termed the 'spatial separatist' theme (Sack, 1974), of whether a separate social science focusing on 'the spatial variable' is feasible (see Johnston, 1983a, Chapter 4). But there have also been problems and issues within the positivist approaches themselves.

Behaviour and theory The first of these relates to the nature of the theory being developed in human geography. As already stressed, most of this was derived from other disciplines, and much of it is rather informally structured (either it is expressed relatively imprecisely or, as Haynes 1975, 1977 argues, the formal structure of a mathematical theory may contain logical inconsistencies). A consequence of this has been that the hypotheses derived – via model-building in many cases – from the theories have proved to be relatively poor predictors. The theories have failed to provide convincing explanations; indeed, in some cases, notably central place theory, it has been shown that the initial assumptions of the theories have little basis in reality.

A strong argument in this context has been expressed with regard to those inital assumptions. The behaviourism underlying most of the bodies of theory outlined above has been of a normative form – this is how all people ought to behave. Further, it is a particular type of normative assumption derived from neo-classical economics that states that, as an economic actor, the individual is an entirely rational profit-maximizer, which in a science of spatial relations means an entirely rational transport cost-minimizer. (Some geographers seemed to believe that this is the only form of normative assumption. Any behaviour can be presented as normative, however – see Hay, 1979 – and can be the basis for theory articulation. The basic deductions of central place theory, for example, do not need every consumer to visit the nearest centre, only that there is no spatial variation in the proportion of consumers using the nearest, next nearest . . . etc. centre.) Because hypotheses were being falsified (when they should have been verified if the theory were to remain valid), this led to the argument that theories were being developed on false initial assumptions. New assumptions should be used, so the argument went, which were positive (what *is*) rather than normative (what *should be*; Pred, 1967, also argued that normative reasoning based on neo-classical economics is impossible).

This argument suggested the need for more direct observation of what people actually do, and how they reach their decisions. An inductive approach was therefore argued for. The result was a great deal of positive, behavourist work: empirical studies which sought to measure behaviour in terms of how it came about (though not why). Thus Golledge (1981, p. 1327) notes in reviewing such work that:

> Researchers stressed that factors such as access to information, degree of risk aversion, images of environments, the stage of learning about stimulus situations, attitudes towards place, felt stress, risk aversion, place utility, and revealed preferences were important in understanding spatial activity.

The reaction to this was the development of what became known as 'behavioural geography' which was:

> process oriented. The processes emphasized . . . are human behavioural processes such as learning, perception, cognition, attitude formation, and so on . . . (p. 1327).

Data were collected from individual decision-makers regarding those process variables which it was assumed governed their behaviour: the focus was not on the unique individual but sought to generalize by aggregation of individuals, not in any *ad hoc* manner for its aim was:

> to *find* meaningful units of aggregation about which generalizations *can* be made (p. 1328).

(Note that Golledge's paper was in part a response to a critique by Bunting and Guelke, 1979. They claimed that behavioural work was based on two false assumptions: that identifiable environmental images exist which can be measured accurately; and that there are strong relationships between such images and behaviour. They suggest instead an idealist approach, see p. 55, based on the interpretation of overt behaviour.)

Central place theory, spatial interaction theory and the other elements of the 'new' geography of the 1950s and 1960s clearly influenced the selection of topics in 'behavioural geography', which focused on such issues as shopping centre choice, the decision to migrate and the search for a new home, choice of transport mode for a journey, and so on. The work was positivist in its search for generalizations through rigorous sampling procedures for data collection, measurement of both the attitudes and behaviour, and statement of the results. But it was not so explicitly theory-led, and hypotheses were not central to the research strategy in every case. This suggested inductivism to some (a charge also levelled at positivist work in general: Slater, 1973). The counter was that an inductive stage was a necessary precursor to the development of any viable theory, given the failings of the deductive theories with regard to explanation and prediction of behaviour. (Normative theories had been built on invalid membership laws.) The failings, it was stressed, lay in the assumptions on which those theories were built:

> The examination of human actions required the definition of sets of assumptions . . . and the one most readily accepted was that of behavioural invariance . . . It was generally accepted that no proof of any of these assumptions was required, and it was not until behavioural work indicated the existence of substantial variability in perceptions and cognitions of external environments and that different *spatial* behaviours could all be explained by the same decision process, that their shallowness was realized (Golledge, 1981, p. 1326).

As Golledge admits in the same review, no powerful new theory has emerged as a result of this behavioural work but he does claim 'substantial increments in the level of the understanding of human spatial activity' (p. 1339). The path to theory is a long one. . . .

Verification Apart from the issues regarding behavioural assumptions underpinning geographical theories, substantial difficulties have been encountered in testing the validity of those being used. In brief, the problem can be reduced to the simple question 'What constitutes a verification of a geographical hypothesis?' (since almost all geographers ostensibly follow the verification rather than the falsification strategy). Answers to this question were never suggested, and just as Ayer could argue that many hypotheses are vaguely stated, so it could be suggested that many are vaguely tested. The criterion of verifiability, according to Ayer (1964, p. 35), is:

> We say that a sentence is factually significant to any given person, if, and only if, he knows how to verify the proposition which it purports to express – that is, if he knows what observations would lead him, under certain conditions to accept the proposition as being true, or reject it as being false.

Human geographers who take the positivist stance know that observations are needed, but have been far from clear as to the conditions for acceptance/rejection of a hypothesis: in commenting on this, Harvey (1969, p. 105) notes that:

> Statements derived from theory may turn out to be empirically insupportable, while empirical statements which intuitively appear to be of great significance sometimes cannot be linked to any existing theoretical structure . . . when we try to determine whether a particular statement is or is not a scientific law. The degree of theoretical support required, the degree of empirical support, the degree of confidence in the theoretical structure as a whole, and so on, may vary significantly from one person to another . . . The precise nature of the criteria may be obscure, but this does not mean that they are useless and insignificant.

For most human geographers using the positivist approach the criteria for hypothesis acceptance/rejection have been statistical, derived from the theories of probability. Thus, for example, if a correlation coefficient could be shown to be statistically significant at an (arbitrarily derived, usually 0.05) appropriate probability level, then this could be taken as evidence of the veracity of the hypothesis (assuming that the sign of the coefficient was as expected). As outlined above, the theory of probability can be used in two ways in such contexts. One states that the relationship observed in a sample is very likely to be present in the parent population (but at an unknown strength according to the methodology of most tests). The other states that in random orderings of the data set being studied, that particular relationship would occur only rarely by chance; since the relationship was predicted and is unlikely to occur by chance, it can be taken as 'real', and thus confirming the hypothesis (Hay, 1985b).

Both of these approaches to statistical testing raise problems. With regard to the first, there are issues relating to the nature of the population and the sample. A hypothesis, and a theory from which it is drawn, must relate to a specified population from which a sample can be taken. What are the populations for geographical theories? They are far from clear in many cases. Thus what do the samples refer to? (Is a study of rural Wiltshire, comprising 200 settlements, a sample of *one* area in which central place theory is supposed to apply? Or is it a sample of 200 settlements, in which case it is surely not a properly constituted random sample?) If the nature of neither population nor sample is clear, then the validity of statistical significance tests must be very much in doubt.

If the sample-to-population approach to inferential statistics is dubious in much geographical work, then the reliance on probability theory must be based on the second of the ways outlined above. If this is so, then in each study the question being asked of the data is whether the expected relationship exists in that sample of one. (The expected relationship is usually vaguely stated. A correlation may be predicted; but how large? Or distance should have a negative exponent in a regression test of the gravity model; again, how large?) But if it is a sample of one, how far does it advance geographical knowledge if the finding is statistically significant? How many separate (independent) studies must report similar results before the hypothesis is verified? And if the studies are separate, do they together constitute a random sample of all possible studies?

The problems of verifying geographical hypotheses are considerable, therefore (more so, perhaps, than if the criterion of falsifiability were adopted). Because of this, although hypotheses derived from theories can be tested, the strategy of testing suggests that the accumulation of results may be little better than an inductive format. Whereas hypotheses in the natural sciences may be universal in their content, and can be tested in controlled conditions anywhere, many social scientific hypotheses are partial, and are set in contextual situations where proper experimentation is impossible. As such, the process of developing theories through contact with empirical reality is a slow one.

The geographical individual The third major problem stems from the previous one. The subject matter of human geography is exceedingly complex; many laws are operating in the same place at the same time. As a result, simple cause-effect hypotheses are difficult to isolate and test, because, as just suggested, it is not easy to abstract two elements only of a complex world and test for the anticipated bivariate relationship. This was recognized early by geographers, who postulated multivariate hypotheses involving not only several independent variables acting on a dependent variable within a closed environment, but also those independent variables acting on each other, and thence on the dependent variable. Technical expertise was developed to handle such situations (Johnston, 1978) but a further problem was raised: can classical methods of inferential statistics be applied in spatial analysis? The problem of spatial autocorrelation raises a variety of technical and substantive issues. The technical issues, relating to the validity of inferential tests with data that are not from independent samples, because the value of one observation is related to that of its neighbours, have been tackled (e.g. Cliff and Ord, 1980), but the substantive issues have been largely ignored, raising doubts in a few minds about the validity of many statistical analyses.

In much research, a further problem has been associated with defining the geographical individual, the focus of study. Few people have addressed this directly. An exception is Chapman's (1977) discussion of the entitation problem, of the fact that 'Geography has consistently and dismally failed to tackle its entitation problems, and that in that more than anything else lies the root of so many of its problems' (p. 7). The spectrum of objects available for study ranges from the atom, through the plant and animal to the nation and the world–economy (which is a single unit). Somewhere along this continuum lies the geographer's object of study. Although he or she may collect data for, or use data collected from, individual units – be they people, shops or factories – the geographer is usually interested in some aggregation of these individuals, i.e. the population of a place (just, for example, as sociologists are interested in aggregations into classes and other groups). But what aggregation? As Chapman points out, the geographical concept of a region is somewhat vague, and gives little lead. (See also Simmons and Cox, 1985.)

This issue of entitation raises two problems. The first concerns populations and samples. If geographers are unsure what it is that they are studying, then this makes the design of experiments to test hypotheses extremely difficult. Secondly, there is the question of statistical validity. The results of, for example, a correlation analysis of the relationship between two variables is independent of neither the scale of the aggregation nor the actual aggregation at any particular scale. As Openshaw and Taylor (1980) have shown, the modifiable areal unit problem is such that with one data set (in this case the 99 counties of Iowa) it is possible to get a correlation between the percentage of the population aged over 60 of and the percentage voting Republican varying from -0.999 to 0.999 if the observations are aggregated into six 'regions' only, or between -0.949 and 0.745 if 36 'regions' are defined. (There is a very large number of ways in which 99 counties can be aggregated into 36 regions, let alone into six.) Which is the right correlation? If the geographer is not clear on the object being studied, answering this question is virtually impossible.

Systems analysis

A major conceptual and technical issue that has faced human geographers wishing to apply the positivist conception of science to their discipline concerns the difficulties of articulating theory about, modelling and experimenting on an exceedingly complex world organized by humans. The work discussed previously, on topics such as central place theory, presented and tested very simple hypotheses in the main, many of them straightforward cause-and-effect (or stimulus-response) sequences, involving single-cause models. Increasingly it was realized that the lack of convincing verification for these hypotheses reflected an over-simple view of reality, a belief that explanation could be advanced by the isolation of a very small section of the interrelationships that comprise the empirical world.

A realization that human geographers needed to tackle the complexity of their subject matter was associated with a developing interest in *systems*. Simply defined, a system is a set of elements, each with certain attributes, that are linked together in a particular way. Activation of the links (flows of some type between elements) operates the system, so that the analogy between system and organism (see p. 8) is a close one. The nature of the links between the elements governs not only the operation of the system but also, where relevant, its evolution. Processes of change are built into the system.

Any system is a simplification, since it represents an abstraction of a part of reality from its encompassing environment (which might be represented as other systems). The justification for any system is that it is relatively self-contained and thus presents a sensible focus for study. Links between the system and its environment will probably activate it, and in turn the system may deliver certain outputs to the environment. As such, the concept of a system has been advanced as a valuable perspective on the complexity of those aspects of reality studied by human geographers (see Bennett and Chorley, 1978).

The argument for the systems approach has been made by several writers, including Harvey (1969, Chapter 23). One of the strongest advocates has been Chorley, who has argued that, among other things, it provides a valuable means for integrating human and physical geography. By focusing on systems of interrelated components, which interact on each other, rather than producing simple cause-and-effect hypotheses:

> systems methods have illuminated thought, clarified objectives and cut through the theoretical and technical undergrowth (Bennett and Chorley, 1978, p. 540).

(Some geographers were attracted by general systems analysis which, in line with the logical positivist view on the unity of science, proposes that there are considerable similarities between the organization of many types of systems, and that investigation of these could well provide useful analogies for the study of geographical systems: see Chisholm, 1967; Harvey, 1969.) Fundamental to the systems approach is the modelling stage of the positivist procedures, for the aim of systems analysis is to provide a faithful representation of the interactions within a system rather than to extract a few simple relationships that can be submitted to empirical testing procedures. (A full description of systems modelling is Huggett, 1980.) Such modelling recognizes that most functional laws are not of the simple form $B = f(A)$, which states that the value of B is a function of the value of A, unless an over-simplified abstraction is to be undertaken. A system could well be structured in the following sequence (i.e. they operate after one another in time):

$$B = f(A)$$
$$C = f(B)$$
$$A = f(C)$$
$$D = f(C)$$
$$B = f(D)$$

which is represented diagrammatically in Figure 1.

If a simple hypothesis were to be extracted from this sequence it might well postulate a linear relationship between B as the dependent variable and A as the independent. This could be tested, using the positivist procedures. But by embedding that relationship in the structure of five equations which describes the entire functioning of the system, it is possible to realize that, in effect, $A = f(A)$, mediated through B and C. (In addition, D influences A through B and C, so that $A = f(A)$ is not a complete statement.) This is a feedback effect, with the state of A at one time partly influencing its state at the next.

The advantages claimed for the systems approach are several. First, by studying wholes rather than parts of wholes – the operation of an entire

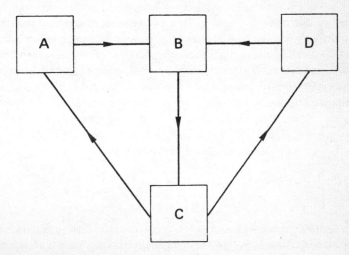

Figure 1

system rather than a few elements of it – geographical study is more
realistic. From this, secondly, flows the argument that explanation is more
comprehensive, because it is all-encompassing. Thus:

> whatever our philosophical views may be, it has been shown that
> methodologically the concept of the system is absolutely vital to the
> development of a satisfactory explanation (Harvey, 1969, p. 479).

And finally, stemming from more satisfactory explanation, is the greater
utility of the output. If systems analysis in geography can provide better
predictions and explanations than the other applications of the positivist
conception of science, then it is providing better tools for manipulating
systems – for social control.

Within human geography, attempts to introduce systems analysis and
the modelling of complex interrelationships have characterized certain areas
of economic geography, notably those concerned with economic growth in
an international, regional, or urban context. (A good example is the work
of Pred, 1977a, on the dynamics of urban growth, whose basis lies in the
input-output formulation of the structure of an economy. His initial
statements showed that urban growth becomes self-generating because of
the nature of the system. Expansion in one industry in a town generates
expansion in others through the extra purchasing power that it provides and
its increased demands for the products of other industries; such first-round
expansion generates even more in a second round – the other industries in
turn contribute extra purchasing power to the local economy – and so on.
He showed how such self-generating growth favours certain places –
mainly the large ones – and discriminates against others, leading to
alterations in the relative importance of settlements within the regional or
national system.) Much of this work on systems has stopped at the model-
building stage, because of problems of obtaining data to test the models as
wholes rather than as series of separate hypotheses. (For some examples, see
Bennett and Chorley, 1978.) Hence the introduction of a systems approach
has led to considerable acquisition of technical expertise by the discipline.

Systems of linked equations, such as those above, raise a number of
problems in calibration (fitting them to data), especially if understanding of
the system is incomplete and data and are not available for all of the links.
Thus the equations above (Figure 1) included:

$$B = f(A)$$
$$C = f(B)$$
$$A = f(C)$$

which could be simplified to $A = f(A)$, except that it must be made clear
that $A_t = f(A_{t-x})$, which states that the value of A at time t is a function of
the value of A at a previous time $(t - x)$, x units earlier. (It could be

extended to $A_t = f(A_{t-x}, A_{t-2x} \ldots .).$) Such a relationship is sometimes termed a 'black box', and sometimes as *instrumentalism* (Gregory, 1980). The investigator knows that A affects something else, which in turn affects A; that 'something else' cannot be isolated so the researcher merely calibrates a model which says that A affects A (somehow) and which thus provides a predictive device for estimating/forecasting future values of A. (For an introduction, see Bennett, 1979b.)

A major input to geography as spatial science has been the introduction of spatial components to systems analysis. Derived in particular from work on spatial interaction – especially with regard to diffusion (see above, p. 37) – geographers have argued that not only is:

$$A_t = f(A_{t-x})$$

which states that the value of A at time t at any point is a function of an earlier value of A there, but also:

$$A_{it} = f(A_{jt-x})$$

where the value of A at place i at time t is also a function of the value at place j at time t – x; the nature of the function – the degree to which the value at j influences the value at i – is usually assumed to relate to the distance between the two points i and j. Addition of a spatial to a temporal component extends the equations to:

$$A_{it} = f\left(\sum_{k=1}^{x} A_{i,t-k} \right) + f\left(\sum_{j=1}^{n} \sum_{k=1}^{x} A_{j,t-k} \right)$$

in which the value of a at place i and time t is a function of its value there at each preceding time (x units of length k: the first term of the equation) and at each preceding time at each other place (n) in the system (the second term in the equation). Such a systems model can be used to represent spatial variations in prices at agricultural markets, for example, with the price at one market being related both to the price there at previous dates and the price at adjacent markets, with the influence of the latter reflecting their distance from the market being studied (Martin and Oeppen, 1975). Calibrating such equations (i.e. fitting them to data) is technically demanding on data (Bennett, 1979b).

The systems approach is one, therefore, in which *the entire model is the hypothesis* rather than the source of separate hypotheses. As such, it offers a greater stimulus to the explanation of events because of its more holistic approach. Because of its technical problems, however, its application has not been widespread. This is particularly so if the models are not deterministic, so that they can only provide conditional predictions – because of either incomplete specification or randomness as an element in the system. Thus any realization – the actual pattern in the world – is but one of a very large number: from this, Chapman (1977) argues that a system is a set of objects for which a large number of potential states is feasible, and that the task for a human geographer involves identifying the nature of that feasible set and the likelihood of the observed situation arising. This approach has been taken furthest by Wilson (1970) in his work on traffic flows, which uses certain information about the system (where the workers live, where the jobs are, what the transport links are) to provide a best-estimate of 'unknowns' about the system (the commuting flows). His model is thus a prediction which can be tested. If it is a weak prediction (again, the problems of what is a satisfactory verification are paramount) he returns to the model and recalibrates it to try and improve its fit. (Other applications of this procedure now have estimating unmeasured attributes of a population from those that are known: Johnston, 1985b.)

The systems approach makes more explicit the naturalistic assumption underlying the positivist conception of social science. Systems of interest to human geographers are treated *as if they were machines*, comprising linked working parts which have little or no independent existence and whose positions in the system are predetermined. This is associated with the structural-functionalist approach to sociology advanced by Merton (1957). According to this, a system (e.g. a society, or a component of a society such as an individual organization) comprises a set of elements, each of which has a fixed place and function related to the system's goals. The nature of the system is fixed, therefore, and should be dissected readily. Also fixed is its dynamic of change. The relationship between elements may not be unalterable. The changes that occur result from the operations of the system itself (which may be exceedingly complex, as recent mathematical work in human geography has indicated: Wilson, 1981), however, so that change results from the operation of internal, not external, forces, which implies teleology. Identification of the forces for change provides a basis for even more sophisticated systems' control, and is the goal of work on the research frontier.

Positivism, empiricism and empirical research

In human geography (as in other social sciences: Platt, 1981) the term positivism has been used pejoratively by some, to attack those whose research – according to the critics – adopted the 'positivistic attitude'. In particular, quantification has sometimes been equated with positivism (as, implicitly, in Sayer, 1984), so that quantitative research (some of it undertaken by those who call themselves 'quantitative geographers': Bennett, 1985) has been a focus of the anti-positivist critique. The response to this has been to stress that although much empirical analysis is indeed rigorous in its use of certain methodological procedures derived from the natural sciences it does not promote the search for universal laws. In the terms of Giddens' (1974) definition of the 'positivistic attitude' (see p. 18), therefore, the first supposition (basically the assumption of realism; p. 28) is accepted; the second (the formulation of law-like generalizations) is not; and the third (the assumption of social engineering) may be.

A strong case can be made in support of this counter to the anti-positivist critique, if its foundation is a misplaced equation of quantification with positivism (Johnston, 1986b). Quantification is a tool that can be used in any of the approaches discussed in this book, as illustrated by Ley's (1974) humanistic study of a Philadelphia neighbourhood and Archer and Taylor's (1981) realist analysis of United States presidential elections. As Taylor (1981) expresses it with regard to factor analysis, it is

> best considered as simply a measurement technique . . . any research employing this tool is ultimately to be assessed not on technical grounds but in terms of the overall social model underlying the research (p. 251).

Indeed, Chouinard, Fincher and Webber (1984) argue that there is a great deal of similarity in the empirical research procedures of both positivist and realist approaches (see p. 111); each produces hypotheses regarding the empirical world being studied, and may evaluate those hypotheses using statistical procedures, but only the former applies the results of such evaluation in a law-building procedure.

Those who defend quantitative research against the charge that it is necessarily positivist argue that such a simplified representation involves a gross distortion of much empirical work. That some of it was indeed set in a positivist mould is not denied: Bennett (1981a), for example, admits that it

> consciously sought objectivity, technical expertise, spatial description and inductive approaches directed towards revealing universal laws which might be used to plan and control (p. 13).

His own case is that objectivity, technical expertise and applied use are desirable aspects of human geography (hence his call for an 'applied quantitative geography': Bennett, 1985), but that the search for laws is not. But if there are no laws – or generalizations – how can the results of the technical expertise be applied?

A similar, eventually paradoxical, argument has been presented by Golledge. In responding to a critique of behavioural geography by Bunting and Guelke (1979), he argued (Golledge, 1981) that

> there are substantial differences between the philosophy of logical positivism and a positivist philosophy. The latter, although entrenched firmly in scientific procedures is nowhere as epistemologically constrained as logical positivism (p. 1333).

He does not indicate what those constraints are, however, nor clearly distinguish the 'analytic geography' that he prefers (Couclelis and Golledge, 1983) from the positivist programme. Entrikin (1976) is quoted favourably, defining 'scientific geography' as

> an approach based upon empirical observation, public verifiability of conclusions and the importance of isolating fact from value (p. 616)

which is clearly not the full 'positivistic attitude'. But Entrikin is also quoted as saying that

> description, explanation, and prediction are important aspects of the scientific method (p. 631)

which introduces, through the terms explanation and prediction, all of the suppositions of the 'positivistic attitude'. Golledge's (1980) own words support this interpretation, for he has defended behavioural geography with the argument that

> by uncovering individual behaviour patterns and improving one's understanding of the reasons for such patterns, the researcher could aggregate populations into meaningful and significant sub-groups such that significant generalizations could be made about those particular sub-groups (p. 16).

And finally, he and Rushton argue (Golledge and Rushton, 1984) the need to reorient behavioural geography. In a seminal paper, Rushton (1969) distinguished between the study of *behaviour in space*, defined as the empirical description of observed choices, and that of *spatial behaviour*, defined as the search for the rules by which alternative locations are evaluated and choices consequently made. The former is empirical research; the latter, with its use of the term 'rules', implies a positivist approach. And Golledge and Rushton (1984) clearly favour the latter. They criticize a trend which seems 'to be emphasizing the behaviour in space paradigm once again' and bemoan that

> The *reasons* for behaviour – the forces of learning, choice, preference formation, cognition of opportunity sets and so on – have to a certain extent become somewhat neglected again (p. 29).

In recent work, Golledge *et al.* (1985) have promoted the use of artificial intelligence modelling in the depiction of behaviour, clearly implying that general rules of behaviour are present.

Quantitative empirical research need not be positivist, therefore, but the defences offered by Bennett and Golledge are perhaps unconvincing in their attempt to distance much of that research from the claim that it is indeed positivist. It is certainly the case that a substantial volume of research can probably best be described as 'quantitative empiricist' rather than positivist, in that it clearly accepts the first of Giddens' three suppositions regarding the 'positivistic attitude' but is equivocal on the other two. The development of such an orientation was at least in part a reaction to the perceived failings of the normative models that were popular in the early years of the 'quantitative and theoretical revolutions'. Industrial geographers, for example, abandoned the location theories that were the catalysts for earlier work (see p. 36) and turned instead to descriptive analyses of such topics as the desertion of inner cities by manufacturing industry (e.g. Lloyd, 1979), the impacts of government policies on the regional distribution of employment (e.g. Keeble, 1976), and the growth of industry in small towns (Fothergill and Gudgin, 1982). Such work was *ad hoc* and pragmatic and its hypotheses (if any were stated) were not deeply embedded in any theory; certainly there was little attempt to establish any law-like generalizations. In the view of Chouinard, Fincher and Webber (1984), and also of Sayer (1982, 1984), it was atheoretical research; the lack of a clear theoretical direction makes the meaning of the results difficult to interpret. It has

> raised novel issues for geographers to consider but its independence from prior theory guarantees that these issues and facts are problematic – precisely what variables should be investigated and how should the results be interpreted? The idea of evaluating theory with reference to evidence forms no part of this tradition (p. 351).

It is, then, quantitative empiricism, producing findings that may be valuable inputs to other research enterprises (p. 46) but in itself of no substantial value in the acquisition of knowledge – as against information.

Nevertheless, some at least of these quantitative empiricist studies are oriented towards application, and thus fulfil the third of Giddens's suppositions. In his work on *The geography of public finance*, for example, Bennett (1980) presented both a descriptive

> *who gets what* benefits from public finance is a function of *where* the individual lives (p. 1)

and a normative component

> Public finance in general and in its geographical components in particular, is aimed at eliminating, or at least reducing, the unequal treatment of individuals in society (p. 7).

His work has normative as well as positive ends, it seeks to prescribe as well as describe – as in the application of control theory to suggest the optimal distribution of government grants in England and Wales (Bennett, 1981b). It is part of a general orientation in which systems are modelled so that control strategies can be devised and implemented 'to manipulate socio-economic systems' (Bennett and Chorley, 1978, p. 443); this implies both the assumption of behaviourism and that of social engineering, thereby meeting all three of Giddens' suppositions.

Empiricism, positivism and empirical research are not the same thing, and quantification is not exclusive to any single philosophy. But much research using quantitative methods in human geography has been closer to the positivist than to any other approach. A considerable volume of it has been empiricist, assuming that reality can be observed and described in a neutral manner, but the theory underlying the empiricism has often been weakly developed. (All empiricism is theoretically based, for without a theory of knowledge it is impossible to classify observations according to agreed concepts. The problem, as Sayer (1985) and Chouinard, Fincher and Webber (1984) make clear, is that poor theory results in observations that are difficult to interpret; Sayer (1984) illustrates this with reference to the all-embracing category 'service industry' which covers such differing activities as plumbing and international finance.) Some of the work has explicitly been oriented to the development of generalizations. Other pieces have not, but the claim that they can be used in a policy context, in manipulating the future, implies acceptance of empirical generalizations.

The critique of positivism only focuses substantially on the use of quantitative procedures because of the concept of explanation that characterizes their use in that context. According to the 'positivistic attitude', application of the methods of natural science involves a particular concept of explanation: that any event can be accounted for as an example of a class of events. The test of a proposed explanation is the regularity of its outcome, and much quantitative work implies such regularity. For a realist such as Sayer (1985), however

> what causes something to happen has nothing to do with the matter of the number of times it has happened or been observed to happen and hence with whether it constitutes a regularity (p. 162)

for regularity implies continuity in the environment surrounding the event. It is, then, on the implications that are drawn from a quantitative empirical analysis that the critique of positivism focuses, and not on the nature of the procedures used: tools and goals, means and ends, must not be confused.

Summary

The positivist conception of science is a particular approach to knowledge based on clearly defined epistemological and ontological positions. Its epistemology – its statements regarding the nature of knowledge and how it can be obtained – is based on the evidence of experience and how that evidence is obtained; explanation of the world is to be achieved via structured (i.e. theory-led) observation of the world as examples of general categories (membership laws) and relationships (functional laws). Its ontology – its statements of what exists – backs this up, with arguments that only what is directly observable (and measurable, to many) is acceptable as evidence. Its methodology is the hypothetico-deductive progress towards explanation, with its emphasis on verification in replicable 'experiments' as the only evidence of the veracity of hypotheses.

The validity of such a philosophy for natural sciences is clear. Theories about nature can be developed, models of particular aspects of it built, hypotheses about certain relationships derived, and experiments designed to test their validity. Successful experiments, properly conducted and reported so that other scientists will accept their findings, have two outcomes. First, they increase the store of knowledge, of information structured in such a way that it can be related to other information: they provide the basis for universal laws and general theories. Secondly, they provide the means of predicting, of saying what will happen next in certain circumstances. This allows not only foresight but also manipulation. If one knows that to do something will produce something else, then one may be able to avoid the latter if it is unwanted or to produce it if it is desired.

The attractions of this conception to the social sciences are that it can advance explanation, providing knowledge of society rather than accumulations of fact. It can predict, which gives society foresight about itself. And it can provide the means for social control, for engineering society towards certain ends. In addition, there are many other, lesser features which appeal to social scientists, such as the ability to make valid statements about behaviour. Thus the positive social science advocated by Comte in the nineteenth century has become increasingly attractive, not only to those social scientists who have sought to advance knowledge, their disciplines, and themselves, but also to the employers of social scientists, who have perceived the potential of obtaining useful information.

In human geography, as outlined here, the adoption of the positivist conception of science after the Second World War led to a major reorientation of geographical work. Certain aspects of the approach were emphasized – such as measurement, data collection, and the statistical testing of hypotheses – whereas others were relatively ignored. The result has been a great volume of work seeking to establish relationships in space, to display the correlations between distributions and to account for the characteristics of particular places in the light of those correlations. In terms of knowledge – as against information – the value of much of this work is questioned by some, because of its lack of theoretical articulation and its apparent irrelevance to real explanation. (To others, as indicated above, this is seen as a benefit.) Technically, work has become much more sophisticated in a short space of time. Substantively, a large number of topics has been tackled. Description is precise, but has understanding been advanced far?

The problems of the positivist approaches to geography are grouped into two categories. The first reflect Keat's (1981) list of positivist claims discussed above. Is the positivist conception of science the only approach to knowledge? Does positivism offer rational solutions to social problems? And is positivism value free? The second group, linked to these, relates to epistemology and ontology. Is experience (structured via experiment) the only means of knowing? Is the phenomenal environment the only source of evidence for explanation? Is explanation feasible? Are mechanistic models valid for the study of people? Is social control via science desirable? The philosophy which some human geographers have adopted is that of the positivist conception of science. The philosophy of logical positivism is that knowledge is only attainable in this way. Although human geographers have in general not accepted the latter, it is still possible to ask whether the subject matter that they have studied positivistically is properly studied in that way. Is too much human geography set in the positivist mould? Should any of it be?

3

Humanistic approaches

The basic feature of humanistic approaches is their focus on the individual as a thinking being, as a human, rather than as a dehumanized responder to stimuli in some mechanical way, which is how some feel people are presented in the positivist and structuralist social sciences. There is a variety of such approaches, for which there is no agreed collective noun. Their common element is a stress on the study of people as they are, by a researcher who has as few presuppositions as possible. The aim is to identify the true nature of human action, and this end, and the means proposed to achieve it, represents the development of philosophies of and for the social sciences, rather than the adoption of philosophies developed for other realms of investigation.

Varieties of humanistic research

There is a wide variety of humanistic approaches within the social sciences, which differ in many ways but which are in general agreement about the main subject matter of the social sciences: the subjectivity of both observer and observed. Their goal is to examine that subjectivity (especially that of the observed) as objectively as possible; the exact nature of that goal and the means by which it can be pursued have been the subject of considerable debate, both between and within the major humanistic schools. This chapter, like the previous one, does not set out to review the history and nature of those debates in any detail. Rather it is a presentation of the major elements of four main humanistic approaches, which in varying degrees have all been presented as relevant to work in human geography.

Idealism

Idealism is a philosophy with a long history and deep tradition. Its basic tenet, that all reality is in some way a mental construction so that the world does not exist outside its observation and representation by the individual, has long been posed against the positivist epistemology and its emphasis on objective evidence. To some, as Ewing (1934) points out, idealism involves the belief that human ordering of the universe is determined by spiritual values. This he claims is a restricted definition, however: idealism embraces a wider range of philosophies that

> have in common the view that there can be no physical objects existing apart from some experience, and this might perhaps be taken as the definition of idealism, provided we regard thinking as a part of experience and do not imply by 'experience' passivity, and provided we include under experience not only human experience but . . . the experience of a God (p. 3).

This requires a definition of physical objects. Ewing argues that the position ascribed to an idealist depends on the acceptance of one or more of the following three arguments:

> (a) because of a general theory of knowledge which implies that no object can exist apart from a knowing mind, (b) because he holds that the particular characteristics of matter logically imply an experiencing or thinking mind, or (c) because he holds that physical objects, while not implying a mind on which they depend, are themselves of the nature of experience or are physical entities of some kind (p. 5).

According to the idealist view, therefore, people build up their own pictures of the world, within which their actions are predicated. The nature of those pictures is to some extent determined by the purpose for which they are being constructed, but:

> we are active in cognition and never arrive at a fact merely by sensation or by passively receiving data but always understand it in terms of preconceived, though not usually explicitly formulated, theories . . . . We cannot . . . apprehend the real without thought (Ewing, 1934, p. 235).

People, as active beings, develop theories to guide their actions. Such guidance includes the direction of future thinking, the interpretation of perceptions, and the nature of decision-making. The theories are developed inductively, by a learning process in which new knowledge is incorporated within theories.

For theories to be developed, and for evidence to be assessed and interpreted, criteria must be used. Central to idealism, therefore, is its coherence theory, which includes: a definition of truth; an account of the nature of reality; and a criterion of truth (Ewing, 1934, p. 195). To positivists, a proposition is correct when it accords with the objective evidence; to idealists it is correct when it coheres with accepted theories. Coherence implies a systematic view of the world:

> (a) that everything is causally determined; (b) that everything is, directly or indirectly, causally connected with everything else, so that there is no series of events in the universe which is causally independent of all events outside that series; (c) that the relation of causality involves a relation of logical entailment,

so that whatever is causally impossible is also logically impossible relative to the rest of the causal system (Ewing, 1934, p. 231).

Thus all new knowledge must fit into the orbit of existing theory – it must be logically related to it – because that theory is of an interdependent world. Eventually, therefore, for a theory to be coherent it must be comprehensive. This, however, is a goal to be sought rather than a reality – en route:

To assert separately from the rest is not to deny the rest (Ewing, 1934, p. 234).

Theories are built up (and if necessary modified) through learning; because knowledge within a theory must cohere, the test of a theory lies in a dilemma: 'Believe this or believe nothing'. One holds on to a belief until it appears that holding such a belief creates incoherence in theories of other parts.

Idealism, then, is a philosophy which proposes that knowledge is entirely subjective. It is ordered by individuals according to their own theoretical systems, which are modified in the light of new knowledge but whose criterion of truth is internal to the theory – 'Does it all fit together?' – rather than external to it. To study human decision-making, according to this view, involves studying the decision-makers and the personal theories that guide them.

This idealist philosophy has received favour among some historians, who have argued against the positivist view, which to some suggests a pre-determined plan by which history unfolds, if it is to be subject to laws and generalizations. Thus, according to Collingwood (1965, p. 36):

The plan which is revealed in history is a plan which does not pre-exist prior to its own revelation; history is a drama, but an extemporized drama, cooperatively extemporized by its own performers.

Pursuing this analogy, Collingwood argues that every piece of history has its own plot, and it is the task of the historian to discover that plot:

To look for a plot in history means seeing history in its individuality, seeing every incident in it as an irreplaceable and unique element in an irreplaceable and unique whole; whereas looking in history for instances of general laws means failing to group the individuality of history and seeing every incident in it as a mere reduplication of a ready-made type, and the whole as a chaotic assemblage of such reduplications (Collingwood, 1965, p. 210).

Collingwood's philosophy of history, therefore, is of a discipline which:

seeks to study the activities of the human spirit not by setting up imaginary instances of them, like the artist, nor yet by substituting for them a mechanical play of abstract types, like the psychologist, but by apprehending them in their full actuality (p. 47).

He studies human decision-making as the outcome of individual theories.

In Collingwood's philosophy of history, idealism refers not only to the objects of the historians' study but also to the individual historians. They, too, are developing personal theories of past events, assimilating new knowledge and applying a coherence theory and its criterion of truth as the method of assessing interpretations: 'Does it all fit together?'. In part they must do this because of the lack of certainty about historical 'facts'. The historian erects a skeleton of theory:

> some working hypothesis as to the things especially worth noticing, especially crucial in their revelation of the nature of the process in which they occur. In reality . . . history has no skeleton; when we fully understand any historical event, each element in it appears as crucial as the rest; but the optical illusion that it has a skeleton is inevitably generated by our own ignorance (p. 39).

The skeleton is always likely to be partial, however. Indeed, there will be many skeletons, representing the views of individual historians, all exercising individual judgement on the information available to them and how it fits with their interpretations and reconstructions of the events of earlier periods. Thus:

> Everyone brings his own mind to the study of history . . . The attempt to eliminate this 'subjective element' from history is always insincere – it means keeping your own point of view while asking other people to give up theirs – and always unsuccessful (p. 138).

Collingwood's philosophy of history, therefore, is one based on what he calls the historical imagination. Each event in the past has what he calls an outside and an inside (Collingwood, 1946, p. 213). The outside comprises the observable conditions relating to it, whereas the inside involves the thoughts behind it. An historian must study both:

> His work may begin by discovering the outside of an event, but it can never end there; he must always remember that the event was an action, and that his main task is to think himself into this action, to discern the thought of its agent (Collingwood, 1946, p. 213).

The study of history, then, involves 'knowledge of mind', which involves the historians putting themselves in the context of the relevant actors so that they can re-enact both the thought and the action.

This idealist history is more than what Collingwood terms 'common-sense history', which is based on memory and authority: memory involves the statements of the actors, as in the various surviving texts; authority implies that the memory is believed. But the historians must not take such statements at their face value. They must subject them to criticism, testing the extent to which they fit into their 'web of imaginative construction', their theory of how and why the actors did what they did. To stress this point, Collingwood draws an analogy between historians and novelists, and uses a detective story as illustration:

> Each of them makes it his business to construct a picture which is partly a narrative of events, partly a description of situations, exhibition of motives, analysis of characters. Each aims at making his picture a coherent whole. . . . The novel and the history must both of them make sense . . . Where they . . . differ is that the historian's picture is meant to be true (Collingwood, 1946, pp. 245–6).

To approach truth, the historian is constrained by three rules: the subject matter must be localized in place and time; the pieces must be consistent with one another; and the construction must be consistent with the available evidence.

Idealist history involves the reconstruction of the context of actions. The historians rethink the thoughts of their subjects, in a way which is consistent both with their conception of the whole of which those thoughts are a part and with the available evidence. On these criteria, it is argued, all inquiries are historical, whether they are concerned with individuals seeking to reconstruct their own ideas or with the study of others. Once performed, all human action is history, and it can only be accounted for by application of the idealist method and the exercise of the historical imagination. (See Hirst, 1985.)

Pragmatism
The philosophy of pragmatism was developed in the United States during the late nineteenth and early twentieth centuries, initially by Charles Peirce and William James (Ayer, 1968), and later by John Dewey, C.I. Lewis and George Herbert Mead. Like idealism, it is based on the belief that actions are structured by meanings, by subjective interpretations of the world. Those interpretations are evaluated in terms of their practical implications, so that truth is defined as that which it is satisfactory to believe, either because the belief is fulfilled or because (like certain aspects of religious beliefs) it contributes to the believer's level of personal satisfaction. This leads to the simple definitions that

> pragmatism . . . defines meaning and knowledge in terms of their function in experience, with reference to adjustment and the resolution of problematic situations (Beck, 1969, p. 515)

and

> pragmatism is a doctrine holding that the meaning and truth of thought is determined (somehow) by criteria of practical usefulness (Thayer, 1973, p. 5).

The latter is an inaccurate generalization, Thayer contends, for the criterion of utility characterizes much older philosophies. His own definition, in full, is

> A theory of knowledge, experience and reality maintaining: (a) that thought and knowledge are biologically and socially evolved modes of adaptation to and control over experience and reality: (b) that reality possesses a transitional character and that thought is a guide to the realization and satisfaction of our interests and purposes: (c) that all knowledge is evaluative of future experiences and that thinking functions experimentally in anticipations of future experiences and consequences of actions – thus in organizing conditions of future observations and experience. Thought is a behavioural process manifested in controlled actualizations of selected, anticipated and planned possibilities of future experience (p. 227).

Thus society changes as beliefs are actualized. Possibilities are addressed and meanings attached to them with 'reference to the ordinary situations and conditions in which actions occur' (p. 225). Choice is then made, according to criteria of utility (ideas are instruments, and 'one understands instruments by getting to understand their uses'), and as a result certain future possibilities are closed down whereas others are opened up. Thus we live in a 'plastic world', one about which we make conjectures and act accordingly: knowledge is developed via practical trial and error. (Thus Ayer, 1968, p. 15, claims that 'the theory of scientific method for which Professor Popper has become justly celebrated in our own times was very largely anticipated by Peirce'.)

Truth, to Peirce and the pragmatists, is not synonymous with belief, however. The cause of beliefs is what he terms the *real*, that which is (Thayer, 1973)

> unaffected by what we may think about it, influences our sensations, which in turn cause thinking (p. 65).

To every question, therefore, there is a true (i.e. real) answer, and it is towards that answer – the final opinion – to which human thought, with all its inaccuracies and limitations, is moving. That movement is undertaken via the scientific method that uses hypothetico-deductive argument and tests its propositions empirically but (Thayer, 1973)

> since we have no access to the Real except by means of conceptual interpretation, pragmatically the real *is* what, in the final opinion, thought represents it to be (p. 66).

We seek the final truth – but can never be sure that we know it!

The practice of pragmatism, of experience, experiment and evaluation in the continual reconstruction of beliefs, is a social and not an individual activity, according to the social behaviourism of George Herbert Mead, which built on Peirce's pragmatism. Thus (Mead, 1934)

We are not, in social psychology, building up the behaviour of the social group in terms of the behaviour of the separate individuals composing it. . . . We attempt . . . to explain the conduct of the individual in terms of the organized conduct of the social group . . . the whole (society) is prior to the part (the individual), not the part to the whole; and the part is explained in terms of the whole, not the whole in terms of the part (p. 7)

so that

the behaviour of an individual can be understood only in terms of the behaviour of the whole social group of which he is a member, since his individual acts are involved in larger, social acts which go beyond himself and which implicate the other members of that group (p. 6).

This interactionist perspective strongly influenced the Chicago School of Sociology founded by Park and Burgess (see Jackson and Smith, 1984), and was the basis for the many detailed ethnographic studies conducted there (using the method that Burgess and Bogue, 1967, termed 'sympathetic introspection', which is similar to participant observation). The social inter-action through which attitudes and beliefs are learned and developed occurs in places, producing what Park termed 'natural areas': a 'unit in the physical structure of the city, typified by a physical identity and the characteristic attitudes, sentiments, and interests of the people segregated within it' (Zorbaugh, 1926, p. 190). Thus, as later perspectives (such as struc-turation; p. 114) have also suggested, the construction and reconstruction of society – the search for truth in Peirce's terms – is a spatially situated activity.

Participant observation is presented as the methodology for uncovering the contents of those natural areas; it involves the researcher becoming a part of the society being studied, in order to appreciate its beliefs and how they are being reconstructed in the context of the effects of their application. It can take a variety of forms (Gold, 1958). The participant-as-observer, for example, is a researcher who becomes a fully involved active member of a community, developing relationships with others which allows reporting of activities 'from the inside'. The observer-as-participant, on the other hand, obtains access but then observes and records with little, if any, active participation. (Styles vary according to context; the former is relevant to the study of a village community, for example, and the latter to the study of a company board of directors.) The methodology is not tied to specific techniques; observing and reporting, formal interviews, and structured questionnaires (with quantitative analysis of the data) may all be relevant to a particular situation. It raises many ethical problems regarding the conduct and reporting of such research, particularly if access has not been negotiated (see Barnes, 1979; Mitchell and Draper, 1982).

The results of such participant observation could be employed simply as academic voyeurism, as insights to particular case studies but no more. This was not the goal of the pragmatists, however, whose view was that knowledge should be used to guide the future. Certainly this was the case with the work of the Chicago School: Burgess and Bogue (1967) describe their ambition as

> to understand and interpret the social and economic forces at work in the slums and their effect in influencing the social and personal organization of those who lived there. Although the objective was scientific, behind it lay a faith or hope that this scientific analysis would help dispel prejudice and injustice and ultimately would lead to an improvement in the lot of slum dwellers (p. 5).

and Lewis introduced his classic *La vida* (1957) with

> my hope that a better understanding of the nature of the culture of poverty will eventually lead to a more sympathetic view of the poor and their problems and will provide a more rational basis for constructive social action (p. 14).

Phenomenology and its relations

Phenomenology is a philosophy of science based on the same foundations as idealism: all knowledge is subjective. It seeks to analyse and identify the basic features of subjective knowledge, not only to provide an understanding of the individual but also in the practical sense of 'making life itself more significant' (Spiegelberg, 1976, p. 79) by uncovering its meanings and values. Thus its:

> primary objective is the direct investigation and description of phenomena as consciously experienced, without theories about their causal explanation and as free as possible from unexamined preconceptions and presuppositions (Spiegelberg, 1975, p. 3).

The development of phenomenology is associated with the pioneering work of the German philosopher Edmund Husserl (see Farber, 1943; Pickles, 1985). This was based on earlier conceptions of how to study the subjective and spawned a wide range of positions which are generally accepted as phenomenological (see the listing in Spiegelberg, 1975, p. 10; also Wolff, 1979). The common ground to such work includes:

1 The belief that people should be studied free of any preconceived theories or suppositions about how they act. The observer's view of the world should be suspended (put into abeyance – Husserl's term for this is *bracketing*), so that interpretations are not contaminated by concepts and potential explanations that are alien to the subject.
2. The search for understanding (represented by the German word *verstehen* – see below) or appreciation of the nature of an act is the goal of social science, rather than explanation (the term associated with positivism and its emphasis on objective evidence).

3. The belief that for people the world exists only as a mental construction, created in acts of *intentionality*. An element is brought into an individual's world only when he or she gives it meaning because of some intention towards it.

The goal of phenomenology, then, is to reconstruct the worlds of individuals, the phenomena in those worlds which are there as repositories of meaning. This leads to an understanding of behaviour in those worlds, which is not the same as a positivist's explanation, since the latter is a construct imposed by the analyst whereas an understanding uses the terms and concepts of the actor (Entrikin, 1976). But the nature of that reconstruction enterprise varies considerably, and has led Spiegelberg (1975, pp. 15–16) to recognize five types of phenomenology:

1. *Descriptive phenomenology* – the presentation of material (phenomena) in the life-worlds of the individuals studied.
2. *Essential phenomenology* – the identification of essences (the essential characteristics or meanings) of phenomena. This (sometimes known as eidetic intuition) involves moving beyond the surface manifestations of the allocation of meanings to the underlying processes involved, studying:

> experiences that can be analysed in intuition in their essential generality and not
> . . . experiences as real occurrences in the natural world (Farber, 1943, p. 211).

General essences, then, are universals underpinning particular examples (such as colour). Particulars can then be studied as examples of such generalities (with the relationship being defined by the subject and not by the observer). From this, the phenomenologist can then move to the apprehension of essential relationships, the articulation within and between general essences, and the ways in which subjective theories are developed.
3. *The phenomenology of appearances* – the study of how essences take shape, as intentionality operates and meanings are assigned.
4. *Constitutive phenomenology* – essences, and essential relationships, develop as patterns that become part of consciousness. Constitutive phenomenology studies how such consciousness develops.
5. *Hermeneutic phenomenology* – the interpretation of meanings which are concealed in consciousness and which are 'not immediately manifest to our intuiting, analysing and describing' (Spiegelberg, 1976, p. 695).

Not all phenomenologists, Spiegelberg argues, either accept or practise all five of these. Many practise descriptive and essential phenomenology only, arguing that the other three are impossible tasks, since the observer cannot enter into the mind of the subject. These arguments are particularly relevant to the adoption of phenomenology in certain social sciences (notably sociology – see below, p. 68).

The focus of phenomenology, therefore, is the understanding of human action through the study of meanings allocated to the elements of the individual's life-world. This is not subjective empiricism, however, for it is founded on the belief that such meanings, the characteristics ascribed by individuals (including practising scientists) to phenomena, are the products of general essences that exist within human consciousness, and which – some phenomenologists believe – can themselves be appreciated. Further, the aim of phenomenology is not only to understand but, by understanding, to enrich life by increasing human awareness. Thus:

> the phenomenological approach is opposed to exploratory hypotheses: it confines itself to the direct evidence of intuitive seeing . . . it constitutes a determined attempt to enrich the world of our experience by bringing out hitherto neglected aspects of this experience . . . [displaying] an omniverous desire for variety . . . [or] unusually obstinate attempt to look at the phenomena and to remain faithful to them before even thinking about them (Spiegelberg, 1976, p. 700).

It begins, therefore, by the study of the 'natural attitude', the life-world which individuals accept and live in, without questioning, although in all encounters with elements there may be suspicion. Having identified the contents of the natural attitude, it then seeks to articulate the general essences that underlie it and, from those, the absolute knowledge that resides in consciousness.

As to phenomenological method, this is frequently summarized by a phrase of Husserl's – 'to the things' – interpreted as implying that phenomena (i.e. the meanings given to items in the individual's life-world) must be transmitted to the phenomenologist without intermediaries. Access must be gained to the subject's consciousness, therefore. As Spiegelberg (1975, p. 46) recognizes, complete access to the subject's mind is impossible, but:

> This does not mean that our perception of other selves is infallible. It may be subject to the usual, plus some unusual, illusions to which all uncritical, and perhaps even some critical, perception is exposed. All the same, here is the only possible gataway to all knowledge of others.

Several routes to this gateway are suggested by Spiegelberg. It may be possible, for example, for a trained observer to identify (perhaps by inference) certain feelings, and thus meanings, in the subject's actions: this raises the problem, however, that 'We may see his eyes as seeing but we cannot see what it is that he sees through these eyes' (Spiegelberg, 1975, p. 46). Thus, bracketing may not be achieved by the observer. Nevertheless, because we cannot see through the eyes of others, approximate solutions to that problem must be found. Spiegelberg suggests two.

The first of these phenomenological methods is *imaginative self-transposal*, which:

requires that the investigator imagines himself as occupying the real place of the other and view from there the world as it would present itself in this new perspective . . . [the investigator] adapts imaginatively as much as . . . [he or she] can of the frame of mind of the other person. Clues for this adoption are to be derived from firsthand perception of the other and from facts of his available biography . . . the ability to vary oneself in imagination is easily one of the most remarkable capacities of the human self (Spiegelberg, 1975, pp. 48–9).

Thus, it is suggested, essential insights can be achieved by vicarious imagination rather than by perception, by the observers attempting to translate themselves into the subjects' situation and from that position reconstructing their life-worlds. The method is reflective.

The second method is *cooperative encounter and exploration*, a procedure associated with Freud's psychoanalysis. Subject and analyst embark on a joint exploration of the former's life-world, in a relationship of mutual trust and respect. Within this, the subject:

by putting his [i.e. the subject's] own perspective – to the best of his communicative ability – at the disposal of the phenomenological analyst, provides him[the analyst] with a unique extension of his operating base. Now the analyst can really use the eyes of the [subject] . . . Yet he must not be under the illusion that these eyes are his own eyes. They remain at best new mirrors, and by no means undistorting mirrors (Spiegelberg, 1975, p. 51).

The new material gained in this way should not only increase the analyst's insights but also provide a better foundation for exercises in imaginative self-transposal. By combining the two techniques, analyst and subject together should be able to penetrate further into the meanings of the latter's life-world.

The only true phenomenology is first-hand phenomenology: the study of oneself through pure reflection. The methods described above are approximations of true phenomenology only. This raises a number of prolems. Criteria of truth can be applied in self-study, but not in either imaginative self-transposal or cooperative encounter and exploration. Thus two phenomenologists, studying the same subject, may achieve different insights. Furthermore, neither can know which is right. (This last argument applies particularly to descriptive phenomenology – see below.) Perhaps most importantly, phenomenological investigation is dependent upon communication, upon intersubjectivity (the making of one's meanings – the interpretations placed on the elements of the life-world – available to others). Not only does this imply specific problems regarding the communicative abilities of subject and analyst but also, more generally, it raises major questions regarding the nature of the communication text, which is most commonly expressed in language. As Giddens (1979, pp. 40–1) argues:

a gulf divides the text, as a particular articulation of language, from whatever intention an author may have had in writing it.

Thus:

> To argue that texts can be illuminatingly studied as situated productions is to insist that there are connections between the two ways in which 'meaning' is ordinarily employed in English: what someone means to say, write or do, and what that which is said, written or done means.

(The difference is between intention and interpretation.) This creates problems for the procedure of bracketing, with the analysts suspending their own interpretations of words:

> One of the main tasks of the study of the text, or indeed cultural products of any kind, must be precisely to examine the divergencies which can become intuited between the circumstances of their production and the meanings sustained by their subsequent escape from the horizon of their creator or creators. These meanings are never 'contained' in the text as such . . . *the consequences of actions chronically escape their initiators' intentions in processes of objectification* (p. 44).

Given that phenomenological methods can penetrate life-worlds and thence provide insight into general essences, it is then possible to pursue other aspects of phenomenology. Husserl's aims were not merely to explicate individual life-worlds. He sought to identify the nature of that which is left, absolute knowledge, after the empirical individual subject is bracketed away. (This is what Husserl called *epoché*, making 'only such judgements as do not depend for their validity on a spatio-temporal world'; Bauman, 1978, p. 119.) The residue is:

> pure consciousness: consciousness which is not anybody's, consciousness free of all earthly attachments . . . [lacking] tradition, history, culturally pre-defined patterns of cognition, social practice . . . [leaving as a residue] the tough nucleus which is explicable only for itself, and not reducible any more to either tradition, culture or society (Bauman, 1978, p. 121).

It is the content of the human mind which has not been socialized, nor has it received any of the learned meanings of a milieu. Husserl's belief in the existence of such pure consciousness or absolute knowledge is represented as a belief in transcendental subjectivity – a seat of all meanings. Its discovery requires the disposal of empirical meanings and the retention of that which is given to humans *a priori*. Thus he presented phenomenology as a science, as a procedure (transcendental reduction) which would identify absolute truth (hence in the end two phenomenologists could not disagree) rather than provide an alternative focus on the mundane.

To Husserl, transcendental reduction would assist the solution of the problems of hermeneutic phenomenology, involving the interpretation of the meanings of the contents of pure consciousness. Initially, the field of *hermeneutics* involved the interpretation of theological texts. It is now used for the interpretation of all texts, with the goal of understanding their authors' meanings. (Thus hermeneutics is involved in all communication; positivist scientists are presenting their interpretation of the world, for example.)

The term *verstehen* – interpretative understanding – is generally associated with the goals of hermeneutics. According to Outhwaite (1975), four aspects of a person may be studied: physical facts – which may signify aspects of non-physical facts (e.g. a mental state); state of mind; what he or she is doing; and why something is being done, what its motivation is. *Verstehen* is involved in the fourth of these:

> we 'understand' people's states of mind (and make inferences about their motives and intentions) with the aid of: (a) visible signs, voluntary or involuntary . . .; (b) explicit statements . . .; (c) a knowledge of the 'facts of the situation' which leads us to expect one sort of attitude or intention rather than another . . . [by understanding] we mean not that we know what it is to feel these emotions or the force of certain motives . . . but rather that we understand the 'situation' in which these emotions or intentions 'make sense' (Outhwaite, 1975, p. 15).

Thus hermeneutics seeks to explicate the meanings behind actions, to provide an appreciation of why a certain action was taken, rather than to explain it. It is an appreciation of context rather than an attempt at prediction.

Verstehen as a concept is associated with the philosopher Wilhem Dilthey, who differed from Husserl over the issue of pure consciousness (Rose, 1981). It is close to idealism in that it seeks to understand why people did what they did, and do what they do, in terms of their personal theories. It introduces the phenomenological concept of meaning to this context – the life-world is made up of the products of intentionality, the assumptions people make about elements in their consciousness. It is achieved, according to Gadamer (see Outhwaite, 1975, p. 104 and Giddens, 1976, pp. 55-7), through *discourse*. In the study of contemporary events, this is a discourse between subject and analyst. In the study of the past:

> Understanding a text from a historical period remote from our own . . . or from a culture very different from our own is . . . essentially a creative process in which the observer, through penetrating an alien mode of existence, enriches his own self-knowledge through acquiring knowledge of others (Giddens, 1976, p. 17).

The dialogue, via texts, both enriches the analyst's understanding and enables the subject to divulge meanings; the analyst learns to live the life of the subjects by participating in their language. Hermeneutics, then, is basically an empirical science, in that it seeks to explicate meanings at the phenomenal level and does not seek universal truths lying beneath those meanings.

Phenomenology was developed largely as a science of studying the individual, as a counter to certain contemporary trends in psychology. For some social sciences, therefore, notably those involved in the study of society itself rather than the individuals who constitute it, there was a need to adapt the phenomenological perspective to their ends. Such was the task undertaken by Alfred Schutz, whose research focused on what is described in the title of his major work, explicating *The phenomenology of the social world* (Schutz, 1972). This was set in the general context of phenomenology, with its goal of advancing intersubjective understanding and its foundation in the subjectivity of the life-world. But Schutz argued that the everyday social world is a 'taken-for-granted' world, which is not normally reflected on when actions occur:

> In the world of routine, everything is taken for granted and therefore unknown . . . most routine tasks of daily life are accomplished without engaging human analytical powers . . . The world of routine . . . is not, therefore, an object of active interpretation or re-interpretation. Unless challenged, we have no 'need' to motivate routine actions to others and to ourselves (Bauman, 1978, pp. 176–7).

Given this foundation, *interpretative sociology* does not seek to undertake hermeneutic discourse, nor to engage in transcendental reduction. Instead, it is looking for general meanings which exist as part of the routine of daily life, in a life-world whose meanings are fixed:

> What we are thus seeking is the invariant, unique, a priori structure of the mind, in particular of a society composed of living minds (Schutz, 1972, p. 44).

The taken-for-granted world comprises a 'stock of knowledge'. Within it – and 'based upon a stock of previous experiences of it, our own experiences and those handed down to us by our parents and teachers' (Schutz, 1971, p. 208) – activity occurs. Such activity is of two types: *action* involves the intent to do something, and when completed it constitutes a performance; *conduct* is spontaneous. Both types of activity involve operating within the taken-for-granted world of implicit meanings. One reacts habitually to certain stimuli (which is not to claim, of course, that all people react in the same way, for the same stimulus may be given different meanings in different life-worlds).

Schutz's proposed methodology for the study of the phenomenology of the social world was based on his appreciation of the sociology of Max Weber, not only their shared belief in the crucial importance of subjective meanings as the controllers of action and conduct but also Weber's analytical procedures. Regarding the former, Schutz (1972, p. 6) stressed that sociology is the 'study of social behaviour by interpreting its subjective meaning as found in the intentions of individuals'. Regarding the latter, he proposed a methodology based on Weber's conception of ideal types:

> Again and again Weber refers to the problem of the ideal type as the central problem of all the social sciences. Our studies have shown how well-founded this conception is. For the world of contemporaries and the world of predecessors can only be comprehended in an ideal-typical way (Schutz, 1972, p. 226).

Meanings can be studied in one of three ways, he argues: those expressing the intentions of a particular person in a particular context (which is the domain of history); those expressed as averages (the domain of statistics); and those expressing the intentions of an ideal-typical actor, which are the subject matter of intepretative sociology. The only social reality that can be comprehended, given the inability to penetrate the mind of others, is that typically comprehended.

The study of ideal types is presented by Schutz as the best of several possible ways of achieving an understanding of the taken-for-granted world and of action and conduct within it. The analysts could seek to study themselves in a similar situation, and project their behaviour on that of the subject, or they could study the subject's behaviour and infer both the effect of the action and its relationships to the intended effect (i.e. the motive). Schutz's preference is for a methodology in which:

> he can resort to his own knowledge of the customary behaviour of the person involved and from this deduce the latter's in-order-to and because-motives (Schutz, 1972, p. 175)

from knowledge of the type to which the subject belongs. Thus the observer identifies types within the population, individuals who have 'one and only one typical motive for a typical act' (Schutz, 1972, p. 188).

Typification is valuable for the analyst both because it circumvents some of the problems of phenomenological method and hermeneutic discourse – especially with regard to a taken-for-granted world whose essences cannot be plumbed – and also because it is a representation of how the taken-for-granted world is structured by subjects. Individuals perform typical acts because they have typified the world, and so the task of the interpretative sociologist is to identify those separate typifications. Such types are not 'formed by social scientists at random without check or restraint' (Schutz, 1964, p. 18). They must comply with four postulates: first, relevance; second, adequacy – 'each term . . . must be so constructed that a human act performed within the life-world by an individual actor in the way indicated by the typical construction would be reasonable and understandable for the actor himself as well as his fellow-man' (p. 19); third, logically consistent; and fourth, compatible – 'The system of ideal types must contain only scientifically verifiable assumptions, which have to be fully compatible with the whole of our scientific knowledge' (p. 19). Together:

> These postulates give the necessary guarantees that social sciences do in fact deal with the real social world, the one and unitary life-world of us all, and not with a strange fancy-world independent of and without connection to this everyday life-world (p. 19).

Thus his phenomenology of the taken-for-granted world can be submitted to positivist evaluation as a true representation of action.

Related to Schutz's work is the field of *ethnomethodology*: 'Schutz supplied theoretical foundations to what ethnomethodology presented as a programme of empirical study' (Bauman, 1978, p. 188). The role of the ethnomethodologist, according to Garfinkel (1967), is to make the ways in which people conduct their daily lives accountable, i.e. 'observable and reportable'. It is, then, the study of the methodologies used by individuals to structure and carry out their daily lives. Such study is intersubjective, in that it involves understanding procedures that are common-sense to the subjects (common-sense involves subjects 'taking for granted that what is said will be made out in accordance with methods that need not be specified': Garfinkel, 1967, p. 30). Thus:

> the anticipation that persons *will* understand, the occasionality of expressions, the specific vagueness of references, the retrospective- prospective sense of a present occurrence, waiting for something later in order to see what was meant before, are sanctioned properties of common discourse (Garfinkel, 1967, p. 41).

Ethnomethodologists study the contents of that common discourse (such as conversations) in order to identify the methodologies of taken-for-granted worlds. They are not academic voyeurs, acting randomly. They aim, like other social scientists who base their research on phenomenology, to get below what Bauman (1978, p. 189) calls 'the technology of life', to identify its basic meanings, even if they cannot comprehend how these meanings are produced. Thus:

> Phenomena best serve the purposes of ethnomethodological empirical activity if reduced to window-panes through which one could look directly to the intricate clockwork which they hide rather than disclose in daily life. But then the ethnomethodologist would not be interested in specific, non-universal and contingent shapes of cog-wheels and catches which made the phenomena as they are: he would try instead to model the 'general', indispensable properties of the clockwork purified as much as possible of all specific content . . . ethnomethodological research is not *of* phenomena, but *through* phenomena (Bauman, 1978, pp. 188–90).

It is in this sense that ethnomethodology is rooted in phenomenology.

These approaches have several elements in common, therefore, as social science philosophies and methodologies. Giddens (1976, pp. 52–3) draws the following four conclusions with regard to interpretative sociologies: first, they stress that *verstehen* is not only a scientific goal but also a basic feature of social life – understanding is the foundation of action and conduct; second, analysts draw on the same resources as their subjects – the former in 'scientific theorizing' and the latter in 'practical theorizing'; third, much knowledge of the social world is taken for granted by the subjects and cannot easily be expressed, especially in the format of positivist science; and fourth, social scientific concepts must be linked to 'those used by laymen in sustaining a meaningful social world' (p. 53). Despite links with positivism, therefore, the interpretative sociologies, starting from their bases in phenomenology and hermeneutics, present a view of the world as it is perceived by the subjects and not as it is structured *a priori* by the observers.

Existentialism

Like most of the other philosophies discussed in this chapter, existentialism is not a unified school of thought. Rather it is a grouping of writers whose works, according to one commentator, might lead a 'bewildered outsider' to conclude 'that the only thing they have in common is a marked aversion to each other' (Kaufmann, 1975, p. 11). The best-known existentialist is the French philosopher Jean-Paul Sartre; Jaspers and Heidegger are included as existentialists by many, as are Kierkegaard, Nietzsche and Dostoevsky. Their existentialism, according to Kaufmann, is 'a label for several widely different revolts against traditional philosophy' (p. 11) displaying 'passionate concern with questions that arise from life, the moral pathos and the firm belief that . . . philosophy has to be lived' (p. 51).

Two key phrases are often used to characterize the tenets of existentialism: 'man makes himself' and 'existence before essence'. Unlike phenomenologists, therefore, existentialists – especially atheistic existentialists such as Sartre and Heidegger – do not believe in general essences, pure consciousness and ultimate knowledge. Reality is created by the free acts of human agents, for and by themselves:

> The self that existentialism seeks is each person's individual self, which he must forge for himself out of such senseless circumstances, such meaningless limitations, as are given him. This self-creation – the making of one's essence from mere existence – is demanded of each of us because . . . there is no *single* essence of humanity (Grene, 1959, p. 41).

This lack of a single essence, Grene argues, reflects the atheism of Sartre and others: it is based on the axiom that 'No God, therefore no essence of man'

(p. 44), which forces the conclusion that human values can only be derived from human existence.

The nature of those values is brought out in the relationships between the individual and, first, the world of things and, secondly, the world of others. With regard to the former, realization of individual freedom produces dread, because of:

> the appalling consciousness that I, and I alone, have, absurdly and without reason, brought order out of chaos; alone, crudely and stupidly . . . have made a world out of nothing: and with that awareness my world itself totters on the brink of the helplessness from which I come . . . It is dread before emptiness – before annihilation – before nothing (Grene, 1959, p. 52).

With regard to others, any revelation of these produces 'annihilation of myself as subject . . . [which] I am bound to try by every means in my power to overcome' (Grene, 1949, p. 79). Further, this revelation of myself to others creates fear and shame because:

> instead of being engaged as a free agent in a project of my own, I am . . . an object in his view . . . I am what *he* makes of me, not what I make myself . . . Fear and shame are the two proper and immediate reactions to the intrusion of another person into my world (Grene, 1959, pp. 80–81).

The only counter to shame and fear is aggression, to threaten the observer with extinction so that one can become a free agent again.

Existentialism postulates atomistic individualism, therefore, which leads to certain attitudes towards the physical world and to others in it. The purpose of existentialism, as practised by Sartre and others, has been to explore these attitudes, particularly their absurd and tragic characteristics. Their explanations have largely involved using fiction to depict these attitudes and characteristics, rather than through any formal methodology. The purpose is to demonstrate how individuals create their worlds, in a context where the only constraints are others doing likewise.

The significance of existentialism, according to Olafson (1967), is in its protest against many elements of modern society. It has sought to heighten self-consciousness and to indicate to individuals that they are 'autonomous moral agents, capable of raising and resolving for themselves all questions about what they are to do' (p. 238). It stresses freedom, decision and responsibility: 'it is through free and responsible decisions that man becomes authentically himself' (Macquarrie, 1972, p. 4). Other basic themes are finitude, guilt, alienation, despair and death, many of which reflect the frustrations people experience in their attempts to create an authentic self and which lead to existentialism being a dominantly pessimistic philosophy. 'They become truly themselves only to the extent that they freely choose themselves' (p. 161) but being part of a society, part of a crowd, hampers choice and generates despair and alienation. If choice is hampered then the individual becomes inauthentic and drifts along at the mercy of events rather than creating a personal future. Societies, like individuals, can experience inauthentic histories. As individuals lose control of their destinies in modern advanced technological societies dominated by large corporations and the state, so alienation increases. Existentialism proclaims this alienation and seeks to replace it by a society in which human dignity is enhanced, and to that extent it is a critique, both political and, to some, theological.

According to Macquarrie (1972, p. 8), 'Most existentialists are phenomenologists, though there are many phenomenologists who are not existentialists'. The agreement comes about with regard to such concepts as intentionality, but phenomenology goes further than individual intentions with its search for essences and universal structures, and the consequent lack of attention to personal idiosyncrasies. Existentialists are not concerned with essential phenomenology (p. 57); they accept some of the phenomenological method but stay at the level of existence for their analyses. Their methodology is one of drawing the individual out from the crowd, from the pressures to conform in society, and to advance the self. This promotes individualism. In existentialist psychiatry (practised by R.D Laing, *inter alia*) the aim is to create authentic beings, for example, whereas existentialist education involves the teacher opening up opportunities for the student, but never leading the way in. In literature, as indicated above, existentialist writers have emphasized tragedy, despair and absurdity:

> reminding us that techniques alone cannot solve the human problem, for this is finally an existential problem. They are not so much pessimists as realists who know that there are utopian solutions to the pathos of existence (Macquarrie, 1972, p. 211).

In ethics, existentialists stress being 'true to oneself' rather than conforming to a law imposed by society which reflects past custom, ensures stability, but promotes human stagnation. And in theology, too, it stresses the moral nature of the authentic individual. To some, existentialism implies atheistic humanism, but to others it can lead to 'those very limits of existence where faith arises' (Macquarrie, 1972, p. 267) without providing any proof of the existence of a God.

Existentialism has many similarities with original Marxism (see p. 102) in its concern with the alienation of the individual within society. It differs, however, in its solution to the problems of inauthentic existence (although again there are common elements between aspects of existentialism and anarchist-Marxism). Its aim is the realization of self and its methodology is to use whatever means are relevant (psychiatric analysis, education, literature, visual art) to illustrate personal inauthenticity to people. It has elements of individualism. It stresses that the individual must learn to live in a society with others, however, but argues that one begins with the individual, not with society, in order to create a more human existence than is experienced at present.

Humanistic approaches in human geography

A common feature of the approaches discussed in this chapter is their focus on subjectivity. To idealists, to phenomenologists and to existentialists knowledge of the world does not exist independent of the knower. Instead, it exists solely in one's experience of the world, and can only be appreciated by sensitive analysis of that experience. Individual behaviour cannot be explained in the positivist sense, therefore, but only appreciated, and the ontology is one of being not of existence. On this definition, a humanistic geography is one which studies people in the worlds that they create as thinking beings. It aims at *verstehen*, at an understanding of people in their environments. (Note that whereas most humanistic approaches are phrased at the level of the individual, Jackson, 1981, has argued that phenomenology can be used to provide insights at the societal level. See also Relph, 1981b.)

The need for a 'subjective' approach in human geography has long been recognized and advanced: Wooldridge (1936) claimed that historical geographers must seek to view the countryside through the eyes of the farmer; Ralph Brown's (1943) classic historical geography of the American Eastern Seaboard in 1810 presented it through the eyes of a mythical inhabitant, Thomas Keystone; and in 1947 John Wright introduced the term *geosophy* as part of his contention that geographical knowledge is part of the mental stock of all humans:

> geographical knowledge of one kind or another is universal among men . . .
> nearly every important activity in which man engages . . . is to some extent
> affected by the geographical knowledge at his disposal (Wright, 1947,
> pp. 13–14).

But these were relatively isolated statements which had little impact on the profession at large: the case for a humanistic geography has only been argued forcibly since about 1960.

Advocacy of humanistic perspectives has taken two forms in the geographical literature. In the first, a general humanistic (or subjectivist) orientation is proposed, usually without reference to any one of the philosophies outlined above; in a few cases, the advocacy is for some combination of elements from two or more of those approaches. The second type consists of arguments for one of the four: idealism, pragmatism phenomenology, and existentalism. (Much of the advocacy has been as much anti-positivistic as prohumanistic, see Jackson, 1981; the latter elements are concentrated on here.) The two types of argument are considered separately.

General humanistic perspectives
One of the first geographers to attract a wide audience with his advocacy of a humanistic approach was Kirk. His position was initially developed in 1951, but most authors refer to a later, revised and more accessible statement (Kirk, 1951, 1963, 1979). He separated what he termed the 'geographical environment' into two components: the phenomenal environment and the behavioural environment. The latter comprises those 'facts of the Phenomenal Environment . . . perceived by human beings with motives, preferences, modes of thinking, and traditions drawn from their social, cultural context' (Kirk, 1963, p. 366); only facts in the behavioural environment are relevant to the study of decision-making. Somewhat similar arguments were put forward by Lowenthal (1961). He argued for the study of what he called 'personal geographies': unique milieux containing information which is 'inspired, edited and distorted by feeling' (p. 257). Lowenthal put greater stress on the interpretations of the elements in such behavioural environments than did Kirk.

In neither of these papers was there any explicit reference to the humanistic philosophies. (Lowenthal refers to a large volume of material on the psychology of perception, however, which may in part explain why some human geographers equate humanistic approaches with the study of perception.) It was only in the 1970s that full reference to these philosophies was made. Thus Tuan (1976, p. 266), for example, argues for a humanistic geography which:

> achieves an understanding of the human world by studying people's relations with nature, their geographical behaviour as well as their feelings and ideas in regard to space and place

and for:

> the study of a people's spatial feelings and ideas in the stream of experience (Tuan, 1974, p. 213).

Such a geography would focus on space and place as they enter human experience, and would enable people to probe their personal geographies more deeply. The utility of such an approach is expressed by Buttimer (1979, p. 30):

> The overall task of geography has often been cited in terms as broad as the drama of human life within its total environmental setting. If the goals of human existence are seen to be the fulfilment of human potential, then state of *becoming* should be more important than *state of being*. If such human becoming can be construed as part of total becoming within the biosphere, then our time-worn

geographic perspective may in fact be one of the most valuable contributions possible towards the resolution of social and ecological issues.

A humanistic (clearly in Buttimer's case very much an existentialist) perspective in geography, it is claimed, will enable people to know themselves better and so improve the quality of their existence. Thus:

> a principal aim of modern humanism in geography is the reconciliation of social science and man, to accommodate understanding and wisdom, objectivity and subjectivity, and materialism and idealism (Ley and Samuels 1978, p. 9).

And:

> Humanism is the conviction that men and women can best improve the circumstances of their lives by thinking and acting for themselves, and especially by exercising their capacity for reason (Relph, 1981a, p. 7).

To some, development of humanistic geography involves linking (or re-linking) the discipline with the humanities (see Cosgrove, 1982). For Meining (1983) this involves literature, in two ways. First, as Pocock (1981a, 1981b) and others have demonstrated, literature can be used to provide 'essential clues about human experience with environment', using literature as a document because

> writers not only describe the world, they help shape it. Their very portrayals establish powerful images that affect public attitudes about our landscapes and regions (p. 317).

The second is to contribute to literature, thereby helping to mould attitudes. Human geographers should not have a parasitic relationship with literature but a symbiotic one

> Only when we write books and essays that are so penetrating and powerful in the elucidation of life and landscape, of the grand themes of geography, that people in the humanities cannot afford to ignore us will we have forged enduring links between geography and literature (p. 318).

The geographer should become a creative artist, therefore, as argued also by Powell (1980) and Daniels (1985), as illustrated in the evocative writings of Estyn Evans (e.g. 1973) and by the poetry of Wreford Watson (1983) who argues for passionate involvement

> Geography can't afford to miss out on passion – far less dismiss it. Geography without passion is about as alive as a body without blood – ready for the grave-diggers (p. 391).

Billinge (1983) cautions against possible linguistic excesses in such work, arguing that

> Academic writers are essentially communicators of ideas – sophisticated journalists whose craft lies in expressing what they believe to be true as clearly and as deeply as possible. They are not writers of 'literature' and to believe that the construction of an academic paper is akin to the art of Tolstoy or Huxley is seriously to misunderstand our functions and concerns (p. 417).

Not for Watson, however, who promotes poetry because:

> The poet gets to the *real* issues, because he is *of* them. He voices them as prime experience. Essentially, he is source material. He is the gut-knowledge that guides the geographer in measuring on the ground the pattern of the mind . . . the whole set of attitudes, goals, feelings and fantasies, the beauty or the beast in us, that give a place its soul (p. 392).

And Tuan (1983) criticizes the development of geography for leaving out human relationships and human individuals, subjects incorporated by novelists who in the nineteenth century 'yearned to accumulate and impart knowledge to educate as well as entertain' and even, in some cases, 'to lift the facade of society and human behaviour to probe the underlying processes and mechanisms' (p. 71).
Thus

> In the capacious mind of a novelist, there is room for concrete details and large generalizations, for complex accounts that aim at realism as well as impersonal, abstract analyses (p. 71).

This, according to Tuan, is because novelists aim at comprehensiveness. Geographers should act similarly

> comprehensiveness – this attempt at complex, realistic description – is itself of high intellectual value; places and peoples do exist, and we need to see them as they are even if the effort to do so requires the sacrifice of logical rigour and coherence (p. 72).

Advocacy for particular humanistic approaches
Apart from the general advocacy outlined above, each of the particular humanistic approaches discussed earlier in this chapter has been presented to human geographers (by human geographers) as a viable philosophy for the discipline; some have been stressed more than others, with phenomenology the most popular. Again, as with the general advocacies, the case presented has frequently been as much against positivism as pro. . . . The aim has been to convert geographers to an alternative perspective because of the failures that were currently espoused (whether positivist or structuralist).

The case for *idealism* has been argued most strongly by two historical geographers who were influenced by Collingwood's (1947) *The idea of history*. Harris (1971) was especially impressed by the argument that historiography is a synthetic practice bringing together, by the perceptive interpretations of documents and other texts, material so that:

Although a complete understanding of complex particular situations may be impossible, synthesis does attempt to find a coherent path through the endlessly complex welter of interrelated facts that lie behind them, and to offer an explanation that is plausible and full (p. 164).

Such a synthessis is achieved by 'an idealist interpretation of explanation in history . . . a historian comes to understand an event as he rethinks the thought lying behind it' (p. 165); Harris argues that a similar approach could be used by geographers:

to understand a particular region, place, or landscape, or to treat a theme . . . bearing on the character of a particular place, is to achieve a synthesizing understanding analogous to that in history. A geographer may have to understand the thought . . . lying behind a great many human actions; . . . he may have to deal with human actions which were not the result of conscious thought, and be able to handle generalizations from social science (p. 168).

In another piece, Harris (1978) presents his appreciation of what he calls 'the historical mind' – representing the idealist conception of historiography – and arguing, in the foosteps of Carl Sauer, Andrew Clark and others, for the development of a parallel geographic imagination which would involve all researchers immersing themselves in a 'region' just as historians do with a 'period': the result would be 'a more penetrating understanding of an intricate part of the world, an appreciation of the complexity of human experience, and much pleasure' (p. 126).

To Guelke (1974), the axiomatic feature of an idealist approach in human geography is that the discipline is concerned with 'the rational actions and products of human minds' (p. 193). Action implies intentions and intentions involve the application of theories. Thus:

The intention behind an action can be regarded as the source of its power, and the theory in it can be considered to be the guidance system (p. 197).

The theory is that held by the actors: it is their view of the world, modified by the data which they receive. Thus to understand actions:

The human geographer simply attempts to reconstruct the thought behind the actions that were taken. He does not need theories of his own, because he is concerned with the theories expressed in the actions of the individual being investigated (p. 198).

Initially, Guelke (1975, 1982) argued for the value of the idealist approach in historical geography. He later extended his case to urban geography (Guelke, 1978) and, by implication, to all human geography.

A case for *pragmatism* in human geography was made by Frazier (1981), arguing that:

It is action-oriented, user-oriented and extends the experimental method to include evaluation and implementation. The research is undertaken for the purpose of solving an immediate problem and results are means to an end for some target population. The researcher gives directives for action and serves as an 'action agent' in the implementation of the results (p. 67).

He notes that space is a composite of knowledge and error, that it changes as our knowledge changes, and is structured and restructured as practical problems are solved; he argues that geographical investigations can change knowledge and so contribute to the solution of practical problems.

Frazier's arguments have had little apparent impact, and pragmatism is rarely referred to by human geographers – though many of the arguments for an applied quantitative geography (e.g. Bennett, 1985) and for the application of 'scientific method' (e.g Hay, 1985a) are closely aligned with it. The interactionist perspective developed by the Chicago School has received more substantial support, however, both in empirical application (e.g. Ley, 1974) and in general advocacy (Jackson and Smith, 1984; Smith, 1984). For the latter, this meant exploring Park's main concerns to draw out 'analytically the dynamic and reciprocal negotiation of identity between geographical space and the social groups occupying it' (p. 356), using the procedures of participant-observation (Jackson, 1983).

One potential danger of such ethnographic studies, identified by Jackson (1985), is that they may provide no more than a collection of particularistic accounts, lacking either social and historical context or any intellectual coherence. There is a necessity for the researcher to provide such context and coherence, developing a theoretical structure that accommodates the empirical findings: as Pickles (1985) expresses it:

> The interpreter of an event, piecing together the picture of what happened, may well come to know that event better than those involved (but in a special way only) (p. 173).

The outsiders' and the insiders' view are combined to give interpretative depth (Johnston, 1986d), as in Ley's (1983) text *A social geography of the city*. Thus a theoretical framework is created that situates the creation and restructuring of the taken-for-granted everyday worlds in the conditions that contain those processes, and provides knowledge that can be used to assist further acts of restructuring, for (Smith, 1984):

> Pragmatic philosophy urges action rather than reflection, not because it is impatient or intellectually lazy but because it is only in practice that the truth of ideas can be realized, thought legitimized, and knowledge constructed. Change is inevitable but progress is not: if we are to appreciate the former and move toward the latter, intellect must become an instrument for action (p. 367).

The case for *phenomenology* has been made by a number of authors. (Some of them amalgamated phenomenology and idealism, see Billinge, 1977, p. 56; Guelke (1978, p. 54) counters this, however, arguing that phenomenologists, in their concern for emotions and meanings, do 'not give us the tools to understand or explain human behaviour in an intersubjective or objective way. . . . The idealist shares the phenomenologist's concern with understanding the different meanings people attach to their surroundings, but at an intellectual rather than an emotional level'.) Relph (1970), for example, provides a brief outline of the nature of phenomenology and notes that some of its concepts have been implicitly incorporated into geographical works (such as Lowenthal, 1961). Fuller development of this approach, he argues, is valuable because:

> Man and the world . . . constitute a unity through their mutual implication, though it is man's intentionality that gives meaning to the world and it is only through an examination of these intentions that we can attempt to comprehend this unity (p. 197).

(See also Relph, 1981a.)

A more detailed evaluation was provided by Mercer and Powell (1972), who reviewed not only the phenomenology of Husserl but also the developments within sociology represented by the works of Schutz and Garfinkel (see p. 68). They discuss the 'points of sympathy' linking phenomenology with idealism but argue with regard to the latter 'that Collingwood's theory of historical explanation underplays the great force of emotional and self-conscious motivation behind much human action' (p. 34; see also Gibson's, 1978, critique of idealism). Note that Guelke (1976, p. 169) argues against geographers asking not only what people thought but why they thought it: such investigations 'fall within the domain of the medical psychological sciences' and are 'clearly outside the scope of human geography conceived as a study of man's activities on the land'. With regard to human geography, Mercer and Powell (1972) conclude, in antipositivist vein, that there is a need for 'a viewpoint which emphasizes the richness of man's experience and his perceptions of the world' (p. 51). Behavioural work (see p. 37), they claim, only goes part way towards this goal, because 'it is deeply permeated by positivistic ideas at all levels'. (See also Cox, 1981; Ley, 1981.)

Of the various phenomenological approaches, those relating to the sociology of the everyday world, to ethnomethodology, and to hermeneutics have received relatively little attention from geographers, even in the form of programmatic statements only. With regard to the first two, Ley (1977) has criticized contemporary social and behavioural geographers for their positivistic psychologism and has investigated whether phenomenology offers 'an underpinning to a reinvigorated social geography concerned with group action which culminates in a landscape effect'. He argues that Schutz's work provides:

a pertinent framework and underpinning for a social geography which examines the social and cognitive contexts antecedent to a spatial fact (p. 507).

because of the important role of place in group and individual action. A social geography of the taken-for-granted world would focus on the meaning of places as created by the intentions of human groups. Smith (1981), too, argues for a methodology based on Schutz's work, allied to a philosophy which admits exploratory hypotheses, generalizations, and explanatory theory. (She excludes 'philosophies adhering to the tenet that inner truth may be divined by reason and trained intuition, for these dispense with the primacy of observational method': p. 293.) Material is gathered through participant observation, by reflection upon and selection from observations and experiences gained 'transactionally' (i.e. through contact with subjects and participation in the activities in their taken-for-granted worlds). Out of this come analytical constructs, understandings of behaviour obtained empathetically, and from them it is possible to move towards generalizations based on 'comparative analysis of the ostensibly unique' (p. 297).

Pickles (1985) has argued that these calls for a phenomenological approach in geography are confused and based on distorted conceptions of the goals of Husserl and Heidegger: thus it is only on page 89 of his book that he can:

> move *from* what passes for phenomenology in the geographical literature, *towards* what is actually the case in phenomenology itself.

He presents phenomenology as the search for and clarification of basic scientific concepts. The foundations of empirical science cannot be identified empirically, but only by reflection, so that:

> a phenomenological geography . . . will not refer to actual experiences, factual places and worlds, but to the formal and universal structures of environmental experience, placehood and worldhood (p. 109).

There is, he argues, an essential relationship between an empirical object and its essence:

> such that to each object there corresponds its essential structure, and to each essential structure there corresponds a series of possible individuals as its factual instances (p. 111).

Consequently, each empirical science is related to an essential structure; what, then, is the essence that provides the foundation for geography? To answer that, Pickles promotes:

> an ontological, existential understanding of the universal structures characteristic of man's spatiality or the preconditions for any understanding of places and spaces as such (p. 155).

The result is an understanding of the fundamental nature of space, a consequence of our making room for settlement and activity.

Regarding *hermeneutics*, Rose (1981) has pointed out the relevance of Dilthey's arguments to a human geography:

> If we accept the premises that: (1) human geography takes place entirely within a sphere of signs, (2) that some of these signs are found together in texts either spoken, written, gestured or acted out, and (3) it is the job of human geographers to interpret such texts as a spectator in order to make certain statements about actors operating within the texts, and further (4) to communicate the meanings of such phenomena as he should deem important back to the actors involved . . . what is required of geographers . . . is not to obtain directly the meanings to which the texts refer but rather the attempt to rediscover those meanings from the text, from the transmitted tradition in the text and from their own worlds (p. 124).

Such a dialogical project has been undertaken by Buttimer (1981; 1983) into the history of geography. She also uses the hermeneutic perspective in arguing for applied geography:

> awakening responsibility among various sectors of society. Does this role of provocateur, of facilitator of such a movement, not require that we eventually allow the 'objects' of our research to become 'subjects' of their own individual and collective lives? We may have expertise to offer . . . but to imagine that we can write the script, set the stage, and manage the production, seems not only pretentious, but could also be destructive of . . . creativity (Buttimer, 1979, p, 33).

An *existentialist* approach to human geography has been argued by Samuels (1978, 1981). Individuals, he claims, define themselves spatially. Part of this creation of an identity, this confirmation of oneself, involves a relationship with the environment. What were objects prior to this process become places:

> a world in which all objects are equally important is anarchical . . . partial space is the assignment of meanings to places and systems of places (Samuels, 1978, p. 32).

Individuals originate in an alienated condition. Their creation of places provides them with roots, so that a landscape is a biography of that creation, a statement of the 'existential origins of spatial arrangements, relations and attachments' (Samuels, 1981, p. 126). Some landscapes are individual, and are the biographies of their creators, but there are general landscapes too, reflecting the experiences of human groups in shared situations, such as the geography of post-Second World War American cities. (See also Cosgrove, 1984.) An existential geography, according to Samuels, would seek to understand those shared contexts:

> Effectively, an 'existential geography' is a type of historical geography that endeavours to reconstruct a landscape in the eyes of its occupants, users, explorers and students in the light of historical situations that condition, modify or change relationships (Samuels, 1981, p. 129).

It is the ability to use existentialist methods to reconstruct societal as well as individual spatial biographies that leads Jackson (1981, p. 303) to argue that 'existential phenomenology [is] more important for social science than either philosophy alone': it allows 'an analysis of the spatial structure of social relations'.

Humanistic geography

In the chapter on positivist approaches in human geography, a large literature was discussed relating to both the methodology of positivism and the products of its applications. The nature of positivistic human geography was indicated by its output. Such an approach is not possible for the present chapter, largely because the output is much smaller. As Relph (1981b) wrote, presumably in about 1979:

> In the numerous geographical periodicals and books published since 1970 there are, to my knowledge, just nine papers which deal explicitly with the relations between geography and phenomenology and six books which use phenomenological approaches to examine geographical phenomena (p. 106).

The numbers are larger now, especially with regard to substantive works (see Jackson and Smith, 1984, p. 44), but Harris's (1978, p. 134) statement that:

> In North America at present, those who call themselves 'humanist geographers' are inclined to philosophical reading and methodological writing . . . whereas cultural and historical geographers tend to pursue their old ways no more affected by the new humanism than by the spatial analysis of the 1960s.

still holds true (although 'programmatic' may be a better adjective than 'methodological' with which to describe the writings). To a considerable extent, therefore, there is relatively little to review to illustrate the nature of humanistic work.

One reason why there is so little to review may be that the programmatic statements have had little effect (note that Relph, 1981b, points out that the language of phenomenology is 'exceedingly difficult to penetrate', p. 102, and that 'without doing phenomenology, it may be impossible to understand it', p. 106), or that the advocacy has been in some ways incomplete. Billinge (1977), for example, writes of the attempts to incorporate a phenomenological approach into human geography as 'witness to a fundamental misconception of the purist nature of phenomenology – at best a misnomer; at worst yet more evidence of the disturbing tendency to adopt terminology the exact meaning of which is manifestly misunderstood' (p. 64; see also Agnew and Duncan, 1981). He concludes that 'phenomenological we have by no means become' (p. 67). More strongly, Entrikin argues that this is because a humanistic approach to replace the positivist is impossible:

> humanist geography does not offer a viable alternative to, nor a presupposition-less basis for, scientific geography . . . . Rather, the humanist approach is best understood as a form of criticism (Entrikin, 1976, p. 616).

In part, he claims, this is because the humanist approach is 'methodologically obscure'; the goal of understanding people's meaningful experiences seems to lead to a situation in which 'any method is acceptable' (p. 629). There is, indeed, relatively little discussion of method in the philosophical literature, let alone the geographical. (Billinge, 1977, p. 63, writes that 'phenomenology has not, in general concerned itself with the details of implementation, but with broader aspects of conception and cogitation. It is not a "practical" philosophy'. See also Billinge, 1983, on the writing styles of humanistic geographies.) Many writers suggest that humanistic work involves thinking rather than practical activity, plus communication, either with the texts or with actors. Thus to Ley and Samuels (1978, p. 14):

> While humanistic methodology is eclectic and the sources for interpretation are numerous, ranging from archival research to participant observation, for the geographer the methods converge upon a group in place and the landscape they occupy.

Doing humanistic research is very largely a personal matter, therefore, involving intuition and imaginative interpretation. It differs from the behaviourist work discussed in the previous chapter in that whereas such work focuses on behaviour, which is observable and quantifiable, humanistic work focuses on experience, which is neither. Participant observation, or experiential field work, is possible for contemporary research into the taken-for-granted world (Rowles, 1978). Nevertheless:

> It is certainly questionable whether any two phenomenologists can ever have exactly the same 'intuitions' of the same phenomenon, or indeed know whether or not they have the same intuitions. It is not possible to *prove* anything by the phenomenological method, and . . . *argument* is impossible (Mercer and Powell, 1972, p. 14).

For such reasons, Entrikin (1976) argued that the eclectic work in humanistic geography provided at best only a form of criticism of positivist work:

As criticism it provides a potentially useful function in reaffirming the importance of the study of meaning and value in human geography, making geographers aware of their often extreme interpretations of science, and making
scientists aware of the social and cultural factors involved in so-called objective
research (p. 632).

Despite these reservations, various authors note that much work has been
done in human geography which adopts the essential stance of the humanistic approaches with regard to the subjectivity of knowledge even if it does
not proceed very far with them – to the identification, for example, of pure
consciousness. Much of this work has been done in cultural and social
geography (Jackson and Smith, 1984), in particular historical geography
(e.g. Baker and Gregory, 1984). The forms of economic geography discussed in the previous chapters have been little affected, despite claims that
they could be (Guelke, 1978; Wallace, 1978). Thus in reviewing the
literature, the emphasis must be on applications to certain aspects of human
geography only. As already stressed, most of these applications are humanistic but have not fully embraced the philosophy and methodology of any of
the four approaches discussed above. Their general orientation is outlined
here, without any discussion of the relative absence of philosophical guidelines.

Historical geography The reconstruction of spatial distributions and
patterns of land-use in the past has long been a popular component of human
geography, presented by some as an end in itself and by others as an aid in
understanding the present. Among historical geographers, there have been
debates regarding whether to study cross-sections through time or changes
over time, for example, but data availability has been a severe limitation on
the questions that can sensibly be asked. In summarizing the preoccupations
of historical geographers, however, Prince (1971) was able to identify 'three
arbitrarily defined, if not truly separate, realms of knowledge' (p. 4):

1 The features of the landscape and human society in the past, which are
verifiable by evidence and so form 'real worlds of the past'.
2 The images of the world held by residents of the past, as influences on
their actions, creating 'imagined worlds of the past'.
3 Reconstructions of past worlds in terms of later models, providing
'abstract worlds of the past'.

The exact nature of these three realms may now be questioned – see the discussion of realism in the next chapter (pp. 111–3) – but the typification is of
particular value here in highlighting the second realm, the behavioural
environments of the past.

In the longest section of his essay, on 'imagined worlds of the past',
Prince notes that once the question 'Why?' is asked regarding the real
worlds:

the full answer can no longer be sought in the external world, because motives, attitudes, preferences and prejudices must be examined as well as works and deeds (p. 24).

The ways in which historical geographers seek to answer that question depend, as Prince illustrates, on the evidence available to them. His bibliography indicates the volume of such work, on a wide variety of themes, times and places.

In terms of the humanistic approaches discussed here, the basic thrust of much of this historical geography has been idealist; the researchers have sought to reproduce the actions of individuals and groups by identifying their theoretical bases. This is illustrated by work on the settlement of the New World where, as Heathcote (1965) and Powell (1970) show for Australia, there was a conflict between two theories, or appraisals, of the environment: the official and the popular. Such studies are almost entirely particularistic, emphasizing the unique, if not singular, aspects of the subject matter, whether theories of the physical or of the social environment (Powell, 1971). Powell (1977) has sought to generalize such enterprises into a framework termed eiconics – the study of images, which are communicated in the settlement process – but although he concludes that:

> Our journey through the changing geography of the New World illustrates sufficiently well that its landscapes have always mirrored the ideas and ideals of its inhabitants (p. 174).

this does not lead him beyond the idealist conception of historical geography to the sorts of generalizations about essences that characterize phenomenology.

As indicated earlier, an existentialist approach to geography sees landscape as the biography of its creator: 'The landscape is thoroughly and permanently imbued with struggle, tension and dialectical conflict' (Samuels, 1978b, p. 293). This theme is illustrated by Samuels with regard to the landscape changes in China stimulated by Mao's 'cosmic battle between man and nature' (p. 294). His general thesis is that 'the created landscapes of men are . . . contingent upon contexts, but the responsibility of authors' (Samuels, 1979, p. 64). Most landscapes are created by key individuals, so landscape biographies can be discerned from the geographies of their authors, whether Mao or Robert Moses (Caro, 1975). Where the authors are not identifiable individuals, then one is looking at the product of a society:

> Our human landscape is our unwitting autobiography, and all our cultural warts and blemishes, our ordinary day-to-day qualities, are there for anybody who knows how to look for them (Lewis, 1979, p. 13).

Thus:

The man-made landscape – the ordinary run-of-the-mill things that humans have created and put upon the earth – provides strong evidence of the kind of people we are, and were, and are in process of becoming (p. 15).

so that the landscape is the text (see also Rose, 1980):

The English landscape itself, to those who know how to read it aright, is the richest historical record we possess (Hoskins, 1955, p. 14).

Although not presented as existentialist, some other work on landscapes also presents them as biographical reflections of past society, and argues that preservation of such landscapes aids human identity. In his essay on the American landscape, for example, Lowenthal (1975a, p. 8) argues that 'simply to know that structures are durable may give residents a sense of being rooted in a place' and illustrates the use of landscape features to create a collective memory of 'a long and glorious past'. He later points out that 'The past we know about is not . . . a present that was ever experienced' (p. 25) so that:

we shape landscapes and artifacts to conform with illusory histories, public and private, that gratify our tastes (p. 36).

Whilst the existentialist uses the landscape to provide information about earlier societies, therefore, Lowenthal claims that society recreates landscapes to present its vision of the past (see also Lowenthal, 1985). This shows a disregard for history, he claims (Lowenthal, 1975b). It also writes a new chapter in the biography and illustrates the nature of a society characterized by that disregard.

The landscape, then, is produced by society, interacting with the environment to create what Cosgrove (1984) calls:

a way to seeing – a way in which some Europeans have represented to themselves and to others the world about them and their relationships with it, and through which they have commented on social relations (p. 1).

so that:

Landscape is not merely the world we see, it is a construction, a composition of that world (p. 13).

As such, it is not susceptible to positivist study, since it is not something that can be studied 'from the outside'. Landscapes are created and interpreted by people in terms of their imagined relationships with nature, their social roles, and their interpretations of the links between others and nature. Thus different societies express their individuality in their characteristic landscapes, as he illustrates in a series of essays on Italy, America, and England.

The sense of place One of the areas of research that comes closest to the

aims of essential phenomenology and its quest for elements of pure consciousness is that concerned with the links between people, individually and
as groups, and places. (It should be noted that most of this work represents
geography with implicit phenomenological content rather than explicit
attempts to 'do phenomenological research'.) This was identified by Tuan
(1976) as one of the main themes of a humanistic geography, the translation
of 'mere space [into] . . . an intensely human place' (p. 269). He presented
such a process as one example of the more general concept of topophilia,
which embraces 'all of the human being's active ties with the material
environment' (Tuan, 1974b, p. 93). Much of his work has explored themes
related to this general concept (e.g Tuan, 1977).

According to one humanist geographer, the sense of place is a fundamental element in the taken-for-granted world. His work is predicated on the
axiom that:

> places are indeed a fundamental aspect of most existence in the world, . . . they
> are sources of security and identity for individuals and for groups of people.

Which is followed by the statement:

> it is important that the means of experiencing, creating and maintaining
> significant places are not lost. Moreover there are many signs that these very
> means are disappearing and that 'placelessness' – the weakening of distinct and
> diverse experiences of places – is now a dominant force (Relph, 1976, p. 6).

(There may be something of a paradox here: if sense of place is an element of
'pure consciousness' – note that Relph does not claim this – then can it be
replaced by a rootlessness created by a changing society?) Relph clearly
believes that a sense of place can be created, or at least facilitated, by landscape planning (or perhaps by a lack of it) to replace the inauthenticity of the
landscapes of industrial and late capitalism, by:

> allowing scope for individuals and groups to make their own places, and to give
> those places authenticity and significance by modifying them and by dwelling in
> them (p. 146).

There are strong links between such work, with its clear base in the
humanistic approaches, and writing on landscape design and 'mental maps'
in the behaviourist/positivist mould discussed in the previous chapter. The
latter drew its inspiration from works such as that of the landscape architect
Kevin Lynch (1960) in *The image of the city* and on the creation of images (see
Downs and Stea, 1977). Whereas such behaviourist investigations obtained
their data from questionnaires and similar surveys, and manipulated these
statistically, however, humanistic approaches have focused on texts and a
presuppositionless approach. The nature of the texts varies widely. As
already illustrated here, the landscape itself has been used by some as the
repository of human meaning (see also Hugill, 1975). Literature, too, has

been used as 'a perspective for how people experience their world' (Tuan, 1978, p. 194). It can provide three forms of aid to the humanist geogapher, according to Tuan: it is a thought experiment revealing modes of human experience; it is an artifact, illustrating the cultural perceptions of an environment; and it is a model of geographical synthesis and writing. According to Pocock (1981a, p. 346) 'it is of the essence of literature to reveal the universal while apparently concerned with the particular': literature is the work (as are all works of art) of artists with particular 'perceptive insight' (Pocock, 1981b, p. 15) regarding contemporary situations.

Sense of place is often interpreted to cover the affective ties between individuals/groups and their (native or adopted) home areas, including their housing; see Duncan (1981). However, it is not only such home areas that are given meanings. For most people, considerable areas of space must be structured to form a life-world, for 'Space is an essential framework to all modes of thought' (Sack, 1980b, p. 4). In a review of the various conceptions of space in social thought, Sack has categorized modes of thought in a two-dimensional framework: the first dimension is a subjective/objective continuum (relating to both subject matter and method of analysis); the other is a space/substance dimension – at one pole the focus is on spatial form alone and at the other on phenomena studied in an aspatial context. He then identifies two dominant modes of thought within this framework:

1 Sophisticated-fragmented modes are characteristic of the arts, social sciences and physical sciences, in that they abstract phenomena from their context, use symbols to represent them (e.g. maps; Blakemore, 1981), and look at parts only rather than wholes.
2. Unsophisticated-fused modes are neither abstract nor based on the use of symbols; nor are they specialized.

The former are not necessarily either positivist or behaviouralist. Sack discusses the analysis of dreams and works of art, although he concludes that:

> Whether there can or cannot be . . . a science [of subjective conceptions of space] is a point we will not engage . . . [but] to abandon the attempt without offering an alternative mode of understanding human behaviour is to despair of knowing (Sack, 1980b, p. 116).

With respect to the unsophisticated-fused modes, he analyses the child's view of space, the normal practical view of the adult, and space as it is presented in myth and magic, and then proceeds to an investigation of the mixture of the various modes within different societies. Such work clearly has strong humanistic foundations. The goal is clear:

> Since our actions on the earth spring from our views of the world, an analysis of the meanings of geographic space in modes of thought will better enable us to explain actual behaviour in space (Sack, 1980a, p. 314).

And because 'geographic space is seen and evaluated in different ways at different times and in different cultures' (Sack, 1980b, p. 3) this means that such explanations of behaviour will be time and place specific.

Associated with the concept of the sense of place and with the structuring of space by individuals and groups is the notion of *territoriality*. This is usually interpreted in much the same way as sense of place – 'the theory that animals, persons and groups identify with and defend territories of various spatial extents' (Seamon, 1979, p. 69) – but to some it implies considerably more. (As such, it could be considered an example of deep structure, as discussed in the section on 'structure as construct' in the next chapter: see pages 97–101.) For geographers, as for many other social scientists, appreciation of territoriality among mammals came with Ardrey's (1969) popularization of ethological work in *The territorial imperative*, and a cognate presentation by Morris (1967). According to Ardrey:

> The concept of territory as a genetically determined form of behaviour in many species is today accepted beyond question in the biological sciences (p. 13).

People, too, map out territories, around themselves as individuals, around their homes, and around their nations, for example. Do they do this because they choose to or, as animals, because they must? (Is territoriality an element of pure consciousness, or a deep structure, as discussed in the next chapter?) He concludes that the latter is the case:

> We act as we do for reasons of our evolutionary past, not our cultural present . . . The dog barking at you from behind his master's fence acts for a motive indistinguishable from that of his master when the fence was built (p. 16).

Most of the geographical use of the concept of territoriality has been based on a general analogy with animal behaviour rather than as the outcome of phenomenological research. (Though see Tuan, 1976, on crowding.) Thus the practice of social distancing at the individual and neighbourhood scales, as well as at the national (with its related concept of xenophobia) has been treated as learned behaviour associated with the class conflict endemic in most societies (Johnston, 1980a, 1982a; Cox, 1985).

The most detailed analysis of territoriality by a geographer has been provided by Sack (1983). He emphasizes the social use of territory as 'a strategy for influence or control' and avoids 'the issue of whether human territoriality is a biological drive or instinct' (p. 55). His definition of territoriality is:

> the attempt by an individual or group (x) to influence, effect or contol objects, people, and relationships (y) by delimiting and asserting control over a territory (p. 56).

Ten tendencies involved in this assertion of control through spatial strategies are identified, showing how territorial assertions of power and influence, using various combinations of those ten tendencies, are used to advance social and individual goals. There is nothing deterministic in their application. Territoriality is a strategy devised by humans and applied as a product of social and individual choice – although Sack accepts that there *might* be:

> Conditions or circumstances in which territoriality is the primary or even necessary means of attaining [certain] . . . advantages (p. 72).

People, nature and landscape The interrelationships between societies and their habitats have always been a source of interest for scholars, as Glacken's (1967) magisterial survey shows. Such a theme has obvious interest for humanistic geographers although it, like so much else, has also been subjected to positivist approaches, as in the search for techniques that will allow generalizations about landscape quality, evaluation and preferences (Penning-Rowsell, 1981).

For humanist geographers, the study of meaning in landscapes is not something which is susceptible to positivistic analyses, although it is possible, according to Appleton (1975, p. vii), to state hypotheses and develop theories. Appleton bases his work on landscape:

> on the assumption that our aesthetic reactions to it are in part inborn, and that they can only be brought into operation if we provide them with sign-symbols of a kind which can be spontaneously apprehended by a mechanism attuned to the natural environment . . . an observer must seek to recreate something of that primitive relationship which links a creature with its habitat (Appleton, 1975, p. viii).

(Thus Appleton assumes, or hypothesizes, that pure consciousness contains certain elements rather than seeking those elements in a presuppositionless way.) Appleton's search for this inborn aesthetic sense begins in animal ethology, from which he derives the main postulate of habitat theory, that animals react to their environments according to their basic needs. For an animal in a habitat he identifies four main activities – hunting, escaping, shelter-seeking and exploring – from which he derives two primitives – seeing and hiding. The environment must provide for these, producing what he terms a prospect-refuge theory, which provides 'a frame of reference for examining the aesthetic properties of landscape' (p. 79), which he makes clear is not the only frame available. (For an alternative, focused on amenity, see Lowenthal and Prince, 1964.) The remainder of his book illustrates Appleton's belief in the viability of this theory, in a wide-ranging survey. Part of the same theme has been investigated by Tuan (1979).

The everyday world The applications of humanistic approaches to studies of people in their daily life-worlds are few. One exception is the work of Seamon (1979), who used phenomenology to explore three themes: movement, rest and encounter. Movement relates to day-to-day environment dealings; rest to person – place attachments; and encounter to observation of the world (p. 17). His methodology involved the use of 'environmental experience groups' (akin to the workshops suggested by Spiegelberg, 1975, and involving cooperative encounter and exploration) which comprised people coming together and sharing their environmental experiences. Seamon recorded, transcribed and discussed the proceedings, and identified his three themes from this procedure. Together, he claims, the three constitute a *place ballet*. This involves:

> Body ballet . . . a set of integrated gestures and movements which sustain a particular task or aim (p. 54)

combined with:

> a time-space routine . . . a set of habitual bodily behaviours which extend through a considerable portion of time (p. 55)

so that:

> Body ballets and time-space routines mix in a supportive physical environment to create place ballet – an interaction of many time-space routines and body ballets rooted in space (p. 56).

Appreciation of the centrality of this integration can lead to a humanistic application, in a dialogue between those who wish to plan places and those who live in them:

> Insiders come to discover one taken-for-granted component of the place in which they live. They recognize through their own experience the value of place ballets; they feel a wish to sustain existing place ballets and foster new ones. At the same time, outsiders recognize the ballets of places under their jurisdiction; they initiate plans and policies to protect place ballets and integrate their dynamics into larger environmental wholes (p. 152)

Whereas Seamon's work on the everyday world was based largely on Husserlian phenomenology (with no references to Schutz, for example), Ley's (1974) study of the everyday world of inner city Philadelphia integrates an idealist view (the interplay of two images: one external to the inner city, the other internal) with that of transactional sociology, arguing that:

> In such a social world it is the daily verbal communication which reinforces the world's reality, and indeed moulds the appearance of the environment (p. 47).

Through communication, residents create and recreate their environments. Ley's participant observation in one inner city area allowed him to identify the nature of those environments, created in situations of considerable uncertainty. (The analogy he uses to describe them is the frontier outpost.) Thus, for example, some streets were perceived as much less safe than others for pedestrians, and were avoided in people's movement patterns, and the area was marked out by graffiti which defined the territories (turfs) of various street gangs (Cybriwsky and Ley, 1974).

Time geography One aspect of the study of the everyday world which became relatively popular in the 1970s was time geography. It was initiated in a paper by Hagerstrand (1970), who argued that in regional science and planning:

> time has to be taken into account along with space . . . time has a critical importance when it comes to fitting people and things together for functioning in socio-economic systems (p. 10).

The constraints on idividual behaviour, he argued, are time-space prisms: the maximum areal extents that can be covered in a given time. Such constraints are threefold: capability, relating to their biological nature (particularly the needs to sleep and to eat) and the tools at people's disposal; coupling, which relates to the conjointness of many activities; and authority, those powers exercised over individuals to keep them in certain places/times and out of others.

Hagerstrand's case was that study of individual biographies would indicate the constraints acting on people, and lead to the potential for better spatial planning. (The affinities with Seamon's work are strong.) It has generated much empirical work on biographies (e.g. Martensson, 1979), which implicitly uses the ideal-typical approach of Schutz and Weber although being much more empirically based. According to Pred (1977b, p. 210), Hagerstrand conceived time geography:

> from a humanistic concern with the 'quality of life' and everyday freedom of action implications for individuals of both existing and alternative technologies, institutions, organizations and urban forms.

and the empirical procedures and findings have been applied in a variety of planning situations in Sweden. Pred suggests that it can also be used in the study of a discipline's intellectual history (see Pred, 1979), in the reinterpretation of historical events, in the study of alienation in society, and in the changing structure of family life. (See also the discussion on p. 114 of structuration.)

Examples of the wider utility of time geography suggested by Pred include a study by Carlstein (1980) which reinterprets the economic geography of pre-industrial societies in terms of time-space resources. However, as developed more in the next chapter, although Carlstein claims that his approach separates essence from appearance (p. 58), the main thrust is structuralist rather than humanist. He makes clear that the approach 'does not . . . subscribe to a phenomenological framework of the 'life-world'. Nor does it entail resting content on an atomistic or behavioural level' (p. 61). Thus time geography has extended much beyond the original formulation, so that in an attempt 'to place time firmly in the minds of human geographers', Parkes and Thrift (1980, p. xi) have adopted a broader perspective which they term chronogeographical. Their treatment is dominantly positivist, indicating a field that is difficult to categorize (as Carlstein, 1980, makes clear); it contains elements, not necessarily integrated in any one piece of work, of all of the approaches discussed in this book.

An evaluation

Humanistic geography is not readily evaluated because, unlike positivist work, it has no explicit criteria by which it can be assessed. The aim is not to increase explanation and predictive power, but to improve understanding, which in a hermeneutical sense is very much a personal project for the observer and, where relevant, the observed. There can be no progress as such, therefore, in that the work is not cumulative. The only real assessment is whether the individuals concerned feel that both their understanding and their future action are better as a result of the work. In an academic discipline this involves a further hermeneutic relationship, between researcher and student, between whom there may be at least one and perhaps several filters (the research paper or monograph; the textbook; the tutor).

Certain humanistic approaches are less atomistic than others, in that they seek to identify 'universal knowledge' or elements of pure consciousness. If such goals were achieved, this would certainly represent an ability to generalize, although it is not clear how such ability would be realized or how the results would be communicated. In any case, as made clear here, with very few exceptions geographers have not attempted to proceed towards 'universal knowledge', and where they have, it has often been in a positivist as much as a humanistic perspective (see Gregory, 1978a). This does not obscure the impact of essays and analyses in the humanistic tradition. As Entrikin (1976) and others have indicated, these have provided a strong critique to the positivist approaches and have indicated the centrality of intentions and meanings in any study of *human* geography.

The problems of doing research in humanistic geography are several, as are those of transmitting its aims and results. One of these, to many by far the most important, is that of communication, in particular the constraints of language. As Olsson has made clear in a number of essays, the human world is full of ambiguity and complexity but language translates much of this into certainty (Olsson, 1978). To him, the humanistic approach:

> allows us to grasp both the certainty of the external and the ambiguity of the internal, of gibberish and silent communication. To speak in aid of ambiguity is therefore not to condone obfuscation but rather to be so precise that the inherent contradictions are retained intact (p. 118).

He seeks to avoid dematerializing 'objects into ideas' (Olsson, 1979, p. 304), to develop a social science in which the constraints of language (which is not the only text) do not distort the message. At present he claims, 'what is judged to be true and just is not independent of the language in which that judgement is phrased' (Olsson, 1975, p. 26), a statement which refers not only to written language but also to the majority of analytical tools. (For example: 'What counts is what can be counted; what can be counted is what can be pointed to; what can be pointed to is what can be unequivocally named. Accumulation of knowledge about the nameable is consequently the point of the scientist's game' – Olsson, 1982, p. 227.) Thus the ambiguities of reality should not be distorted by the languages of mathematics and statistics, for example, not only because this hampers the development of understanding but also because it is used (or may be used) as the basis for social engineering (planning) which will confine the world within present boundaries rather than allowing it to change. (See also Pred, 1981a.)

The problem of language, in its broadest sense, is internal to humanistic geography, just as it is to all humanistic enterprises. Other problems refer to the relevance of humanistic approaches and their orientation. The major criticisms are twofold. The first, largely positivist, presents humanistic approaches as subjective and thus unscientific, of general interest perhaps but having little relevance to the creation of better objective conditions in a late capitalist world. The second, largely structuralist, presents the atomistic focus on the individual in humanistic work as a distortion of reality; it gives individuals freedom to act when if fact they are very much constrained, if not constricted, by external circumstances over which they have little control. A partial response to such criticisms is to claim that some humanistic approaches at least have scientific goals, in that they are seeking to uncover the nature of universal knowledge which governs all individual behaviour. Such goals do not loom large in humanistic geography, however, most of which focuses on the particular and emphasizes the singular. It illustrates the subjectivity and complexity of individuals and drives home the importance of meanings, but remains a relatively diffuse literature, a critique whose alternative has attracted relatively little support.

The epistemology of humanistic approaches, then, emphasizes the subjectivity of knowledge. People are thinking beings whose intentionality creates a world within which they act. The ontology of such approaches, therefore, is that knowledge can only be obtained from what exists in the human mind. This involves a variety of levels: the often unconsidered and accepted elements of the taken-for-granted everyday world; the new elements which are brought into the life-world, or behavioural environment; the theories which link these elements together and provide the frameworks for conduct and action; and the components of pure consciousness which structure those theories and the perceptual processes involved in the creation of behavioural environments. Humanistic approaches seek to explore these various levels, to gain an understanding of the individual. Humanistic geography explores those aspects relative to its major themes: people/environment relationships, and people/people interrelationships in their spatial contexts. The understanding achieved is to be used to help individuals understand themselves, thereby increasing the depth of their self-knowledge and enabling them to improve the quality of their lives.

4

Structuralist approaches

The characteristic feature of structuralist approaches is an axiom that explanations for observed phenomena must be sought in general structures which underpin all phenomena but are not identifiable within them; the explanation cannot be produced through empirical study of the phenomena alone. Such beliefs have a very long history. In many religions, for example, the belief that life was created by a god means that the understanding of life requires an understanding of the god's intentions. Recent structuralism argues that the underlying structures can be appreciated through a combination of theory and observation/analysis.

The term structuralism is very widely used, throughout the social sciences and humanities. Rossi (1981), for example, distinguishes between empirical and transformational structuralism. The former is characteristic of work, especially in sociology, on social structures, which emphasizes interdependence in systems: this is frequently known as structural-functionalism (see p. 48). Transformational structuralism, on the other hand, represents the approaches presented here:

> Transformational structuralists find not only naive but false the positivist and behaviourist assumptions that people's conscious explanations and overt behaviour are to be taken at their face value as objects of scientific analysis . . . we have to go beyond surface structures to find the deep and real structures that account for the variety of observable phenomena or conscious explanations and their apparent contradictions (Rossi, 1981, p. 63).

Thus structuralists believe not only in the need to delve beneath surface appearances to discover explanations but also that such analysis will identify universal structures that provide the motive forces in societies.

Even within the field of transformational structuralism there is a considerable variety of approaches. Not all of these are relevant to the present book. Two types are identified here.

Structure as construct

The basic feature of work in this type is a belief that cultural phenomena – language, kinship rules, myths, taboos, etc. – which appear

extraordinarily diverse when observed are in fact transformations of a few
basic structures which are universal to the human mind. Discovery of those
structures involves identifying the nature of human existence itself:

> Cultural and social phenomena . . . are to be thought of as projections onto the
> world-out-there of structured patterns generated by human minds. It is further
> postulated that, at the most basic, abstract level, the variety of such patterns is
> very limited. The diverse structured patterns discernible in directly observable
> cultural phenomena are all transformations of a narrow range of mentalist
> structures which are common to all humanity (Leach, 1981, p. 29).

Those structures (often called deep structures) are not directly accessible to
social scientific analysis. They must be uncovered through study of their
transformations in observable phenomena and behaviour.

The origins of this form of structuralist inquiry are generally traced to the
work of de Saussure (1966) in linguistics. In this, he stressed the difference
between the signifier – the term used in a particular language – and the
signified – the concept which the term represents. He argued that:

> The relationship between signifier and signified is not natural or fixed but social
> and, hence, infinitely variable. Therefore, the nature of the sign itself is
> completely arbitrary. Since signifier and signified can take any form and since
> signs can be combined into an infinite variety of languages, the proper focus on
> the study of language is on the relational and structural characteristics
> (Heydebrand, 1981, p. 82).

A further difference emphasized in this linguistic work, and clearly building
on the signifier/signified relationship, is that between *parole* (the speech act
of everyday life) and *langue* (the language system whose rules are understood
so that the speech acts are interpretable). The former is a transformation of
the latter: structural linguists analyse speech, in order to identify the
fundamental characteristics of language systems, the rules which govern
communication and which are thought to be genetically imprinted.

The development of transformational structuralism in linguistics is
associated with the works of Noam Chomsky. He argues that the common
principles of languages are so well articulated, and that children can so
readily derive the structural principles of their native languages from
listening to their parents, that language systems must be 'biologically
determined' and 'genetically transmitted from parents to their children'
(Lyons, 1977, p. 7). Thus the study of language should be able to transform
one into another, thereby isolating the general principles. These principles, which are genetically imprinted, are the deep structures whose
identification is the purpose of structuralist inquiry (Smith and Wilson,
1979).

Within the social sciences, the introduction of transformational
structuralism is associated in particular with the work of the French social

anthropologist Claude Lévi-Strauss. His writing was strongly influenced by Saussurean linguistics, and led him to the conclusion that 'human behaviour is preordained by unconscious forces beyond human control' (Kurzweil, 1980, p. 27). Identifying those unconscious forces involves studying each example of a particular phenomenon (e.g. myth) as a transformation of a deep structure. Each is an algebraic transformation of all others, analysis should show, so that each is also an algebraic transformation of the deep structure, the biologically imprinted element of the human brain which is manipulated by cultural agency. Thus one has a superstructure, which is the observed realization, the deep structure, which is the construct, and between them the mediating force, which transforms the latter into the former. As Gregory (1978a) demonstrates, Lévi-Strauss presented the transformation process with the analogue of a camshaft driving the cutting machine producing jigsaw puzzles. Each individual jigsaw may have its own particular pattern, so that the transformation has concealed to the student of jigsaws the common element: the deep structure which gears the cams and produces each individual puzzle. As a structuralist, Lévi-Strauss was intent on identifying and understanding the nature of the gearbox.

Lévi-Strauss's views are somewhat similar to those of essential phenomenologists and their beliefs in 'pure consciousness' (see p. 57). As Leach (1974, p. 26) presents them:

> since all cultures are the product of human brains, there must be, somewhere beneath the surface, features that are common to all.

This argument can be extended to the study of history which 'offers us images of past societies which were structural transformations of those we know' (p. 15). Further, according to some interpretations, because the transformations are represented by mechanical means (as against statistical, or probabilistic, ones in positivist science) once the deep structures are identified prediction should be possible:

> By isolating the deep structures of social systems, mechanical models permit us to relate various systems to each other through transformational operations as well as to predict what changes are produced in the system when one or more of its elements are modified (Rossi, 1981, p. 75).

Lévi-Strauss's methodology developed that employed in Saussurean linguistics, emphasizing the dynamic as well as synchronic relationships between signifier and signified. The resolution of binary oppositions within myths, for example, allows him to identify their basic elements, which can be projected onto those in other phenomena. The transformations necessary to achieve successful projections lead to the identifications of deep structure. The complex nature of this methodology, and certain aspects of Lévi-Strauss's treatment of evidence, have come under considerable criticism (see Leach, 1974, 1981). This suggests that a sizeable gap has still to be bridged between the theory and practice of transformational structuralism in social anthropology: the idea of deep structure has yet to be transformed, according to many, into a convincing scientific concept.

The influence of Lévi-Strauss on social science has been considerable, especially in France (Kurzweil, 1980). But there, it is argued, the ideas no longer have strong support:

> Some readers might consider the discovery of unconscious texts as superfluous or might be bored by the many intricate analyses. Others may deprecate all the structuralisms because they have not answered the questions of human origins and of existence as they originally promised. Perhaps the aims of the structuralists were unattainable: but they did introduce some intriguing and suggestive modes of analysis (Kurzweil, 1980, pp. 244–5).

One other researcher whose work clearly falls into the 'structure as construct' type is the Swiss philosopher/psychologist Jean Piaget. He defines a structure as a system of transformations, incorporating three key ideas: wholeness, transformation and self-regulation. It is the characteristic of wholeness that distinguishes a structure from an aggregate; in the former every member is linked to every other but in the latter, because of its arbitrariness, this is not so. The idea of transformation is similar to that presented by Chomsky and Lévi-Strauss:

> If the character of structured wholes depends on their laws of composition, these laws must of their very nature be *structuring*: it is the constant duality, or bipolarity, of always being simultaneously *structuring* and *structured* that accounts for the success of the notion of law or rule employed by structuralists (Piaget, 1971, p. 10).

Finally, self-regulation implies that the transformations refer only to the structure itself. It is a closed system in which the transformations act to maintain equilibrium.

In his discussion of structuralism and structures, Piaget (1971, Chapter 6) distinguishes clearly between two types. Global structuralism relates to the study of self-regulating wholes, such as social groups: such structures are simply unions of components (and their study is the structural-functionalism referred to on p. 48). Analytical structuralism, on the other hand, refers to wholes whose constitution is derived from some particular source, a deep structure. Global structuralism, then, refers to theoretical constructs imposed on some subject matter, whereas analytical structuralism refers to wholes which are empirically given – they exist.

Piaget's own work is on analytical structuralism and involves the search for structures which govern the development of intelligence in humans. He views the individual as starting with a structure, a mode of intellectual functioning, which comprises the ability to do two things: to assimilate new material into existing schema; and to accommodate schemas to experience of the external world (see Boden, 1979). With these twin abilities learning proceeds as a continuing process of transformation. The result is greater intelligence and an ability to act within the empirical world. Thus:

> Whereas other animals cannot alter themselves except by changing their species, man can transform himself by transforming the world and can structure himself by constructing structures; and these structures are his own, for they are not externally predestined either from within or without (Piaget, 1971, pp. 118–19).

Thus Piaget, unlike some phenomenologists, does not believe that there are certain innate essences to human consciousness. Instead, what is innate is the ability to assimilate and to accommodate. With this ability, which forms the initial structure, learning and behaviour take place and the structure is continuously transformed as a consequence. Piaget has demonstrated how such transformations occur as intelligence is acquired, in particular how children learn.

Structure as process

Whereas transformational structuralists included in the 'structure as construct' type present observed phenomena (signifiers) as representations of deep structures genetically imprinted on human consciousness, those discussed here present phenomena as representations of underlying social structures whose base lies in the material conditions of existence. No attempt is made to link these structures to deep structures. The general argument is the same, therefore, except that: first, the transformations are of a structure that is identified at the societal (the infrastructure or base) rather than the neural level; and second, the structure is itself continually being transformed, hence the designation of the type 'structure as process'. These lead to many other differences in approach to understanding and in the nature of analysis.

By far the largest body of literature characterized by the 'structure as process' typification is that of Marxism; this has had most influence on contemporary geography. A major chronicler of Marxist literature has pointed out 'There is scarcely any question relating to the interpretation of Marxism that is not a matter of dispute' (Kolakowski, 1978, v. 1., p. vi). All that can be done here is to outline the basic features of the Marxist approach to understanding society, plus those of allied developments which are relevant to contemporary work in human geography.

Marxism, historical materialism, and social science

The voluminous writings of Karl Marx – many of them incomplete manuscripts published by others long after his death – have stimulated a great deal of social thought and political practice. The stimuli vary substantially. Giddens (1979, p. 150 ff), for example, has recognized seven different interpretations of Marx's works: as a methodological prescription for historical analysis; as a means of studying human life; as an emphasis on the significance of labour in human society; as a theory of social change; as a theory of the relationships between infrastructure and superstructure; as a theory of human consciousness; and as a theory of the centrality of class relations and class conflict in human society. Followers of Marx have built on these interpretations, separately or in some combination. Sklair (1981) has identified four varieties of Marxism in twentieth-century British sociology, for example. The first two relate to the works of Marx himself – with a break identified around 1857 (Kurzweil, 1980, p. 42). In the first, the 'early' Marx, the emphasis is on problems of alienation and the division of labour; in the second, the 'later' Marx, it shifts to what Sklair terms 'mechanical materialism', or 'analysis of the ways in which the economy determines everything in the last resort' (p. 152). The third, post-Lenin, covers problems of power, consciousness and hegemony. Finally, there was the Althusserian structuralism of the 1960s, which was critical of empiricism, which claimed scientific status, focused on the primacy of the mode of production, and took a holistic rather than an individualistic perspective – the 'humanism' of the early Marx is rejected. This last is usually placed as opposed to much of the content of the other Marxisms. For human geographers, it is much harder to identify clear Marxist schools (though Duncan and Ley, 1982, suggest that Althusserian arguments are typical of certain works: see p. 137). No classification is presented here, therefore, but a review of Marx's major theses and of developments thereon.

The origins of Marx's works lie in his philosophical training and in his own form of humanism. People, according to his observations and analyses, were becoming dehumanized. Marx's goal was to restore their humanity to them, by uncovering the workings of dehumanizing society and depicting them in such a way that they would react and create a new, more human world. Thus his work was:

> aimed at enlightening the proletariat concerning its objective and potentially emancipatory role in history (Sensat, 1979, p. 69)

and:

> Marx's criticism of existing society makes sense only in the context of his vision of a new world in which the social significance of each individual's life is directly evident to him (Kolakowski, 1978, v. 1., p. 131).

Central to Marx's analysis of dehumanization in society was the concept of *alienation*. By this he meant the separation of the workers from their own labour power and from its fruits, as well as from nature (Johnston, 1986c). Labour, under capitalism, is a commodity to be bought and sold, in the market place, and as such is alienated from the worker. Alienation is increased as the division of labour becomes finer. Such dehumanization affects both parties in a capitalist society (i.e. bourgeoisie and proletariat):

> In capitalist production neither the worker nor the capitalist is a human being: their personal qualities have been taken away from them. Thus, when the class-consciousness of the proletariat evolves . . . to a revolutionary consciousness . . . by the same token a worker becomes a human individual once again. . . . As for the capitalists, they cannot as a class take up arms against their own dehumanization, since they rejoice in it and in the wealth and power it brings. Thus, although both sides are equally dehumanized, only the wage-earner is spurred by this state of affairs to protestation and social combat (Kolakowski, 1978, v. 1., p. 287).

It is, therefore, the nature of capitalist society that creates alienation according to Marx. Alienation affects all members of the society, but only the proletariat suffer economic as well as human deprivation, however, so only the proletariat can be stimulated to overthrow the capitalist system and create a newer, more humane society.

The form of economic analysis developed by Marx was based on earlier work by David Ricardo on the labour theory of value (for a brief introduction to Marxian economics, see Smith, 1981). In a capitalist economic system, individuals must sell their labour power in order to obtain a level of subsistence, thereby to reproduce that labour power and to reproduce society as a whole. Labour is sold to a capitalist, who uses it to produce saleable goods. The aim of the capitalist is to sell the goods for as high a price as possible, while keeping the costs of labour as low as possible. The difference between the two, generally known as the *surplus value*, is the return to the capitalist, and is the source of profit. Thus surplus value is the difference between the selling price of a commodity and the production costs, a combination of the costs of labour and those of 'dead labour' (the costs of machinery, materials, etc.) produced by labour earlier in the production chain. The rate of profit is the surplus value divided by total costs (labour plus dead labour).

The aim of capitalists, according to Marx, is to maximize the rate of profit: 'the insatiable appetite for self-increase by the exploitation of surplus labour' (Kolakowski, 1978, v. 1., p. 291). Part of the surplus value accruing to the capitalist class is used for consumption and is spent on the products of the labour process. The remainder is invested in further production, creating further surplus and allowing extended reproduction of the capitalist class. Capitalists seek unendingly to increase their store of wealth, to accumulate.

To achieve their ends, capitalists must hold the costs of labour as low as possible, relative to selling prices. To do this, for any particular commodity, they seek to reduce the unit costs of labour by increasing its productivity (the amount of surplus value produced per unit of labour cost). This is achieved by increased investment in dead labour, in particular in machinery which is more productive than is human labour *per se*. Technological development is therefore vital to the continued expansion of capital. To increase the level of surplus value and the rate of profit the capitalist must always be investing in ways to revolutionize the means of production.

This apparently never-ending process of technological development is far from smooth, however, and the progress of capitalism is punctuated by a series of crises. This is because, as outlined further below, capitalism is characterized by a number of internal contradictions. For example, it seeks to increase the productivity of labour, which means reducing the labour input to the production of each item. At the same time, it seeks to increase the volume of surplus value, which can only be done by increasing the labour force, since labour is the sole source of value (Shaw, 1978, pp. 86–7). The two are only possible if the market for products is increasing, at a rate at least equal to the increase in the volume of production made possible by technological developments. And the market, at least in part, comprises those workers whose wages are being held down by the technological developments that are making many of them under- if not unemployed.

A consequence of these contradictions is the tendency within capitalist economic systems for the rate of profit to decline. This can happen in individual industries and sectors of an economy, as the increased abilities to produce exceed the ability to sell. This leads the capitalists in that sector to withdraw investment from perceived poor potential returns, and to redirect their money into other sectors, where the potential for profitability is perceived to be greater. At the same time, within any sector the more successful capitalist will be able to increase the market share by elimination of competitors. In general, therefore, as the rate of profit in an industry/sector declines so ownership there is concentrated into fewer hands and the surplus realized is redirected into other industries/sectors.

A capitalist system is characterized by flows of capital (the accumulations of surplus value not used by the capitalist class in consumption) from industry to industry in search of high profit rates. The capitalist class, according to Marx, is not concerned with what it produces, and its utility, but only with the profit that it achieves. But this flow of capital produces a tendency for the profit rates in the various industries/sectors to converge on an average. This can lead to crises that are more general than those already mentioned: they affect most, if not all, sectors of an economy and produce a general problem of over-production (or under-consumption). The capitalist system has developed the ability to produce commodities far in excess of its ability to consume them (with the latter in part reflecting the increased concentration and centralization of capital and the relatively small proportion of the exchange value of commodities returned to the proletariat to spend on consumption). It must, then, seek to restructure itself, to create new conditions where profits can be made and investment is worthwhile. (The use of where is crucial here since, as Harvey, 1982, demonstrates, restructuring is of necessity a spatial process.) To some extent, as already stressed, such restructuring is continuous. But not entirely so. There are occasional major crises, according to Marx's interpretation:

> Capital overcomes its contradictions by means of periodic crises of overproduction which ruin the mass of small owners and wreak havoc among the working class, after which the balance of the market is restored for a time (Kolakowski, 1978, v. 1., p. 299).

The havoc wreaked on the working class created what Marx termed its immiseration. He believed that capitalism degrades workers, even though their material conditions of existence may be improved. They become increasingly a commodity to be traded, a minute element in the complex division of labour. Alienation is the result of the commodity fetishism that characterizes capitalism: everything is reduced to monetary terms and human dignity is lost. Such alienation can only be removed by the introduction of communism.

In analysing how this dehumanizing alienation is necessary to capitalist expansion, Marx focused on the *dialectics* of the mode of production, on the resolution of contradictory opposites that is central to capitalism's success. (It is the centrality of these contradictions to Marxian economics which leads to its typification here as structure as process: the structure contains ongoing processes.) Thus Marx's approach to analysis, usually known as *historical materialism*, is based on understanding the dialectics at work within the structure.

The concept of dialectics was developed by Marx from his work with Hegel's phenomenology. It is usually presented as a sequence of thesis, antithesis, synthesis, with the sequence being replicated as each synthesis in turn becomes a thesis. The thesis is something of only limited value which generates opposition to itself: the antithesis. The struggle between the two eventually leads to an accommodation, a synthesis that incorporates elements of the two but which, in turn, generates its own opposition. (For an introduction to dialectics in philosophy, see Popper, 1972, pp. 312ff.) Such oppositions, or contradictions, appeared to Marx to characterize capitalism (as exemplified above). Their resolution, through the creation of new syntheses, provided the generative force for continued capitalist accumulation. (In Marxist dialectics, the term contradictions is not used in the same way as it is in everyday speech. Heilbroner (1980) notes, for example, that dialectical contradictions are not the same as logical contradictions (i.e. assertions each of which denies the other). Rather they imply incompatibility; as Heilbroner (p. 35) puts it, 'the unstable coexistence and successive resolution of incompatible forces'. Things begin as the resolution of incompatible forces, but they immediately set up a new pair of such forces.)

In Marx's work, the major dialectic identified was that between the productive forces and the relations of production (Shaw, 1978, p. 8). It is realized in the falling rate of profit:

> the urge to maximize the rate of profit defeats its own object by increasing the amount of constant capital [dead labour] and so causing the profit rate to fall steadily (Kolakowski, 1978, v. 1., p. 322)

which in turn creates inter-class (proleteriat–bourgeoisie) antagonism. In Hegelian dialectics, every synthesis took one closer to pure consciousness (in the phenomenological sense of that term: see p. 62). In Marxian dialectics, the uncovering of every successive synthesis should reveal its real conditions to the proletarian consciousness (as against the false consciousness that capitalism itself creates), and lead to the revolutionary explosion that will finally remove capitalism.

The concepts of productive forces and relations of production are central to historical materialism and its analysis of capitalist development. The *productive forces* are the elements of the production process. They combine the means of production, the objective conditions of labour, and labour power (within which is incorporated scientific and other knowledge). The *relations of production* comprise the conditions within which the productive forces are brought into operation. These create the work situation and are based on ownership relations; the capitalist owns the means of production and buys the labour power of the proletariat in order to create commodities and surplus value. These relations (for a full exposition see Shaw, 1978) are fundamentally class relations: each society has a privileged class with regard to ownership of the productive forces, and an underprivileged, exploited proletariat.

The dialectic between these two elements involves the resolution of the contradictions which capitalism necessarily creates, as the desire to create surplus value founders on the falling rate of profit, the replacement of labour (the source of surplus value) by dead labour, and the limits to markets. To overcome these limits to the accumulation of wealth, the capitalist class uses the relations of production to reorganize its use of the productive forces, seeking ways out of crises by creating new forms of profitability. This setting of the productive forces in motion involves exploitation of the proletariat by the bourgeoisie, and the antagonism which this generates is itself a continuing problem in the realization of surplus value. Resolution of this antagonism, or at least its containment, involves the creation of a social formation, a societal structure (including a state) in which there is sufficient harmony that the relations of production are able to employ the forces. (Such a structure legitimizes capitalist relations.)

Historical materialism, as developed by Marx, thus involves a dialectical process. The social formation comprises a series of oppositions or contradictory forces, which frequently hinder the achievement of its goals. Such contradictions must be circumvented, by the creation of new situations that will encourage and allow further pursuit of the goals. The restrictions on the use of the productive forces are in some way removed, so as to allow surplus value to be appropriated. But, because the capitalist system permanently comprises contradictory tendencies, this new synthesis is of necessity short-lived. It soon generates its own opposites, and creates further crises of over-production and under-consumption. Thus capitalism is continually transforming itself. (Note that historical materialism as an academic discipline cannot predict the way in which any individual contradiction is resolved. Thus the processes of change cannot be subject to a positivist analysis, since they cannot be expressed as a functioning system, p. 45: the forces of change are not exogenously determined.)

The whole of Marx's work was organized to indicate the crucial role of the economic structure of capitalist society – in particular the various contradictions involving the productive forces and the relations of production – as determinants of human consciousness and being. To some, this led to an interpretation that denied human free will and relegated culture and politics to the status of dependent categories: such as interpretation is frequently associated with the writings of Louis Althusser (1969, 1970). Marxist structuralism separates the infrastructure (the economic determinants) from the superstructure (the religion, culture, polity, etc.) of a society. It does not entirely relegate the latter to a position of total dependence on the former:

> Marxist structuralists insist that the different structures which constitute any given social formation all have a certain autonomy, and that while the economic structure (the mode of production) has to be conceived as ultimately determinant, other structures may nevertheless be *dominant* in constituting and reproducing a particular form of society (Bottomore, 1978, p. 137).

Thus, the nature of the state in a particular place at a particular time may influence how a current economic crisis is solved, and those controlling the state may pursue policies not linked to economic forces. But the state does not determine the nature of society, it can only influence the realization of the processes that are embedded in the economic infrastructure.

Historical materialism is not, therefore, a crude form of economic determinism. Marx argued that economic forces dominate capitalist society, but not that there is no freedom for human interpretation of those forces in the resolution of particular antagonisms. Thus the much quoted statement from *The Eighteenth Brumaire of Louis Bonaparte* that:

Men make their own history, but they do not make it just as they please; they do not make it in circumstances chosen by themselves, but under circumstances directly found, given and transmitted from the past.

The unfolding of history is the result of the conscious behaviour of individuals. Marx's case is that the nature of that consciousness is determined by the economic circumstances, which in turn, as the result of successive dialectic syntheses, are determined by earlier economic circumstances. Thus:

great individuals who appear to shape the course of history actually come upon the scene because society needs them. Alexander, Cromwell and Napoleon are instruments of the historical process; they may affect it by their accidental personal traits, but they are unconscious agents of a great impersonal force which they did not create. The effectiveness of their action is determined by the situation in which it takes place (Kolakowski, 1978, v. 1, p. 340).

Marx's aim, then, was to uncover the general laws of history – its immanent forces, which he located in the economic infrastructure – and not to account for specific events. As Kolakowski (p. 339) puts it, historical materialism:

is not and does not claim to be a key to the interpretation of any particular historical event. All it does is define the relations between some, but by no means all, features of social life.

One of those essential features is the class division of society, so that the whole unfolding of history, including the development of the superstructure of individual social formations, reflects the antagonisms of that division. This is often interpreted as history being created by the class struggle. To some, the validity of this general concept of history means that 'Marx's approach is still the only one which enables us to explain the whole span of human history' (Hobsbawm, 1972, p. 282).

Because historical materialism as conceived by Marx is not concerned with the details of history, it differs from the structure as construct type discussed earlier, within which the nature of the structure can be identified by analysis of its transformations in particular empirical situations:

For Marx, the scientific understanding of the capitalist system consists in the discovery of the internal structure hidden behind its visible functioning (Godelier, 1972, pp. 335–336).

This hidden structure, Godelier argues, cannot be apprehended in its realizations, because capitalism is not a thing but a social relationship. As a result, the structures which are sought by historical materialists are relationships (hence the definition 'structure as process'). What is observed by empirical social science research is an outcome of those processes, which cannot themselves be apprehended.

Because historical materialism is concerned with hidden structures, its 'explanations' are not subject to empirical verification. Its method is the development of conjectural theory (Saunders, 1981, p. 17). This proposes certain relationships within society which, if correct, would account for empirical appearances. The theory is consistent with observation. This is termed the retroductive method (Sayer, 1979), which is neither deductive (there are no laws which are ahistorical, only historical processes) nor inductive (regularities in the world of appearances provide no basis for implying regularities in the causes). Thus Marx's historical materialism involves the development and refinement of plausible theories about the dominant forces in society, plausible both as explanations and as guides to action:

> Marx's method can be used fruitfully to generate theories that are plausible to a greater or lesser extent but can never finally be demonstrated, and it follows that there is no necessary and compelling reason to accept such theories other than one's own political values and purposes. Marxism, in other words, is as much a guide to political practice as a method of scientific analysis (Saunders, 1981, p. 18).

The 'test' of such theories is provided by the success or failure of actions founded upon them.

Developments on Marxism

The published works of Marx (and of his collaborator, Engels) have been more influential than those of most other scholars, over a very wide field. The impacts can be divided into two types. The first involves Marxism as a guide to political practice, with regard to both the revolutionary potential of the proletariat and the criteria for a society in which human dignity is not degraded. A large number of revolutionaries and would-be revolutionaries have based their programmes on Marx (see, for example, the review in Kolakowski, 1978, v. 2), although, as Kolakowski (1978, v. 3) argues, attempts to apply Marxist ideas have largely abused them, in part because they have been allied with nationalist ideology:

> Wherever Communism is in power, the ruling class transforms it into an ideology whose real sources are nationalism, racism or imperialism . . . Nationalism lives only as an ideology of hate, envy and thirst for power (Kolakowski, 1978, v. 3, pp. 529–30).

Because of this, he claims, Marxism as practice has lost contact with the other main stream of Marxist literature identified here: Marxism as a theoretical base for the social sciences. The latter is in general a relatively recent development, with the volume of Marxist scholarship expanding very substantially since the Second World War, especially in the English-speaking world.

To many Marxists, the distinction made here between Marxist practice and Marxist social science is unreal. Adoption of a Marxist approach implies that scholars are working not simply to provide a proper understanding of the course of human history, but also to achieve a transformation from capitalism to socialism. To others, however, whereas the former task is quite acceptable the other is not (for a variety of reasons). These may be termed Marxian writers, in that they use the basic methods of Marxist analysis. The lack of commitment to Marx's political programme is sometimes explicit, but often only implicit.

Work in the Marxian mould has considerably extended the original analyses, which is not surprising, if the theory of historical materialism is correct, since the continued dialectic of the structure as process has created many new social forms that were unforeseen by Marx. To some, the fact that these were unforeseen is indicative of the failure of Marxism as a theory. Popper (1972, p. 37), for example, claims that many of its predictions have been tested and refuted, but:

> instead of accepting the refutations the followers of Marx re-interpreted both the theory and the evidence in order to make them agree. In this way they rescued the theory from refutation; but they did so at the price of adopting a device which made it irrefutable.

To him, Marxism failed to meet the criteria for designation as a science. (See also Popper, 1945.) To others, Marx never made any prediction of a socialist revolution, beyond claiming that it would be generated by 'the catastrophe towards which capitalism is swiftly yet unconsciously tending' (Kolakowski, 1978, v. 1, p. 306). According to Marx's thesis:

> Only the proletariat can intervene to redress the conflict between the productive forces and their relations of production. . . . In the absence of this, the productive forces will continue to push for more compatible relations of production (Shaw, 1978, p. 113).

The analysis of these pushes for 'more compatible relations of production' has been the focus of much recent Marxist social science, concerned with such topics as the rise of the state, the changing structure of ownership, the evolution of late capitalism, and the growth of 'intermediate classes', all of which were only dimly perceived by Marx in the mid-nineteenth century.

While some practising Marxists seek to create the socialist revolution, therefore, and some academic Marxists seek to generate the conditions for it by their analyses and teaching, the main impact of Marx's work on academic social science in the capitalist world has been via the introduction of Marxian perspectives, in some cases modified to incorporate aspects of others. (That individual social scientists, as social scientists, appear to be Marxian rather than Marxist, as defined here, does not involve comment on their political philosophy. It simply indicates that their social science work concentrates on historical materialist analysis and makes little or no reference to any political philosophy. Of these perspectives, three are outlined here because of their usage in and relevance to the literature in human geography.

Realism, more properly transcendental realism, to distinguish it from naive or direct realism (p. 26), is a philosophical position associated with the works of Bhaskar (1975, 1979) and Keat and Urry (1975). Set in a clear structuralist mould:

> The basic principle of realist philosophy of science, viz. that perceptions gives us access to things and experimental activity access to structures that exist independently of us, is very simple (Bhaskar, 1975, p. 9).

Underlying this basic principle is a belief that mechanisms are independent of the events that they generate. Constant conjunctions of events may provide the bases for empirical laws, but not for process or mechanism laws (those which create the conditions for the operation of the empirical laws). Such process laws are:

> the real things and structures, mechanisms and processes, events and possibilities of the world; and for the most part they are quite independent of us. . . . They are the intransitive, science-independent, objects of scientific observation and discovery (Bhaskar, 1975, p. 22).

Thus, according to this view, in much scientific activity the relationships identified reflect the nature of the experiments conducted, which are at the level of appearances and not that of the mechanisms which produce those experiences. (Gravity exists independently of experiments that show its relationship to the rate of acceleration of falling bodies, for example. The results of those experiments are neither necessary nor sufficient for an understanding of the causal laws producing gravity; they are illustrations of it.) Thus transcendental realism involves the study of a 'law-governed world independent of man' (p. 26):

> Science, then, is the systematic attempt to express in thought the structures and ways of acting of things that exist and act independently of thought. The world is structured and complex and not made for men. It is entirely accidental that we exist, and understand something about our bit of it (p. 250).

In *A realist theory of science* Bhaskar (1975) argues that the purpose of science is to isolate the general laws of nature that operate independently of human existence and its creations (including scientific experiments). In this sense they are laws of the structure and not of the relationships in the superstructure (see Keat and Urry, 1975, pp. 30–1, who argue that the answers to 'why' questions are to be found in 'how' and 'what' questions: 'to explain why is partly to say how' – p. 31). In *The possibility of naturalism* Bhaskar (1979) applies these ideas to what he terms 'the contemporary human sciences'. In that context, the realist philosophy involves:

> the movement from the manifest phenomena of social life, as conceptualized in the experience of the social agents concerned, to the essential relations that necessitate them (p. 32).

Thus the focus is not on people and what they do (and why they say they do it) but rather on the structures of the societies of which they are part and which provide the necessary conditions for their activity: structure is separated from action. (The former, according to Bhaskar, are the psychological sciences; the latter are the social sciences.)

In developing his realist approach to the social sciences, Bhaskar is clearly influenced by the content of Marxist analysis ('if Marxism without detailed social scientific and historical work is empty, then such work without Marxism (or some such theory) is blind' – p. 56) and its retroductive methodology (see p. 109). He argues against both idealism – separation of the superstructure from the infrastructure, or effects from their causes – and reductionism – which represents the superstructure as a mechanical outcome of processes in the infrastructure. If the infrastructure is the economic base (complete with its antagonisms, as identified by Marx) and the superstructure contains its individuals and their multifarious organizations, then not only does the society guide the actions of individuals, through the processes of socialization, but in addition the actions of the individuals are part of the process of the reproduction and transformation of society. In this way, human agency is incorporated into the dialectic, so that there is both a dialectic within the infrastructure (between the productive forces and the relations of production) and between the infrastructure and the superstructure (between the process and its realization). Thus a transcendental realist philosophy of social science seeks the causes of phenomena in a structure which is constantly being transformed but, more so than is the case in many Marxist presentations, argues that the outcomes of these causes in turn influence the processes of transformation within the infrastructure. The individual cannot exist without society (so the superstructure is dependent on the infrastructure) but in addition society can neither exist nor be continually re-created without the activities of individuals.

The basic argument of transcendental realism, therefore, is that the empirical world is the result of the actions of mechanisms that cannot be directly observed in particular contingent circumstances. This has been summarized by Chouinard, Fincher and Webber (1984) as follows.

1 Causal mechanisms are real structures that exist independently of any knowledge of them.
2 Although those mechanisms exist, only their effects can be observed.
3 The causal mechanisms will only produce empirical regularities (that can be expressed as scientific laws) in closed or controlled systems. Since social science deals with open systems, empirical regularities cannot be expected, so that its study is of the tendencies inherent in the causal mechanisms only.
4 In the study of tendencies only, social scientists cannot guarantee any particular outcome. They cannot predict, and so knowledge of the mechanisms can be gained only theoretically, not empirically.
5 The mechanisms themselves are not fixed, but are social products created by societies as means of organizing the reproduction of human life. They can be changed, and so further prevent the possibility of predicting empirical outcomes.

There is, then, a major difference between realist social science and realist (sometimes termed post-positivist) physical science. In the latter, the mechanisms are fixed and are not affected by human action so that the results of empirical experiments are replicable. This does not account for the mechanisms, however, only demonstrate that the empirical world is consistent with theories of their existence. Thus the same conjunction of events (an empirical experiment) can be created many times, with the same outcome.

Realist social science is not experimental, however. It cannot assume constant conjunctions, for two reasons. First, the contingent conditions through which the general tendencies of the mechanisms are filtered are continually changing (Sayer, 1984), for no other reason than that human societies have memories (individual and collective: Smith, 1984) so that present interpretations of the mechanisms (decisions on how to act) are influenced, not necessarily consciously, by interpretations of the outcomes of previous decisions. The context for decision-making is always changing. Secondly, the tendencies themselves may be influenced by the empirical outcomes, as part of a feedback from superstructure to infrastructure. Thus realist social science, which includes Marxism, is necessarily anti-positivist. It also rejects systems analysis, presented by some as a means of integrating physical and social science (e.g. Bennett and Chorley, 1978), because that assumes fixed sets of relationships and a fixed trajectory (Gregory, 1980). (Of course, the use of positivist social science, including systems analysis, within society seeks to impose such fixity – we live in a 'pseudopositivist world'; Johnston, 1986b – which creates tensions over the use of social science, as made clear by Harvey, 1973, 1984.)

Bhaskar's realist philosophy has much in common with the theory of **structuration**, developed by the Cambridge sociologist Anthony Giddens. This theory was developed, he indicates, because of:

> the lack of a theory of action in the social sciences. . . . In their eagerness to 'get behind the backs' of the social actors whose conduct they seek to understand . . . [Marxist and related approaches] largely ignore just those phenomena that action philosophy makes central to human conduct (Giddens, 1979, p. 2).

Human action takes place within structural contexts, however, and the relevance of Marxist work to the understanding of these is made clear: 'Marx's writings still represent the most significant single fund of ideas that can be drawn upon in seeking to illuminate problems of agency and structure' (Giddens, 1979, p. 53; see also Giddens, 1981). But the problem with much structuralism – both Marxist, or 'structuralism as process', and 'structuralism as construct' – he argues, is that it gives too little attention to the role of human agency:

> The production of society . . . is always and everywhere a skilled accomplishment of its members . . . [but it is necessary] to reconcile such an emphasis with the equally essential thesis . . . that if men make society, they do not do so merely under conditions of their own choosing (Giddens, 1976, p. 126).

The aim of Giddens's work is to fuse structuralist approaches to society, with their focus on the constraints to behaviour, to humanistic aproaches, whose foci are the intentional acts of human agency. This fusion is achieved through his concept of structuration:

> the duality of structure, which relates to the fundamentally recursive character of social life, and expresses the mutual dependence of structure and agency . . . the structural properties of social systems are both the medium and the outcome of the practices that constitute those systems (Giddens, 1979, p. 69).

Thus rather than see structure as a constraint to action, Giddens presents it as *simultaneously both constraining and enabling*, whilst at the same time it is being reproduced and transformed by individuals. (Any approach which denies the role of individual actors is teleological according to Giddens and 'implies a derogation of the lay actor[s] . . . [who] are regarded as cultural dopes or mere 'bearers of a mode of production', with no worthwhile understanding of their surroundings or the circumstances of their action', Giddens, 1979, p. 71).

Giddens's theory of structuration is based on a series of clearly stated 'rules of sociological method', which can be taken as axioms. They are (Giddens, 1976, pp. 160–2):

1 'Sociology is not concerned with a "pre-given" universe of objects, but with one which is constituted or produced by the active doings of subjects.'

2 'The production and reproduction of society thus has to be treated as a skilled performance on the part of its members not as merely a mechanical series of processes.'

3 'The realm of human agency is bounded. Men produce society, but they do so as historically located actors, and not under conditions of their own choosing.'

4 'Structures must not be conceptualized as simply placing constraints upon human agency, but as enabling.'

5 'Processes of structuration involve an interplay of meanings, norms and power.'

6 'The sociological observer cannot make social life available as a "phenomenon" for observation independently of drawing upon his knowledge of it as a resource whereby he constitutes it as a "topic for investigation".'

7 'Immersion in a form of life is the only and necessary means whereby an observer is able to generate such characterizations.'

8 'Sociological concepts thus obey what I call a double hermeneutic.' (The first is the nature of scientific activity itself; the second involves using science to interpret a different conception of the universe held by the individuals being studied.)

9 'In sum, the primary tasks of sociological analysis are the following: 1 The hermeneutic explication and mediation of divergent forms of life within descriptive metalanguages of social science; 2 Explication of the production and reproduction of society as the accomplished outcome of human agency.'

For such a merger of the 'structure as process' and humanistic approaches, he identified three concepts regarding society: first, the *system*, or set of regular social practices; second, the *structure*, the (changing) rules and resources which guide the system; and third, *structuration*, the conditions whereby members of systems govern the continuity and/or transformation of structures, and thereby influence the reproduction of the systems themselves. What Giddens is proposing, therefore, is the development of a mode of analysis which pays substantial attention to the role of human agency in the transformation of structures. (Gregory, 1978a, p. 89, claims that the concept of structuration is taken directly from Marx, 1976, p. 283; the statement there, however, refers to a dialectic between people and nature rather than people and structure.) Structuration accepts part at least of the Marxist arguments regarding the role of the infrastructure, but argues for the important role of human agency in both the realization of the structural processes (i.e. the observed world of the empirical researcher) and the modification of the processes themselves. Further, in his recent writings Giddens (1984) has agreed that structuration is undertaken in *locales*, and he uses Hagerstrand's time-geography (see p. 93) to demonstrate how human agency is contextual because interaction is constrained to local milieux.

Critical theory This 'school of thought' is also associated with Marxism in many ways and has the same basic goals. It is not a single body of work associated with an individual scholar, but rather a large body of linked material produced by a group of scholars frequently known as the 'Frankfurt School'. This is divided into two groups, the first focused on five scholars working at the Institute of Social Research at Frankfurt before the Second World War and the second centred on the work since the 1950s of Jurgen Habermas.

The common aims of the critical theorists are similar to those of Marx: the creation of a society lacking domination. Individuals must be emancipated, therefore, by a process:

> involving the active participation of everyone in the control of social phenomena; in other words, people must be subjects and not objects (Kolakowski, 1978, v. 3, p. 392).

This emancipation from domination, Habermas argues, must be achieved through:

> self-reflection, [whereby] individuals can become aware of forces which have exerted a hitherto unacknowledged influence over them. Thus, the act of knowing coincides with the goal of the interest (Held, 1980, p. 318).

The emancipatory interest, then, is achieved by increasing individual awareness. Successful self-reflection leads to a greater conscious understanding of the nature of one's position in society and therefore to an increased ability to realize emancipation through changing society.

Only self-reflection, according to Habermas, can create the conditions for the achievement of real, material freedom (conditions which are necessary but not sufficient). The role of critical science is to pave the way for this process. Self-knowledge is hindered, it is claimed, by the various interests of individuals and groups within society, which are expressed ideologically. Positivist science, for example, advances certain technical interests based in the desire for domination, whereas the hermeneutic sciences seek to advance intersubjective understanding. With regard to the latter, much communication within a social system is distorted, in part because of 'the semantic structure of communication itself' (Sensat, 1979, p. 27). Critical theory seeks to remove those distortions by the creation of what Habermas calls the *ideal speech situation*. In this, there is:

> equal opportunity for discussion, free from all domination, whether arising from conscious strategic behaviour and/or systematically distorted communication (Held, 1980, pp. 343–44).

Critical theorists have examined a wide range of phenomena to demonstrate the variety of distortions in communication which manipulate knowledge to particular interests. (Studies of aesthetics, for example, illustrate the influence of bourgeois culture.) The aim is to extend Marxism, and to show, as in Habermas's (1976) *Legitimation crisis*, that the transformations of society since Marx wrote have created new conditions relating to the maintenance of a capitalist structure. This involves studying the role of the state (a topic largely ignored by Marx):

> In order for the system to function, there must be a general compliance with the laws, rules, etc. Although this compliance can be secured to a limited extent by coercion, societies claiming to operate according to the principles of bourgeois democracy depend more on the existence of a widespread belief that the system adheres to the principles of equality, justice and freedom. Thus the capitalist state must act to support the production process and at the same time act, if it is to preserve its image as fair and just, to conceal what it is doing. If man's loyalty is threatened, a tendency toward a legitimation crisis is established (Held, 1980, p. 291).

The act of concealment is part of the systematically distorted communication identified by Habermas. Emancipation will enable people to overcome this situation, to provide enlightenment via self-reflection and undistorted discourse. Thus:

> The Frankfurt school and Habermas sought to extend and adapt the insights of Marx's work in order to reveal the complex factors which hinder people coming to consciousness of themselves as capable of different action (Held, 1980, p. 363).

Critical theory, then, is Marxist both in its analysis and in its commitment to practical goals. It seeks to uncover what the processes are within a society (hence it is realist) and to communicate the results to individuals so that they will better realize how they are manipulated in a society and as a result wish to change that situation.

World-systems analysis is a project devised and promoted by a single scholar, Immanuel Wallerstein, although his followers have generated considerable debate concerning the details of the research agenda. His goal has been to rewrite the history of capitalism from its origins in the late fifteenth century, and two of the projected volumes, bringing the story up to 1750, have so far appeared (Wallerstein, 1974, 1980). It is a development on nineteenth-century Marxism.

Wallerstein's foundation is in the identification of the basic economic organizing units – what he terms world-systems. There are three types of system. In the *mini-system*, there is only limited division of labour, exchange is organized reciprocally, and age and gender are the main differentiating characteristics within societies. In *world-empires*, exchange at one level is reciprocal (between artisans and food/raw material producers) but at another it is redistributive, with a surplus being appropriated by a military-bureaucratic ruling class. Finally, in *world-economies* production and exchange are organized through the market place.

Wallerstein's historical project is concerned to understand how a particular world-economy, the capitalist world-economy, has developed, temporally and spatially, from its northwest European base into first an international and then a global system. (This raises important issues regarding the position of the presumed non-capitalist countries: Chase-Dunn, 1982.) Its development has not been a simple linear progression, but it has had six consistent, defining characteristics (Taylor, 1986a): a global market for commodities; a competitive state system, with no one political unit able to control the market; a core – periphery organization of space; an economic class division which interacts with both status groups and the spatial organization; a cyclic economic process, dominated by long waves; and the secular spread of the system until it becomes truly global. As with other 'structure as process' writers, Wallerstein's goal is to transcend the disciplinary divisions of social science, including history, thereby to promote a holistic understanding of capitalism and to advance the transition from that mode of production to socialism. (A short statement of his ideas is provided in Wallerstein, 1983.)

Structuralism in human geography

As with the positivist and humanistic approaches, the introduction of structuralist ideas to human geography came via the other social sciences, most of which were either the source of structuralist developments or had been influenced by them earlier than geography. And, as also with the other two approaches, it is possible to find examples of the importation of some structuralist ideas to human geography long before the main impact in the 1970s (see Johnston, 1983a, Chapter 6). Indeed, two early anarchists – Peter Kropotkin (Breitbart, 1981), and Elisée Reclus (Dunbar, 1981) – were both practising geographers.

With regard to the schools of work depicted here as 'structuralism as construct' there has been little attempt to relate most of them to the research interests of human geographers. Gregory (1978a) has presented a brief outline of Lévi-Strauss's work and related it to human geography, but this has not been taken further. Perhaps surprisingly, the structuralist work in social anthropology has not had any impact on cultural geography, as illustrated by the absence of any reference to it in either a review essay by Mikesell (1978) or a programmatic essay on the economic geography of non-industrial societies by Jones (1978). ('Realist' anthropology – as in the work of Leeds, 1984 – has similarly had little impact. See Duncan, 1980, on the interpretation of culture by some geographers as a determinant of human agency.)

The only 'structure as construct' work to have had much influence on geographical research is that of Piaget on the acquisition of intelligence as a process of structural transformation. This developmental psychology work included studies of how the child learns about space and geometry. He found that each stage of development is qualitatively different from that preceding it, and that at each stage new material is integrated with that already held, that all material is consolidated and coordinated – this is the self-regulating feature of the structure in that all of the material is fitted into schemata (it is not random information). Piaget's experiments suggested that there are four major stages in the development of a child's conception of space (a review is provided by Hart and Moore, 1973; see also Golledge *et al*; 1985). These experiments did not extend to the traditional subject matter of geography. Gould (1973, p. 185) notes that:

> Though much of the pioneering work of the child psychologist Piaget is directly concerned with the way in which children learn about space, the world around them, and geometrical and topological concepts . . ., it does not deal with the essentially *geographic* images that children hold or the way they learn about them.

Gould's own work was very largely concerned with 'preference surfaces' (see Golledge, 1981), the attitudes of respondents to particular places (Gould and White, 1974), but others have been more concerned with the child's acquisition of geographical knowledge (Blaut, McCleary and Blaut, 1970; Blaut and Stea, 1971). Golledge (1981) claims that such work involves 'anchoring of many of the concepts of cognitive mapping in the structuralist theories of Piaget' (p. 1329) but most of it (e.g. the review by Downs and Stea, 1973) pays very little attention to the structuralism arguments and focuses rather on what people know and how they acquire it; it has a strong positivist quaity. (The analytic behavioural geography proposed by Couclelis and Golledge (1983) – they term it constructivist-transactionalist – appears close to Piaget's arguments.)

It may be that there are other deep structures in human consciousness that are particularly relevant to geographers but are as yet virtually unexplored. An obvious example of this would be the way in which people organize spatial information and represent it pictorially (and cartographically). Lewis (1981) has shown that the ways in which Amerindians organized spatial information were very similar to those proposed by modern geographers, which has led Blouet (1981, p. vi) to wonder:

> to what degree humans are genetically programmed to organize knowledge about the earth's surface in common ways? Are many geographical concepts

cross-cultural in the sense that all humans have the capability to generate them as part of their inherited mental equipment, in rather the same way as migratory geese are born with a sense of space that allows them to navigate vast distances by instinct rather than instruments?

The potential for more work in the Piagetian mould is clearly considerable, but as yet relatively little is being done which is truly structuralist, as indicated above. (Pickles's, 1985, identification of spatiality via essential phenomology – see p. 81 – indicates similar agenda items for future research.)

For the remainder of this chapter, the focus is on 'structure as process', in particular the various forms and derivations of Marxism which have been introduced to human geography in recent years. As Peet (1977) indicates, the adoption of Marxist perspectives grew out of an increasing frustration with the current structure of western society and the inability to achieve major change within it by research in the positivist tradition (see Johnston, 1983a, Chapter 6). This transition is exemplified in the work of David Harvey, one of the major stimuli to the development of Marxist work in geography, who outlines in the introduction of *Social justice and the city* (1973) the transformation in his own conception of problems and their solutions from an initial 'liberal reform' position (which was positivist; Harvey, 1969) to one based on Marxism, because the latter is holistic, stressing the interdependence of economic and social issues (of production, consumption and distribution).

The introduction of Marxist thought to the mainstream of human geography literature in the early 1970s has led to considerable debate over its relevance and to a variety of responses. Several writers have adopted certain aspects of Marxist thought – notably those relating to the economic workings of capitalist society (as in Smith, 1977, 1979) – but without embracing a full Marxist approach. This has been criticized by, for example, Asheim (1979) who argues that such liberal (Marxian rather than Marxist?) formulations fail because: first, they continue to separate production from distribution/consumption, and thus economic from social geography, when Marxist works make it clear that the two are inseparably linked; second, they allocate too much autonomy to the individual as decision-maker instead of focusing on the constraints of structural relations within the mode of production; and third, they give too much autonomy to the role of space (what is sometimes termed 'spatial fetishism') as a determinant of behaviour, apparently believing that there are immutable 'spatial laws', rather than recognizing that space and spatial relations are part of the structure of the mode of production (space is structured by society, not the other way round). (Mercer, 1978, calls such workers 'philoMarxists'.)

A full Marxist geography, therefore, is one which accepts the fundamental importance of the organization of production in the creation and structuring of all social processes:

> it is that part of a whole science which specializes in the dialectical relations between social processes on the one hand and the natural environment and spatial relations on the other (Peet and Lyons, 1981, p. 202).

But it is more than a method of analysis, more than a holistic viewpoint based on the primacy of the economic:

> it is aimed at changing the fundamental operation of social processes by changing the social relations of production. Social revolutionary changes are necessary to solve endemic spatial and environmental problems, for these problems originate deep in the capitalist social formations (p. 202).

To Marxists, theory cannot be separated from practice; understanding leads to a programme for change. How Marxist geographers should work to achieve a revolution, from capitalism to socialism, is not made clear by many. The consensus would appear to be the gradualist one suggested by critical theory (see below), whereby appreciation of reality as depicted by Marxist analysis will increase the powers of self-reflection and lead to emancipation from domination. Thus:

> Marxism and Marxist geography provide a powerful theoretical and political base for resistance. They are theories constructed on behalf of the mass of 'ordinary' people of the world to aid to our struggle against an international ruling class and a destructive and exploitative form of social life (Peet and Lyons, 1981, p. 205).

For Harvey (1973), the division of labour within society requires academics to provide the knowledge whereby a revolution in practice is set in motion:

> We are academics. . . . As such, our task is to mobilize our powers of thought to formulate concepts and categories, theories and arguments, which we can apply to the task of bringing about a humanizing social change. . . . Empirical evidience . . . can and must be used here. But all of those experiences and all of that information means little unless we synthesize it into powerful patterns of thought (p. 145).

His Marxist geography is:

> concerned with the total reconstitution of geographical thought and practices and the ultimate fusion of geographical studies . . . and other subjects under the umbrella of historical materialism (Harvey, 1981, p. 209; see also Eliot Hurst, 1980),

and he argues that:

> geographers inevitably practise politics while politicians just as inevitably engage in geographical practics. Marxists freely acknowledge that link and seek to strengthen rather than hide it (p. 210).

Harvey (1984) crystallized his views regarding the practical use of Marxist geography in presenting a 'historical materialist manifesto', designed to expose the material base of society in a people's geography that:

> must have a popular base, be threaded into the fabric of daily life with deep taproots into the well-springs of popular consciousness . . . it must also open channels of communication, undermine parochialist world views, and confront or subvert the power of the dominant classes or the state (p. 7).

It would be an 'applied peoples' geography', not linked to narrow and powerful special interest groups (as outlined in Harvey, 1974) but democratic and able to promote the transition from capitalism to socialism.

To some, the nature of the holistic perspective of Marxism, as expressed through historical materialism, and of the practical goals of Marxist work means that the division of the social sciences into separate disciplines is counter-revolutionary. Eliot Hurst (1980), for example, argues against any redefinition of human geography. Instead, he argues for a de-definition of all social sciences, replacing them by a single discipline – historical materialism:

> the science of human society ranks alongside mathematical and natural sciences as the only tenable scientific practices (p. 13).

Indeed, he finds Harvey's call for a 'people's geography' paradoxical, in that its transdisciplinary claims are nevertheless rooted in a particular discipline (Eliot Hurst, 1985).

Others disagree, arguing that although the holistic perspective must be retained, the individual social science disciplines are valuable in their provision of particular foci for attention. Dunford (1980), for example, has argued that disciplines can still be identified by their 'distinctive objects' within a historical materialist framework. For human geography, the specific objects of analysis are:

> the spatial forms of human appropriation of nature and of human social organization (p. 84)

producing the definition that:

> Geography is the study of spatial forms and structures produced historically and specified by modes of production (p. 85).

(The definition is from Scheibling, 1977.) Further, this particular focus has a practical value too. According to Asheim (1979, p. 17):

> The concept of space as the property of the object makes human geography more politically (and practically) relevant, in that the actors become more precisely identified as groups in regional social structures.

The proposition that there is a valid geographical focus within the social sciences is in part related to the concept of structuration. This has been introduced formally to the geographical literature in a few places (e.g 'man is obliged to appropriate his material universe in order to survive and . . . he himself has changed through changing the world around him in a continual and reciprocal process'; Gregory, 1978a, p. 89), but it implicitly used by many more writers. (See for example, the argument of Massey and Allen, 1984, that 'geography matters' and that of Johnston, 1986d, that 'places matter'.) Within Marxist literature, there is considerable debate between proponents of a 'structure as construct' approach (such as Althusser), who present the economic infrastructure of the mode of production as both dominant and determinant and the elements of the superstructure as dominated and determined (although there is no mention of a deep structure), and proponents of a 'structure as process' approach who identify dialectics not only within the infrastructure but also between infrastructure and superstructure. Interpretation of the latter, according to Gregory (1978a, p. 120), means that:

> Spatial structure is not, therefore, merely the area within which class conflicts express themselves . . . but also the domain within which – and, in part, through which – class relations are constituted, and its concepts must have a place in the instruction of the concepts of determinate social formations. (See also Gregory, 1981, p. 11).

(To Gregory, and others, structuralism implies the 'structure as construct' formulation presented here, so that most interpretations of Marx are not structuralist. A broader definition of structuralism to incorporate 'structure as process' is clearly being advanced here.)

The concept of a dialectic between levels (between superstructure and infrastructure) creates what Soja and Hadjimichalis (1979) term the spatial problematic. Following Lefebvre (see Kurzweil, 1980), they argue that:

> The class struggle itself is seen as embedded in the structure and contradictions of socially organized space. No social revolution can therefore succeed without being at the same time a spatial revolution (p. 5).

Thus they argue for a need to introduce spatial analysis into Marxist work which, with a few exceptions, displays 'a deep tradition of anti-spatialism' (p. 6). This leads Soja (1980, p. 208) to define a socio-spatial dialectic:

> The structure of organized space is not a separate structure with its own autonomous laws of construction and transformation [this is positivist spatial fetishism], nor is it simply an expression of the class structure emerging from the social (i.e. aspatial) relations of production. It represents, instead, a dialectically defined component of the general relations of production, relations which are simultaneously social and spacial.

(This is presented later as a concept of *spatiality*: Soja, 1985.) Such a view is represented in a variety of works (e.g. Peet, 1975, on the maintenance of poverty) and provides a clear example of a geographical perspective within Marxist theory. The continuous transformation of capitalism reflects not only the dialectics inherent within the mode of production but also the dialectic between it and particular spatial realizations. (An outline of research on this theme is given below: p. 126. Note that Eyles, 1981 – quoting Peet – doubts whether the 'spatial dialectics' studied by some Marxist geographers are contradictions in the Marxist sense.)

Human geography is often presented as having a twofold approach: the horizontal, which stresses spatial relationships; and the vertical, which stresses people-environment interrelationships. The latter has also been interpreted in Marxist perspective. Sayer (1979a) has provided a historical materialist discussion of the concept of nature (jointly with the concept of people: 'people and Nature are not separate: we are part of Nature', p. 22) as that which provides the objects of labour (the things worked upon). The transformation of nature is part of the dialectic of the mode of production, according to this view:

> In constructing a building we both transform parts of Nature (sand, wood, stone), objectify human knowledge and reproduce or modify certain social relations (p. 31)

so that:

> in any given historical period the interaction with Nature is locked into a determinate structure of social relations and the eternal necessity of labour (in abstract terms) misleadingly gives the appearance of an eternal necessity of those social relations (p. 32).

Harvey (1974a) has illustrated this in another context, showing how conceptions of resources and hence of overpopulation represent a particular conception of nature, that embedded in capitalism. (See also Quaini, 1982, on society's interrelationships with nature under different modes of production, O'Riordan, 1977, on various conceptions of the environment, and Smith, 1984, on conceptions of nature.)

The general theme of all of this work is clearly realist (p. 111) in that it sees the explanation of the phenomena of human geography as lying in hidden mechanisms rather than in the phenomena themselves. Realist philosophy *per se* is explicit in relatively few pieces of geographical writing (e.g. Sayer, 1981, 1984, 1985; Chouinard, Fincher and Webber, 1984), but its tenets provide the implicit foundations for much interpretation. Cox and McCarthy (1982), for example, round out their empirical analyses of the social and spatial correlates of neighbourhood activism in Colombus, Ohio, by presenting such behaviour as an element of false consciousness. It is, they argue, a form of behaviour emanating 'from the structure of social relations in the society as a whole, and not merely from forces unique to the living place' (p. 214), but because most analyses deal only with the observable outcomes of social conflict (the particulars) rather than the determinants (the relations of production) this *real* nature of the behaviour is not revealed. (See also Sayer, 1979b.)

The explication of these hidden mechanisms is the goal of not only a realist philosophy of science (Bhaskar's 1975 presentation of which includes statements such as 'men must be causal agents capable of acting self-consciously on the world', p. 20, but contains no firm guide as to practice) but also critical theory. This, too, has not been discussed in much of the geographical literature. Lewis and Melville (1975, p. 98) introduced it as:

> recognizing the centrality of the relationship between theory and practice by allowing for the effect that knowledge has on those whom it is about . . . a critical theory allows for the fact that hypotheses about society are 'tested' by the development of the class struggle,

and this has been developed more fully in Gregory's (1978a) chapter on 'Committed explanation in geography'. To him, the subjects of geographical study must be made more aware of the results of investigations, and indeed be made part of those investigations, through hermeneutic encounters (as in the geographical expeditions in Detroit, Toronto and elsewhere organized by Bunge: Bunge and Bordessa, 1975). But this may compromise the process of self-reflection by focusing it on particulars rather than generalities. Geographers must present:

> (a) a critique of the concepts through which the discipline has sustained its image of the world; and (b) a critique of the processes through which the social formation has sustained its relations of production (p. 165).

(To encourage self-reflection in society as a whole, and to provide the materials for that, geographers must reflect on the nature of their own discipline.) As expressed by Harvey (1973, 1984), the task of academics is to develop their powers of analysis, thereby to assist others to develop theirs.

Structuralist geography

Like the humanistic approaches, quite a considerable proportion of the geographical writing in the structuralist mould comprises critique, emphasizing the deficiencies of other approaches (both of those discussed in the two previous chapters.) The focus of that critique (as in Massey's, e.g. 1979, of industrial location theory) is that work which is concerned largely with the outcomes of social processes (the locations of industries) and with the impact of individual decision-making (behaviourism) cannot identify the real processes that underpin the creation and re-creation of geographies.

The retroductive approach, with its focus on the infrastructure, presents an alternative, but this is one which is hard for those accustomed to empirical work to appreciate, because its theories are not testable against empirical evidence in the positivist sense (see p. 109). This is not to argue that empirical work is neither possible nor valuable. Massey and Meegan's (1979) analyses of industrial reorganization illustrate how historical situations influence individual decision-making behaviour but they argue that their findings cannot be generalized away from that specific context. S. Duncan (1981) has illustrated the problems of forging links between empirical research and theoretical articulation; the theories have provided considerable insights to the study of all aspects of human geography although, as illustrated below, the impact has been greater in some areas of the subject than others.

Economic geography: uneven development A major substantive impact of structuralist work has been on aspects of the geography of development and underdevelopment, transforming this from a subject dominated by ideas relating to unilinear growth sequences (derived from Rostow's work; see Keeble, 1967; Taylor, 1986c) and a deterministic spatial spread of 'modernization' through a country (see Abler, Adams and Gould, 1971) to one thoroughly permeated by, and extending, Marxist political economy. The stimulus for such work comes from the writings of a variety of scholars (for a critical review, see Brewer, 1980; a geographer's review is Brookfield, 1975; see also N. Smith, 1979, 1984).

Although the various authorities involved in the study of development differ on the relative importance of certain causative factors, there is general agreement that spatial variations in levels of development between countries are an integral aspect of capitalism:

> the unequal development of regions and nations is as fundamental to capitalism as the direct exploitation of labour by capital (Soja, 1980, p. 219)

is a fundamental axiom of such work (though see Browett, 1984). It has been built upon by analyses showing the relationship of imperialism (plus neo-imperialism and neo-colonialism) to the accumulation of wealth in certain parts of the world (usually termed the metropolitan cores). One reaction to the falling rate of profit in those areas is to seek cheaper labour and extended markets in other, relatively weak, areas. (Harvey, 1982, has made a major theoretical contribution to the understanding of the changing pattern of economic activity by incorporating the geography of development with Marxist theories of capitalist crises.) Thus a thriving core-area bourgeoisie is complemented by an impoverished dependent proletariat in the periphery. At the world scale, this allows a classification, basically of countries, into core and periphery, with an intervening semiperiphery. The core comprises the developed countries and the periphery the underdeveloped or dependent; the former absorb surplus value and the latter export it, with the flows being articulated through the urban system (Johnston, 1980a).

At a finer spatial scale, individual countries can be subdivided into cores, peripheries and semi-peripheries; even the least developed country of the international periphery has its local bourgeoisie concentrated into a certain region, usually a single place (Santos, 1975). Structuralist analyses have shown how such intra-national spatial structures have developed, and have then reproduced themselves, as an example of the socio-spatial dialectic. Again, the emphasis has been on demonstrating the inevitability of such uneven development, particularly with the centralization and concentration of the ownership of capital which characterizes recent trends in the transformation of capitalism (Johnston, 1982a), and Massey (1984) has related the changing spatial structure of the United Kingdom to the strategies of capitalist investors.

During the present century, there has been much work in many of the countries at the core of the world economy of what is almost universally known as the 'regional problem'. The major manifestation of this has been (relatively) high unemployment rates in certain regions characterized by a dependence on industries which are in decline. The decline may be a result of a fall of demand for their products or, more likely, a consequence of a shift of investment in those industries to areas where production costs are lower and the potential for accumulation consequently greater (such areas may be in other countries, in some cases several thousand miles from the markets; Thrift, 1986). As with the study of international variations in development, structuralist analysis has sought to relate the regional problem to spatial switches in the pattern of investment, and thus as part of the dialectic between the productive forces and the relations of production. Again, this involves a socio-spatial dialectic. The outcome of one moment of the class struggle in one place (perhaps higher wages for labour, or the implementation of environmental controls: Storper, Walker and Widess, 1981) can reduce business confidence there and lead to a redirection of investment (Massey, 1984).

Recently, descriptive analyses in a number of countries (such as the United Kingdom and the United States of America) have identified a new spatial dimension to the pattern of uneven development, the so-called inner-city problem. Initially, it was argued that this reflected deficiencies in the environment of those areas, but later, structuralist-inspired, analyses have argued that the inner cities are merely the latest areas to be deserted by capital as the transformation of the mode of production continues (Thrift, 1979; Hall, 1981a). Thus:

inherent in capitalist social relations is an unevenness of spatial, political and economic development . . . The emergence of the inner-city problem should be seen in this light. It is not, as such, a new problem in that uneven development has always existed, its novelty lies rather in its promotion to the status of a problem (Forrest *et al.*, 1979, p. 114).

Recognition of this leads the analysts, as in the case of the regional problem, to question the utility and viability of spatial solutions, policies which are area-based in their attempts to boost investment and thereby stimulate employment (Holland, 1976).

As noted above, the articulation of the flows of capital and surplus value takes place through the system of urban places. In addition, of course, the concentration of population into urban places has proved necessary to accommodate the means of production under industrial capitalism. Thus structuralist analyses of urbanization very much follow those of regional variations outlined here, as in Harvey's original analysis of urbanism (Harvey, 1973, Chapter 6; see also Johnston, 1980a, 1982a) and in his later work on capital circuits (Harvey, 1978). Whether the urban area is a sensible focus for analysis – whether there is a specifically urban phenomenon – is, however, a topic of current debate (Saunders, 1981; Dunleavy, 1982).

All of this work illustrates how uneven economic development and its concomitants, at any scale, are necessary consequences of the processes inherent in capitalism. A framework is provided for understanding such phenomena, and that framework could readily be applied in all aspects of economic geography even though it is not as well developed in some branches (agricultural geography, for example) as others; central to the argument is the claim that the study of economic geography cannot be isolated from the more general study of socio-spatial structures. What is not provided is an explanation for which areas become the cores, and which the peripheries, nor for which areas are likely to decline and which to grow, and so on (Johnston, 1982b). Once the spatial structure is established, the socio-spatial dialectic seeks to maintain it. 'Structure as process' provides a *post facto* rationalization for the actual in terms of theories of the real. Because those theories cannot predict how the dialectics will unfold, certainly not in fine spatial detail, they cannot say what will happen where. Realism provides a general understanding within which details about particulars must be fitted.

Social geography: residential segregation As in the work summarized under the previous heading, the introduction of a structuralist approach to social geography, mainly urban social geography, brought about a considerable transformation in research orientations. (Compare, for example, two books on urban residential patterns: Johnston, 1971; Bassett and Short, 1980.) As indicated in Chapter 2 (p. 36), the pre-structuralist work on who lives where within urban areas drew its stimuli from ecology and multivariate statistical analysis. This, it was pointed out (e.g. Eyles, 1974), assumed: first, a given set of social relations; second, no change of a qualitative kind in those relations; third, a consensus within society regarding the 'rightness' of those relations, of the ways in which individuals are allocated to positions within society, and of the ways in which they may seek to change positions; and fourth, free competition for housing, in which all have free choice as to where to live. Against this view, it was argued that society is ever-changing (as the relations of production are constantly transformed), is characterized not by consensus but rather by dissensus (and sometimes outright conflict; Johnston, 1980c), and contains a variety of mechanisms which constrain both choice of housing and choice of residential area.

These themes were introduced to many social geographers by two of the chapters, on ghetto formation and on urban land-use theory, in Harvey's (1973) *Social justice and the city*. These set the determinants of land-use patterns not in the abstractions of the 'frictions of distance' nor in the results of free bargaining in choice, but rather in the class relations characteristic of capitalism. Regarding ghettos, Harvey (p. 135) concluded that:

> the rich group can always enforce its preferences over a poor group because it has more resources to apply either to transport costs or to obtaining land in whatever location it chooses.

The explanation for residential separation of socio-economic and other (e.g. racial) groups therefore lies in the infrastructure. Its appearance in the superstructure can be described and modelled, but not accounted for.

Harvey developed his ideas regarding the forces creating residential segregation in a series of general essays plus a detailed study of the housing market in inner Baltimore. In one of the former, he set out four hypotheses (Harvey, 1975, pp. 362–3):

1 Residential differentiation reflects the reproduction of social relations under capitalism.
2 Residential areas provide milieux within which individuals are socialized.
3 Residential fragmentation into separate communities fragments the class consciousness of the proletariat, thereby hampering the transformation to socialism.
4 Patterns of residential differentiation reflect the contradictions within a class-based society.

From these, he concluded that the creation of urban social areas:

> is produced, in its broad lineaments at least by forces emanating from the capitalist production process and it is not to be construed as the product of the autonomously and spontaneously arising preferences of people (p. 368).

Those preferences are created by the capitalist forces, in the socialization process within community milieux (see also Harvey, 1985b).

Harvey identified a variety of institutions operating with the capitalist economy to assist in the creation of residential separation and thereby to serve the interests of the bourgeoisie and their associates. Analysis of these institutions, the urban gatekeepers and managers, has been the focus of a considerable volume of empirical work (usually termed urban managerialism: Leonard, 1982). Increasingly, however, it was realized that although such work presented useful empirical insights into the workings of housing markets it was not a realist approach in that it focused attention on the decision-makers rather than the context. Thus, stimulated by such works as the translation of Castells's book *The urban question* (1977), a more overtly Marxist approach was adopted (e.g. Bassett and Short, 1980).

As in the work on uneven economic development, much of the realist analysis of the production of residential separation into urban social areas provided rational accounts of why spatial patterns emerge but not of the details of those patterns. Such details are, as pointed out elsewhere in this chapter, irrelevant to the general themes of Marxist work which focus on the major processes rather on the means by which they are realized. Nevertheless, some Marxist analyses of the morphology of social areas have been produced, most notably Walker's (1978, 1981) detailed work on suburbanization in the United States of America, which he associates not only with the desire of the bourgeoisie and their associates to distance themselves from the environmental and social negative externalities of the inner-city but also with the need within capitalist industry to create a demand for 'suburban arcadia'. (See also Johnston, 1984c, for a specific case study of the manipulation of residential space to promote socio-economic goods.)

Political geography revived A comment by Brian Berry in 1969 that political geography was a 'moribund backwater' (Berry, 1969, p. 450) has been much repeated, both within the small subfield and without. Berry's comment was stimulated by his observation that the 'quantitative revolution' of the 1950s and 1960s made little impact on political geography, which remained a combination of (unrecognized) idealism and pre-positivist empiricism (apart from grand environmentalist theories, such as Mackinder's heartland concept). Despite a major growth in the application of positivist approaches in electoral geography (Taylor and Johnston, 1979), a revival in political geography had to await the stimulus of structuralist approaches.

The conflict focus of the structuralist approaches has provided a number of valuable research themes for political geographers (as illustrated in Burnett and Taylor, 1981; Cox and Johnston, 1982). Many of these centre on the role of the state within capitalist and other modes 'of production. Until the late 1970s, the nature of the state had not been considered a research problem for political geographers, but work since has tackled the major theoretical issues and has sought to integrate such theory into not only political geography (e.g. Johnston, 1982b) but also human geography in general. Clark and Dear (1981, 1984; Dear, 1981) have made major contributions to this task, with their book on *State apparatus* providing both a theoretical analysis of the state and its division into various state apparatus and empirical analyses of the American state. (The two are extended in Clark, 1985.) They provide no treatment of why the state is a territorial unit, however, a topic pursued by Mann (1984; he claims that the state is, of necessity, a place with fixed spatial boundaries) and Harvey (1985a; see also Sack, 1983).

The major contribution to the development of a realist political geography has been made by Taylor (1985a), whose work is firmly located in the theoretical framework of Wallerstein's world-systems analysis (p. 117). He focuses on the international system of states and the inter-relationships among states (including war; see also O'Loughlin, 1986), on the state and nationalism, and on the locality as a context for political learning (see also p. 115). He links the three, and believes that he has answered a sceptic's view of the world-systems project (Pahl, 1979) that a:

> theory that the world capitalist crisis is responsible for everything from dirty streets to the closure of teacher-training colleges is inadequate (p. 42).

(For a similar attempt to link the three scales, see Short, 1984.)

Wallerstein's (1984) ideas on politics and the state further inform this particular revitalization of political geography (Taylor, 1986b). With Harvey (1985a), he suggests that states have evolved to protect and advance the interests of a territorially defined bourgeoisie against those of other bourgeoisies. (Harvey suggests that class alliances may develop, probably within the context of a state, to promote the interests of both bourgeoisie and proletariat there, but that such an alliance is likely to be short-lived. On the inability of the state to counter the growing global hypermobility of capital, see Johnston, 1986f.) In this way, the roles and functions of the state with regard to the promotion and legitimation of capitalism can be appreciated (Taylor and Johnston, 1984). For the critical theory perspective, the lesson to be drawn from this understanding, and one promoted by Wallerstein, is that the transition to socialism cannot be achieved state by state; it requires a global politics to produce a single world order.

Historical geography For historical geographers, structuralist approaches offer a realist method of interpreting patterns in the past, just as they do for the economic, social and political geographers of the contemporary scene. Apart from the temporal context, therefore, little may separate them from other branches of geography. If, however, they are interested not in the patterns at one time period but in the processes and patterns of change, then the structuralist approach may be especially appropriate since the changing landscape is presumably a reflection of the dialectics of the mode of production (Cosgrove, 1984). Such an approach is particularly valuable for the geographical study of major changes, such as the transformation from feudalism to capitalism (Butlin, 1978) and the subsequent onset of industrialization (Gregory, 1978c; Dunford and Perrons, 1983), but if one accepts Blaut's (1961) dictum that space is process then it is relevant to all studies of change. (See also Quaini, 1982.)

The process of change has been analysed by Pred (1978) using the concept of structuration and the insights of time-geography. Individuals move along daily and life paths as they pursue their individual and collective projects. As they do so, they encounter others, and accumulate mental experiences which shape intentions and influence future movements. In this, individual and society are in a constant dialectic, so that everything that affects an individual affects society, and vice versa. The result is that (Pred, 1981a):

> the details of social reproduction, individual socialization, and structuration are constantly spelled out by the intersection of particular paths with particular institutional projects occurring at specific temporal and spatial locations (p. 10).

He has illustrated this in a variety of ways, including essays on his own academic career (Pred, 1979, 1984a), and has shown how changing institutional structures – working practices – led to a restructuring of family life (Pred, 1981b). His interpretation of structuration is set out as a sequence of five statements (Pred, 1984b, pp. 280–281);

1 In any place, social reproduction is continuous and inseparable from everyday life in all institutions (such as the family).
2 Socialization, through participation in institutional activity, provides skills appropriate to the given social contexts and leads to local rules of behaviour being absorbed as part of the taken-for-granted world.
3 Thus people's consciousness is shaped by the (place-bound) societies of which they are part, while at the same time society is shaped by the individual's consciousness, so that:

> socialization and social reproduction (and transformation) always become one another (p. 280).

4 There is a continual dialectic between practice and structure, which lies at the heart of structuration.
5 Structuration is characterized as:

the structural properties of any social system express themselves through the operation of everyday practices at the same time that everyday practices generate and reproduce the micro- and macro-level properties of that social system (p. 281),

Thus, as the title of the paper indicates, place is a 'historically contingent process' or, as he expresses it elsewhere (Pred, 1984c):

Societies and biographies are never in frozen states of being, but always and everywhere are in the process of becoming. People produce history and places at the same time that people are produced by history and places.

People do not produce history and places under conditions of their own choosing, but in the context of already existing, directly encountered social and spatial structures (p. 251)

a theme which he develops with reference to the elite group who promoted the development of Boston as a major international centre of mercantile activity in the early nineteenth century.

The institutions that comprise the social structure are, of course, themselves human productions. Understanding their creation, and their role in the reproduction of societies, is the goal of Harvey's (1985b, 1985c) two-volume study of the history and theory of capitalist urbanization. The first volume – *The urbanization of capital* – follows from his earlier reconstruction of Marxist economic theory, incorporating the production of space (Harvey, 1982), by seeking to understand how urbanization is produced through the operation of the laws of motion of a capitalist mode of production. The second volume – *Consciousness and the urban experience* – investigates the impact of this process on social relations and political consciousness in particular instances (see also Castells, 1983 and McDowell and Massey, 1984, on spatial variations in gender relations). Five loci of consciousness formation are identified (Harvey, 1985c), so that:

Individuals draw their sense of identity and shape their consciousness out of the material bases given by the individualism of money, the class relations of capital, the limited coherence of community, the contested legitimacy of the state, and the protected but vulnerable domain of family life (pp. 261–2).

All five intersect in particular places:

within a produced urban milieu that institutionalizes and reifies the social and physical patterning of all such human relations in space and time (p. 262)

thereby providing the contingent conditions within which the general tendencies of capitalist urbanization are worked out. The landscape itself, then, is both a representation of the institutional foci and a contingent condition for the future development of capitalism and consciousness. As Cosgrove (1984) argues, each social formation (an historical representation of a mode of production) unifies economic, social, political, religious and cultural practices in a particular local consciousness, and he claims that the 'landscape idea' is a part of that consciousness; landscape is one of the cultural products of a social formation – like literature, painting, poetry and drama – which, between the fifteenth and nineteenth centuries in Europe, implied:

> a particular sensibility, a way of experiencing and expressing feelings towards the external world, natural and man-made, an articulation of a human relationship with it (p. 9).

The basic thesis of the 'structure as process' approaches, that the mode of production is continually in transformation as a result of both processes within itself and interaction with the products of earlier transformations, makes it an attractive framework for the study of historical geography. Indeed, it suggests that there is no such thing as historical geography, since change is continuous. The methodology is the same, whatever the time and place of the topic. The data sources and contexts vary, and must be understood by the scholar, but this requirement differs little from the need to understand the spatially varying cultural contexts of the contemporary world.

Summary

To a considerable extent, initially the major impact of structuralist works in human geography, as with humanistic, was as critique. The epistemological and ontological bases of other approaches, notably the positivist, have been laid bare and practitioners have been forced to reflect more on the nature of their work. Thus, as indicated in the next chapter, even if the introduction of the 'structure as process' arguments has fully not achieved the revolution in geographical practice that some hoped for (e.g. Harvey, 1973, p. 145) it has at least identified some of the problems of the other approaches.

But this is an insufficient achievement, especially for those who argue a strong Marxist line and who see other approaches as counter-revolutionary, both in the sense of the development of understanding and with regard to changing society. To them the only valid epistemology is the realist one: knowledge is obtained not by the accumulation of evidence but by the development of theories which account for the driving forces within society, provide understanding of our experience within that society, and indicate the intellectual tools that can be used to achieve real (i.e in the sense of the mechanisms) social change. Such an approach is difficult for many people to accept, because it is not verifiable/falsifiable against evidence in the positivist sense. The test of a theory to a Marxist is not whether it accounts for a certain phenomenon or event but whether it can form the basis for a viable practice, one which will produce change that releases people from domination.

To achieve the Marxist end, especially if this is by the route advanced by critical theorists rather than that of others (not necessarily geographers) which involves revolution and the imposition of a new mode of production, it is necessary for the theories to suggest an acceptable practical route. In the short term, therefore, the work which is done, the theories erected and set against the empirical world, must be interpreted as sensible by others. As illustrated in this chapter, such work is as yet relatively underdeveloped and there are still many topics to be tackled, many debates to be resolved, and many sceptics to be convinced. The contribution so far has involved demonstrating the need for a structuralist approach, indicating that processes must be studied realistically, that a main component of such study is theoretical articulation, and that the activation of the revealed mechanisms must inform the appreciation of events in historically and spatially contingent circumstances. To some extent, the actual outcomes of the theories are irrelevant to their understanding. They are relevant, however, to those experiencing the outcomes, whose willingness to accept the structuralist theories may be influenced by their ability to relate outcome and process. In the long-term, the success or failure of the structuralist approaches will depend on the dialectic between theory-producers and 'world residents'.

5

Conflict and accommodation

The preceding three chapters have outlined, albeit briefly, the epistemology, ontology, methodology and substantial contributions of the three approaches that dominate contemporary human geography in North America and the United Kingdom. Each has been presented separately, though clearly there are links between them. The concern with this final chapter is arguments over the extent to which the three, or two of the three, or parts of the three, can be brought together. The focus, therefore, is on the debates over whether accommodation is possible.

As with all debates, positions tend to be polarized. At the one extreme are those who argue a pluralist position; at the other are those who contend that accommodation is impossible, and that geographers must make a choice.

Typical of the pluralist position is that of Golledge (1972) who contends that:

> There is . . . one thing of which we can all be sure – that there is no single way to obtain knowledge (p. 16).

which is not debatable since, as illustrated here, there is no single definition of knowledge. He continues that:

> Perhaps much of the confusion that lies at the heart of geography today results from an awareness that there are simply many geographies and many possible worlds. Uncertainty arises because we know not which geography to choose, nor which possible world we should aim for. We run the risk of becoming dogmatic by trying to force all worlds into one very limited format, and in doing so we ignore, belittle or forget the others (p. 21).

Golledge is against such dogmatism, against attempts to chart a single path for geographical practice: instead:

> Let each of us stress our individuality and our difference, our temperaments, our beliefs, our knowledge levels, our interests, our perspectives (p. 22).

Couclelis (1982) agrees, arguing that:

> Fragmentation of research is not necessarily in itself an evil: the world is after all a very varied place and we need all the different perspectives we can get . . . As long as there are people around with different temperaments, beliefs and

ideologies, and as long as they have something to say, there should be room for positivist geography, for marxian geography, for Vienna-circle geography, for Frankfurt-school geography, for Lyon-group geography, and so on. The more, the merrier (p. 105).

Further, it seems, it doesn't matter too much if those various groups do not readily communicate with each other. So long as we have a common sense of direction which defines 'progress in the field of geography' then:

> the simpletons playing with odd-shaped little pieces of coloured wood could suddenly be seen to be serious people working at different corners of the same jigsaw (p. 106)

In the same book, Gould (1982) believed that he had identified the jigsaw. He argued that:

> we do not have to choose,. . . we do not have to abandon the technical in favour of the hermeneutic, and favour the emancipatory over both. Indeed, our inquiries (I am tempted to say our lives) are diminished by such categorical choices. We can use, *must* use, all perspectives, all traditions of inquiry simultaneously in troikalike parallel (p. 78).

The methodology for this was Q-analysis, a language of structure which reveals structures from observations.

Ranged against such pluralistic views are those which promote one only, frequently through the negative mode of attacking others rather than positively by demonstrating the superiority of that favoured. Thus, with regard to structuralist arguments, Ley (1978) attacks certain forms of Marxism as presenting:

> a world of reductionism, a world of pallid human profiles where the moves of the faceless and mindless ones are determined according to the system of an outside operator. . . . Materialism, reductionism, determinism; there are the characteristics of an epistemology and an ideology of manipulation that has an unauthentic model of man (p. 48)

and he followed this up by proclaiming that (Duncan and Ley, 1982):

> structural marxism has led to a passive model of man that is conservative and results in an obfuscation of the processes by which human beings can and do change the world (p. 54).

Chisholm (1975) also finds Marxism unhelpful, and not apparently worthy of a place in the discipline's literature:

> Harvey wants us to embrace the Marxist method of dialectic. This 'method' passes my understanding; so far as it has a value, it seems to be as a metaphysical belief system and not – as its protagonists proclaim – a mode of rational argument (p. 175).

And Muir (1978) was even more scathing, equating academic Marxism with Eastern European political practice and characterizing it by:

> the commands from such little men as Marx, Lenin, Trotsky, Stalin and Mao concerning the primacy of activism, the obligations of party membership and the necessity to subordinate individual judgement to the will of the party (p. 126).

Other approaches have come in for similar criticisms. There are positive arguments too, as in Berry and Marble's (1968) case for a positivist approach:

> building accurate generalizations with predictive power by precise quantitative description of spatial distributions, spatial structure and organization, and spatial relationships (p. 6)

and Abler, Adams and Gould's (1971) linking of this to an applied goal:

> Like it or not, geography and the other social sciences have pressing social and moral responsibilities. We see no alternative to practising geography as a science if we hope to meet these obligations (p. 28).
> . . . explanation and manipulation are the focus of our discipline today and will continue to be in the future. Because of our wish to manipulate events, we must explain both process and structure to ourselves so we can intervene in process to produce the spatial structure of activities we desire (p. 88).

Finally, there are those who seek to transcend the pluralism, not by rejecting one or more of the approaches but rather by combining them in some way. Both Herbert (1978) and Johnston (1980b), for example, noted that realist approaches involve work at several levels – empirical, actual, and real – and advocated associating them with the separate methodologies of positivism (identifying spatial order), humanistic approaches (studying individual actors, such as urban managers), and Marxism (identifying the mechanisms that drive society). Thus (Johnston, 1980b):

> there is a strong case for using positivist/behavioural approaches within modern human geography, to describe and explain the particular realizations which form the world in which we live. . . . Work should be set within, and be guided by, the structural mould, but this is insufficient to be truly geographical (p. 411).

In response, Eyles and Lee (1982) argued that:

> There appears to be an assumption . . . that these 'approaches' are in some way alternatives; that we can select this concept from one approach, that method from another, and the perspective from yet another. Unfortunately, this desire for eclecticism rests on the false assumption that these approaches are above all techniques for analysis rather than epistemologies (p. 117).

Hudson (1983) makes a similar point, and extends it by promoting one approach:

> It is correct to identify different levels of analysis but equally incorrect to suggest that these have to be dealt with separately within different theoretical frameworks, and then welded together; historical materialism itself provides the necessary methodological framework for such multi-level analyses (p. 33).

Fincher (1983), too, argues against eclecticism, particularly an eclectic usage of Marxian concepts. She notes that:

> Concerned social scientists, interested in the insights of Marxian analysis but accustomed to working with other theories, occasionally comment that some Marxian ideas are useful and may be grafted onto other modes of analysis without requiring adoption of the whole Marxist 'package' (p. 606).

But, she argues, such eclecticism is unjustifiable, on two grounds. First, Marxian abstract categories cannot be equated with empirical concepts; their theoretical and vernacular meanings are not necessarily synonymous. Secondly, Marxist work has an explicit political purpose, and use of Marxian terms implies an acceptance of that purpose. Thus, although:

> Marxian science is similar to other sciences in its attempts to impose order on reality (p. 608)

it differs from them in both its epistemology and its ideology; without acceptance of both, Marxian terminology is improperly used.

So, is it necessary to choose? Can choice be avoided by the eclectic creation of a hybrid approach, somehow integrating the various elements of the menu into a single dish? To address these questions, it is necessary to be explicit on the contents of the menu, which is the goal of the next section.

Three approaches?

The writings just reviewed suggest that some geographers deny the relevance of one or more of the three approaches outlined here, that some seek to bring them together in a variety of ways, and that some merely promote all, in the expectation that, eventually, each will contribute to a unified body of geographical knowledge. Particular concern in the rest of this chapter will be with the 'bringing together' arguments. The dismissive arguments stand or fall on their own grounds, the pluralist arguments cannot be tested, though they can be dismissed. Only the middle ground can be explored. Before doing that, however, it is necessary to clarify briefly the differences between the three approaches. This will be done in the context of analyses of their underlying ideologies.

Ideology is a widely-used but hard-to-define term. Some present it in positive terms, such as Larrain's (1979) definition of it as:

the expression of the world-view of a class . . . the opinions, theories and attitudes formed within a class in order to defend and promote its interests (p. 14).

According to this view, it is a framework for looking at the world – and one to be imposed on others, some would argue. But it is also, because of that imposition, a negative concept, defined by Larrain as:

a critical concept which means a form of false consciousness or necessary deception which somehow distorts one's understanding of social reality (pp. 13–14).

The one framework can be both positive and negative, because it is used to advance the interests of one group in society and obscure those of others. (Thus under capitalism, it is argued, an ideology that favours the interests of the capitalist class is imposed on the proletariat – in a variety of ways, many by the state – in order to obtain its acceptance of the capitalist mode of production.)

Here, the origins of an ideology – and hence whether it is positive or negative – are less important than its contents. An ideology is defined, following Scarbrough (1984), as a system of beliefs divided into two components:

1 the core beliefs, the assumptions, values and goals 'which hold steady in the face of the flow of events' (p. 39); and
2 the principles of action, which are the empirical outcomes of the core and which guide the response to particular situations.

Each of the three approaches outlined here is thus to be equated with an ideology. Its core beliefs are presented here, as metaphors (or 'models of man') which lead to different conceptions of the principles of action – the conduct of inquiry, and its purpose.

Metaphors are 'at the heart of the nature of scientific understanding' (p. 13) according to Harrison and Livingstone (1982), because language is the means by which scientists express their (often imperfect) understanding of newly-discovered phenomena. They argue, following Mepham (1973), that scientific activity does not produce a language to describe the aspect of the world being studied: the language comes first, a culturally acquired mode of organizing and expressing experiences. Thus new experiences can only be communicated in the context of the existing language, which requires meanings to be transformed through metaphors. In this way, the metaphor is a key element in the expansion of understanding; it may be developed systematically, in which case it is akin to a model, or it may be less structured, in which case it is closer to a myth (see also Berry, 1980).

Harrison and Livingstone identify three separate axes to contemporary geographical thought (Figure 2), each with a set of associated metaphors. Central to them all is the metaphor of *form*, representing the major focus of human geography as areal differentiation. On the functionalist axis (empiricist-positivist in the present volume) – which Harrison and Livingstone identify as 'Much of what passes for orthodoxy in contemporary geography' (p. 15) – the dominant metaphors are *machine* and *organism*. The mechanistic metaphor presents society, and the individuals comprising it, as a system functioning according to pre-defined rules, with stimuli producing predictable responses. Organism has a similar purpose, presenting a holistic metaphor of a functioning system with a place (i.e. a defined territory and its contents, including physical environment and people) reified as a complexly ordered machine.

The metaphors associated with the structuralist axis are *construction* and *domination*. The former represents the theoretical goal of structuralist work, which is to understand, through the construction of viable theories, the mechanisms that drive society but which cannot be directly apprehended. Domination reflects the impact of those mechanisms on individual behaviour:

> the structures of society are not neutral but can be seen as oppressive and exploitative – in short, they are seen as instruments of domination (p. 23).

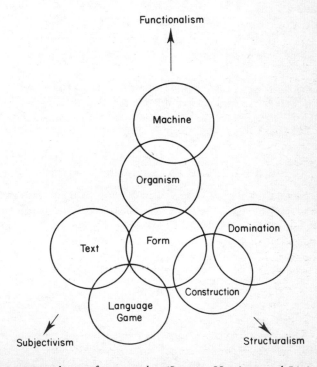

FIGURE 2 Metaphors of geography (Source: Harrison and Livingstone, 1982, p. 18)

The individual is thus constrained by the mechanism, according to this metaphor. But along the subjectivist axis (the equivalent of the humanistic approaches as outlined here), works:

> differ from functionalism, on the one hand, by focusing on understanding the nature of social realities through asking questions of meaning and intentionality, and from structuralism, on the other, by emphasizing the intelligibility of human thought and action without recourse to determinant, deep, universal structures (p. 24).

The associated metaphors are *language game* and *text*. The former derives from Wittgenstein's depiction of social activity as a game of thoughts, words and actions – we understand what people do, and why, through their mode of expression (words); meanings are conveyed through language which, as Olsson (1982) has reminded geographers, is a major constraint to expression. The textual metaphor expands the language game, arguing that meanings are conveyed in a variety of ways – hence Meining's (1979) arguments for 'reading the landscape' to understand its creators' meanings.

Harrison and Livingstone present these three groups of metaphors as the underlying organizational frameworks for much modern human geography. They are the models within which scientific activity is organized, the core beliefs of various geographical ideologies. Others have suggested alternative sets of models – they term them 'models of men', and that wording will be used here when referring to such works, despite its unfortunate sexism.

Van der Laan and Piersma (1982) have suggested that most models present either an active or a passive image, and that debate may involve one being posed as the dual of the other – as in the environmental determinism vs possibilism debate. In the passive image:

> the acting individual is seen as an 'object' that is fully controlled by external stimuli . . . man is reduced to a *homme sans tête* (p. 414)

whose mental capacity can be modelled in a mechanistic way. In the active image, on the other hand, 'external stimuli alone do not explain behaviour', for the source of action is inside the actor, not in the stimuli. Thus science presents two basic models:

> the mechanistic-materialistic view of man as a complicated programmed machine . . . susceptible to the scientific approach peculiar to the natural sciences and mathematics . . . [and] the humanistic approach, which studies man through human behaviour . . . [and] emphasizes man's internal creative processes in explaining spatial behaviour (p. 415).

The former image is the one associated with the quantitative movement, they argue, because of its 'lifeless' presentation of the human being through numbers, whereas humanistic work – with its focus on the mental climate within which actions are decided – promotes the active image. In what they term 'goal-critical' work (as in Marxist geography), both images can be found. They quote from Marx (1971) that:

My own existence is a social activity. For this reason, what I myself produce I produce for society and with the consciousness of acting like a social being; the individual is a social being. The manifestation of this life . . . is therefore a manifestation and affirmation of social life (pp. 46–7).

This could be read as presenting a passive image, of a socially determined individual, but it could be allocated an active image, with the individual playing a creative role within society. Van der Laan and Piersma argue that the former is the correct interpretation of classical Marxism, because of the necessities implied by the mechanisms of a capitalist society, but that critical theory combines the two:

Within the societal context, man is considered to be active and passive at the same time: active in giving form to society, passive in undergoing social influences (p. 422).

An alternative set of 'models of man' has been presented by Claval (1983). He identifies three as prevalent in recent geographical writing.

1 *Homo rationalis* is the classical 'economic man' of much normative theory, able to argue logically and to learn without cost (and thus, presumably, not needing education!); the result is perfect decision-making. This model has important geographical consequences, according to Claval:

The environment has no influence on decisions since reason is inborn and information is free. It also means that *homo rationalis* has no childhood: it is not necessary to study his development since the result is independent of the family, of the local milieu, and of the hazards of existence. Man has no destiny, since he is reduced to intellect (p. 3).

Thus places should be the same, and geography is only relevant to the extent that distance is a variable about which logical decisions are made.

2 *Homo historicus* does not accept that the individual has innate reason, independent of society and civilization; people develop over time, within the constraints of natural and social environments. But, Claval argues, this development is collective and not individual:

Homo historicus has a history, but it is a collective one, the history of his class and of the situation of this class in the whole society; he has no individual destiny (p. 5).

For geographers this too implies that place is irrelevant, that spatial variations arise from differences in society alone.

3 *Homo roboticus* is a person with:

practically no inborn capabilities except the aptitude to construct ideas and feelings out of experience. He is a product of the environment (p. 6).

Thus individual development is a process of acculturation; the person is a machine programmed to assimilate that which is taught. Of the three models, this has the most interest for geographers, since individual change is environmentally produced:

Man is a product of his social environment; he changes when the values of the group change. . . . He has a history, but not a personal one. His life is not a true destiny; its features are shaped by the general conditioning he has received (p. 7).

Thus in all three, the model of man is really a model of society: human diversity is no more than social diversity, if it occurs (according to *homo rationalis*, it shouldn't).

These three sets of models (note that there are others, linked to them, as in Couclelis, 1982) identify the core beliefs, or ideologies, that provide the structuring frameworks for contemporary human geography. Can these ideologies be merged in any way, or must we choose?

Integrate or choose?

The three approaches to geography outlined in this book are underpinned by three separate ideologies – represented by metaphors, or 'models of man'. To some, as implied earlier in this chapter, the best way forward within human geography is to advance all three, which will make their own contributions to understanding (or will atrophy, because they have no contributions to make); this 'let's agree to differ' stance is idealistic – will people who have invested intellectual capital in an approach recognize that it has no contributions to make? – and potentially cowardly, since it retreats from fundamental debate. Others are prepared to engage in that debate – though often from entrenched ideological positions – and reach a conclusion about a single, viable way forward. A third group wishes to explore all three approaches, in the hope of discovering some combination that they find superior. It is on such explorations that the present section focuses.

One early exploration was undertaken by Hay (1979), the title of whose essay – 'Positivism in human geography: response to critics'– indicates his starting-point (and possibly his preferred destination). He notes that both humanistic and structuralist approaches have been involved in a critique of the positivist, though contends that they have tended to 'brand all "scientific" epistemologies as "positivist" ' (p. 2). Four basic criticisms are identified:

1 The abandonment of any study of meanings, that cannot be evaluated in a positivist methodology;
2 The reification of individuals (i.e. passive 'models of men');
3 Reductionism in that systems are treated as no more than aggregates of individuals; and
4 Lack of self-criticism in considering the ideological underpinnings of positivism, especially as they refer to the utility of its findings in an unequal society.

These are tackled by stressing five misconceptions about the nature of the (so-called?) positivist work. First, Hay does not claim that all topics can be studied according to the rules of 'scientific dialogue' (p. 4): he accepts the distinction between science and metaphysics, and does not argue for the elimination of the latter. (In Keat's terms – p. 13 – therefore, he rejects scientism.) Secondly, he points out that positivist work should not be equated with normative theory, so that abandoning theories based on *homo rationalis* does not mean abandoning the 'positivistic conception of science'. Thirdly, he argues that positivist approaches should not be equated with the search for general (time and space invariant) geographical laws. Its goal, he argues (following Popper), is:

> identification of the *problem situation* (practical or political) which the individual or group was trying to solve, the identification of the *decisive* elements in that situation, and an explication of why the historical action was adequate to the situation. Such an approach is capable of falsification . . . In such a way it may therefore be possible to speak of an objective and logical analysis of human behaviour which is in no sense nomological (p. 5).

(This is close to the philosophy of pragmatism – p. 59; see also Hay, 1985a, for a development of this idea). Fourthly, he argues that prediction should not be equated with prophecy. In positivist work, prediction is the way in which hypotheses are tested with regard to accounting for the unknown, it can only provide the basis for prophecy, in an 'as if . . .' context, assuming that the conditions that applied in the test situation recur. Finally, he argues that any postulated explanation is likely to be incomplete, but that the

> question to be asked of a geographic theory is not 'does this theory *totally* explain the observed variation?' but the more modest question, 'does this theory contribute an explanation of a part of the observed variation which would other- wise remain obscure?'. If the claims of location theory are couched in these terms the critique ceases to be important (p. 9).

What Hay has done, therefore, is to extract a problem-solving method- ology from the positivist conception of science; he presents an empirical evaluation procedure, which some may see as valid (as pragmatism per- haps – p. 59), but not positivism (see Johnston, 1986b). He then sets it, following a review of the other two approaches, into an attempted reconciliation of the three. In this, the terminology is that of Habermas (1972), who identifies three types of science: the empirical-analytic or nomological (including positivist); the hermeneutic; and the critical. Geography spans all three, Hay claims, so that human geography could embrace at the same time:

> a *nomological* geography which seeks, for example, to understand the workings of urban rent theory as positivistically observed, a *hermeneutic* geography which seeks to identify the meaning of the urban rent system for those who are participants (active or passive) within it, and a *critical* geography which points to the extent to which present urban rent systems are themselves transformations of the capitalist system, but which admits that some of its features may indeed be 'invariant regularities' (p. 22).

The terminology is somewhat unfortunate, since nomological is usually interpreted as 'concerning or involving laws'. In his context, Hay appears to argue for positivist-inspired empirical analyses that may identify 'invariant regularities'– though the range of invariance is not specified.

Hay's arguments have been echoed by others. Christensen (1982), for example, makes very similar points when she contends that:

> phenomenology constitutes a rejection of *positivism*, but not a rejection of a *positive*, that is to say *empirical*, science. But this point is lost in human geography, because human geographers have not consistently differentiated between positivism and empirical science (p. 43).

The latter 'yields factual knowledge that is precise, exact and certain' (p. 47) – but no more. It is not antagonistic to a human science:

> The descriptive, interpretative, and empirical components are all necessary if a human science is to develop an intersubjectively valid theoretical framework that has relevance to the human phenomenon studied. Each component presupposes the theoretical attitude, yet each proceeds according to its own distinctive method. The empirical component proceeds through the method of hypothesis testing; the descriptive part develops by means of descriptive analysis; and the interpretative component employs the canons of hermeneutics (pp. 50–1).

(Note that there is no mention of the structuralist perspective.) In such an approach, the potential value of quantification is recognized; as Taylor (1981) and Walker (1981b) make clear, its use in precise description can be substantial – though Sayer (1984) disagrees – and any definitive equation of quantification with, and only with, positivism is false (Johnston, 1986b).

Hay's presentation has also been mirrored in a recent argument for a revival of regional geography. Scargill (1985) notes the diversity of approaches within geography as practised in recent years, and illustrates them with reference to the Fenland area of Eastern England.

The historical geographer looking at this region might be interested primarily in recreating its past landscapes, the periods chosen for study corresponding with those of major changes in the evolution of the drainage system. The spatial-analytical geographer, by contrast, seeks to fit Fenland phenomena – crops, farms, drains, etc. – into his statistical models of distribution, at the same time observing the diffusion of selected phenomena from centres of innovation. To the physical geographer the Fens are first and foremost an example of a controlled ecosystem and interest lies principally in the response of plants and animals to the hydrological situation. The literature and folklore of the region provide the starting point for the humanist who will probably have read Dorothy Sayers's novel *The Nine Tailors* and will be interested in this as a portrayal of the life and character of the region. Some, however, could prefer a landscape approach, noting how the region has been illustrated in art. Finally, the Marxist might seek to interpret the geography of the Fens in terms of the crisis of capitalist landownership, observing how present patterns of farming are a response to EEC prices (themselves related to the international division of capital) and how wealthy farmers benefit from a system that was not intended for them (pp. 140–1).

All of these approaches are seen as 'of value' and it is argued that:

by noting how the region might be studied in different ways the student will be helped to see how the systematic branches of geography fit together (p. 141).

No framework for fitting them together is offered, however. Scargill's committee was advised by Gregory, who elsewhere (1984) argues that:

All – or at any rate most – of these approaches would, I think, have much to offer [to the study of the Fens] (p. 486)

in an apparently anarchic way which elsewhere he castigates as 'inchoate eclecticism' (Gregory, 1978a, p. 169).

Harrison and Livingstone (1982) proceed a little further, in promoting an accommodation. They argue that metaphors themselves build bridges, because of their basis in a shared language:

by signifying that understanding is never purely individual but communal (metaphor communicates shared meaning), never purely intellectual but experiential (metaphor arises out of share experiences), never purely theoretical but practical (metaphor is practised in a shared context) (p. 30).

Their reconciliation is humanistically-based, bridging the subjectivist and structuralist metaphors, and based on an epistemological foundation that has explored the shared presuppositions expressed through language (Livingstone and Harrison, 1981). These presuppositions provide the framework within which meanings are created and communicated, and on them:

it may then be possible to erect a humanistic geography which is, at the same
time, *critical*, in questioning rather than bracketing our presuppositions, *hermeneutic*, in interpreting the meanings behind action, and *empirical*, in examining the
subjectively interpreted objective world (p. 370).

Thus we identify the metaphors that people use, communicate them to
others, explore how they structure interpretations of the empirical world,
and critically assess how they have been brought about.

Guelke, who had earlier criticized both positivist and structuralist
approaches in his promotion of the idealist (Guelke, 1982, see above, p. 78),
has argued that (Guelke, 1985):

as long as geographers have a commitment to basing their interpretations of
specific geographical phenomena on evidence the possibility of a dialogue exists
among advocates of different philosophical positions (p. 135).

He notes that among historians the study of slavery is a field 'in which
positivists, Marxists and others are all active' (p. 135). Thus questions may
be posed from very different ideological perspectives, but can be empirically
evaluated – as an example he cites 'was slavery abolished because sugar
growing had ceased to be profitable?'. (I am not sure that this is readily
evaluated.) It is not clear whether this question is being posed in positivist
terms, however. Guelke argues that:

One would certainly not anticipate that a major interpretation would be over-
thrown by the first piece of negative evidence that was uncovered, but the
accumulation of new evidence on key questions would certainly call for the
modification and revision of accepted ideas (p. 136).

At best, this is a call for rigorous empirical inquiry along the lines argued by
Hay (though Guelke, unlike Hay, does not accept the criteria of critical
rationalism, it seems); it does not suggest a full acceptance of the 'positivist
attitude'. Guelke argues for a unified geography, clustered around certain
themes, but with philosophical pluralism leading to the posing of empirical
questions. He believes that:

the fact that various geographical phenomena were being investigated by
scholars with different perspectives would put pressure on all to be cautious
about their claims and careful about the quality of their evidence. For example, a
positivist geographer with liberal inclinations might wish to show how well off
the people of a city were or the progress that had been made. This work would
undoubtedly benefit if the scholar engaged upon it knew that it would be subject
to the critical scrutiny of a Marxist, who was very much out of sympathy with
his general ideological orientation (p. 136)

But care in the use of evidence is necessary whatever the context, and results
can as well be scrutinized from within as from outwith a philosophical
approach. And Guelke's equation of description with positivism is a

misrepresentation of the latter term. It is a less convincing attempt to fuse several approaches than that of Jackson and Smith (1984), which draws on pragmatism, interactionism, Weberian stratification theory, and the theory of structuration (but *not* positivism) to offer:

> a means by which to appreciate the meaning as well as the form of space and society, an opportunity to focus on social and spatial boundaries in terms of the power relations which sustain them, and the beginnings of a fuller appreciation of the relationship between structure and action which is as appropriate to the interpretation of spatial relations as it is to the understanding of social interaction (p. 208).

They accept that it will be condemned by some, because it separates the natural from the social sciences and does not deny human creativity and freedom. Yet, they say:

> it is not a perspective that denies the existence of constraint, nor one refusing to admit that constraints are often hidden, inaccessible to those they affect.

It brings together elements of humanistic and structuralist approaches, and – from its base in pragmatism – promotes rigorous empirical analysis.

Claval's (1983) search for a reconciliation is somewhat different, because the models he identifies in the literature are basically all of the functionalist (*homo rationalis*, *homo roboticus*) or structuralist (*homo historicus*) variety. He believes that attempts to develop a new model for the subjectivist axis are uncoordinated, and he seeks to bring them together on the basis of *homo ecologicus*. Crucial to this is his concept of 'individual destiny'; people learn – in the general ways suggested by *homo roboticus* – in the context of particular experiences, especially those of early life, so that understanding requires the study of biography, to illustrate that:

> Man partly chooses the type of identity he develops. The main difference between present studies and positivist ones is that creativity and freedom no longer appear scandalous. The roles we assume are not only the result of our formation. We improve and modify them all the time. We shape our behaviour following models offered by persons we admire or by groups we envy (p. 16).

Thus people are culturally shaped, in the context of local traditions.

Claval's exploration is not for some eclectic mixture of existing metaphors or models, therefore, but for a new one that can transcend and replace them. It has much in common with others that seek to remove the polarization between what Thrift (1983) terms the determinist and the voluntarist approaches to human geography (though Claval's trilogy recognizes no voluntarist approaches, undoubtedly reflecting the context of his work – French geography – which differs from almost all others discussed here; and thereby promotes Thrift's case). Thrift also notes that social theories (i.e. of society) tend to be polarized too. Compositional theories allocate individuals to groups (classes, etc.) within society, and account for their behaviour accordingly – as in much structural Marxism. Contextual theories account for behaviour by its spatial and temporal context – as in the biographical approach hinted at by Claval for *homo ecologicus*. The theory of structuration (see p. 114) brings the two together by situating behaviour in both a local context (what Thrift terms one's 'interaction structure'; p. 41) and a compositional ordering (the 'objective social structure'). The locale is a temporally and territorially defined social system, created by people as their interpretations of the compositional ordering, and creating people in that it is their biographical context; both acts of creation are continuous (see Gregory, 1981), so that the nature of the locale, and those resident in it, are in continual flux.

The structuration model provides a framework for an integrated social science incorporating geography, but one which some see as difficult to operationalize empirically since it is not clear how to 'break into' the continuous recursive inter-relationships of structure and agency in order to undertake empirical research (Gregson, 1986; see also Moos and Dear, 1986; Dear and Moos, 1986). It provides an integrating framework, however, rather than an argument that 'anything goes'. One illustration of how that framework might be used has been provided by Taylor's (1982, 1985a) reconstruction of political geography, based on Wallerstein's world-systems approach (p. 117). In this, the compositional structure is the capitalist global world-economy – what Taylor calls the *scale of reality*. Within it there are many locales, the places in which people live, learn and act – these form the *scale of experience*. Mediating between locales and world-economy are states – what Taylor terms the *scale of ideology*. All three levels are human creations, and all three are changing as a result of human action, which involves interactions among all three. The result is an historical social science within which geography is fully implicated, because change is both spatial and temporal (Taylor, 1986a). Structuralist ideas are present, since they can account for the mechanisms driving the world-economy, humanistic approaches are present, since both states and locales represent meanings and provide the contexts for interpretation; and empirical analyses are present since they allow the evaluation of tentative descriptions of the spatial and temporal components of this historical social science. Positivism is absent, however, since the order identified is not presumed to be universal.

A common thread running through all of these arguments is a rejection, usually explicit, of positivism as that term is normally interpreted (see p. 12). The orientation of that approach towards the formulation of general laws is rejected, for one which is just as rigorous but which does not shift to the other pole of the determinism–voluntarism continuum. This is reflected in recent arguments for the revival of regional geography (King,

1985). In the past, regional geography has been an empiricist practice (and has recently been repromoted as such; Hart, 1982). It falls into what has been termed the *singularity trap* (Johnston, 1985a) with each region, an assemblage of environmental, cultural and other characteristics, presented as an individual phenomenon, the explanation of which is internal to it only. Positivism, which was a reaction to such work, falls into the *generalization trap*, presenting the characteristics of each region as no more than the consequence of an interacting (in predictable ways) set of universal laws. Avoidance of both involves presenting each region as *unique*, as a particular continuing – and hence always changing – interpretation of general mechanisms: the region, in this view, is the intersection of the compositional and contextual approaches, and is the spatial representation of *homo ecologicus* (who is a hybrid of *homo historicus* and *homo roboticus*).

Most of the writings reviewed in this section have implied, if not suggested, that choice between the three approaches is unnecessary because they can be integrated in some way. (The nature of the integration is indicated by some, others just say 'do it all', and presumably hope that something coherent will emerge.) And yet, virtually all have exercised choice because:

1 They have rejected the search for generalizations and laws, which is central to the positivist conception of science.
2 They have rejected the voluntarism that underpins several of the humanistic approaches, notably idealism and existentialism.
3 They have rejected the determinism that is at the heart of certain variants of structuralism, such as some interpretations of Marxism, and (implicitly) of phenomenology.
4 They have rejected the concept of the neutral, disinterested observer-scientist (what Couclelis, 1983, terms the spectator view of science).

Together, these four rejections sum to a denial of the value of almost all of the approaches reviewed here, and a choice of one – that variant of structuralism which incorporates both compositional ordering and context. In itself, this is a large area of work with many variants. Its basic tenets are those of realism (Sayer, 1984, 1985), which in no way incorporates aspects of either positivism or idealism. It is the study of people creating themselves, in the context of both how others (in the locale) have created themselves and the mechanisms of the economic system. It is a further item on the menu.

Doing the Research
As presented here, the choice is a relatively stark one, which should be made prior to embarking on any piece of research. But it is rarely, if ever, like that, because people do not commence research in a discipline by first considering the philosophical arguments for the various approaches. Most

people setting out on a career as geographical researchers do so after a
lengthy period of educational socialization into the discipline which will
almost certainly contain two main elements: a fragmentation of subject
matter, especially at the later stages of education, and an emphasis on
empirical work.

Like most of the social sciences, human geography has a substantial history of empirical inquiry, much of it empiricist in its orientation, and,
despite a much greater awareness of philosophical issues now, that orientation continues in its curricula and syllabuses. The presentation of empirical
material – organized either systematically (usually by topical subdivision,
such as economic, urban, etc; sometimes by spatial form, as in Haggett,
1965) or spatially (regional geography) – dominates the didactic components of a geographical education, and the collection and analysis of such
material characterizes the practical components. Thus potential researchers
in human geography are likely to be socialized into believing that their role
is to add to the empirical store of material.

The orientation towards this work is likely to be towards either the
positivist or the humanistic approaches, with the one emphasizing data,
rigorous analysis and generalizations and the other stressing particularity
and interpretation. Models are available to be followed. In the former, there
is a very substantial volume of journal articles with the following format:
review of the literature on a topic, derivation of hypotheses to be tested,
conduct of an 'experiment', evaluation of the results. As stressed here, this
may be explicitly positivist and phrased as being involved in the search for
generalizations, or it may be rigorous empirical science with no explicit goal
of contributing to a broader development of theory. With regard to the
humanistic approach, the available models will illustrate a research style
characterized by an open engagement with the sources (texts) and an
attempt to transmit the contents of those sources without any reporter-bias
or imposed structure: Buttimer's (1983) presentation of autobiographical
essays to illustrate the individuality of approaches to geography exemplifies
this approach; so do the essays edited by Billinge, Gregory and Martin
(1984), although the geography described therein is almost entirely
empiricist.

When embarking on a research career, therefore, most human geographers will probably display an initial bias towards either the positivist or the
humanistic approach, but their main goal will be to tackle an empirical
problem. Reflection on this, on the reactions of other researchers, and on
the wider literature within which it is set, may then lead to a refinement of
philosophical position, and perhaps eventually to the articulation of a clearly
structured personal ideology. But in most cases, this doesn't happen, and
researchers continue to pursue empirical studies, generally embracing one of
the two approaches but with little explicit commitment.

What of the third approach? Some commentators (e.g. Hall, 1981b) stress the problems of situating empirical research within a structural framework, because its theories of the mechanisms do not produce empirical predictions. This is interpreted as meaning that the theories are of little value – they predict nothing, and so cannot be evaluated formally – and, as all empirical outcomes can be related to them, they also postdict everything. Thus, for example, Lipsey (1979), in reviewing Dearlove's (1979) book on *The reorganisation of British local government*, wrote:

> Dearlove's model is such that nothing contradicts it. . . . The trouble is that a theory that is apparently compatible with any set of facts at all, is ultimately empty, lacking either predictive or explanatory power (pp. 217–18).

Such criticism may suggest either that one sticks to theory about mechanisms and never 'dirties one's hands' with empirical material, or that one works at the empirical level alone, and never bothers about the underlying mechanisms.

The real choice, however, is not about how to do the empirical work, but rather about how to use it. Most empirical research involves the collection and evaluation of material – or data. This is analysed using the best available, relevant techniques – multivariate statistical procedures for numerical data, perhaps, or narrative (Daniels, 1985) for textual material. In general, one would anticipate the former being used within a positivist framework, as a building block in the construction of general models of the subject matter, that can be employed in some form of planning of the future. The latter, one would expect, would be used to explicate conditions described in the text, to add to the stock of understanding (Paterson, 1974) which means a better-informed society, but no more. But both could equally well be used in the context of a structuralist approach – particularly one that combines compositional with contextual – to illustrate the outcomes of particular interpretations of general mechanisms. Empirical material, quantitative or not, hypothesis-testing or not, is not particular to any one philosophical approach in its potential utility, therefore; in particular, much development of structuralist interpretations has drawn on material produced without that explicit goal.

This is illustrated by a research project on neighbourhood activism in Columbus, Ohio, reported on by Cox (1983; see also Cox and McCarthy, 1982). The work focused on which people in that metropolitan area had been involved in neighbourhood activism, defined as discussing and taking steps to counter perceived problems in the local area. It was suggested that the levels of neighbourhood activism would be highest, ceteris paribus: (1) among households with school-age children, relative to other households, because neighbourhood change – actual or threatened – would have an impact on local schools and thus, potentially, on the users of that service;

and (2) among owner-occupiers, relative to renters, because neighbourhood change could have an impact on their investment in property. These expectations were confirmed by the data, leading to the conclusion that (Cox and McCarthy, 1982):

> In sum, what we find on the basis of the survey data examined here is that home-ownership and children do give residents an interest in events on the local residential turf that is expressed in activism where those events become problematic; and these effects are independent of the effects of other possibly related variables . . . (pp. 207–8).

Clearly this was a piece of empirical research closer to the positivist tradition than to the humanistic; the data were collected by questionnaire, and submitted to multivariate statistical analysis. The study was firmly set in the area of behavioural geography (p. 38). This could lead to it being categorized as positivist – as being used to promote the building of generalizations about neighbourhood activism – but nowhere do the authors make any claim as to this goal. Theirs is an empirical case study only. Clearly neighbourhood activism is not confined to Columbus, Ohio, and claims could be made that there is no reason to believe that the situation in Columbus is unrepresentative. But this is not the goal, for Cox and McCarthy are interested in the underlying forces that lead to the development of neighbourhood activism, and are not concerned to establish that the same empirical results hold elsewhere. Their concern with the underlying forces leads them to examine the class relationships that form part of the compositional structure of society, and to postulate that neighbourhood activism is an outcome of those relationships. The forces of capital seek to alter neighbourhoods in order to promote accumulation, while the owners of labour counter such attempts and the potential impact on their lives: for the former, the neighbourhood is a source of exchange values, whereas for the latter it is more a source of use values. The conflict over those values is being played out locally, in contingent conditions which have stimulated that response by the individuals involved, but it is not just a series of local conflicts. Thus (Cox and McCarthy, 1982):

> Neighbourhood activism as a politics of turf, therefore, is a mere semblance of a more fundamental conflict (p. 197).

There is no suggestion that it will always be so; as compositional structure and contexts change, so might behaviour.

In this way, Cox and McCarthy have used the empirical material both to suggest structural interpretations of observed relationships and to illustrate the empirical outcome of structural mechanisms – in given circumstances. There is no implication from their work that neighbourhood activism is a necessary outcome of those mechanisms – except when the contingent conditions are identical to those obtaining in Columbus at the time of their survey. Others may interpret the results differently, and suggest that they are examples of general laws of human behaviour, while perhaps denying Cox and McCarthy's structural interpretation. Empirical research results can be *used* in a variety of ways.

It could be implied from this that the protocols for empirical research are independent of the philosophical approach employed by the researchers. But this is only partly true. The goal of empirical research is to describe a situation, and rigorous analysis is not a characteristic of some approaches only. But the terms of the description are crucial, and to some extent at least the ideology underpinning the research enterprise will influence how its terminology is employed (Sayer, 1984; see, for example, Dunleavy and Husbands, 1985, on the definition of class in British voting studies).

In this context, Chouinard, Fincher and Webber (1984) have made the interesting observation that:

> there are more similarities in the actual *practice* of research in different branches of scientific human geography than statements of the differences between 'positivist' and 'post-positivist' [i.e. realist] traditions would seem to allow (p. 346).

The reason for this, they claim, is that neither type of research can be conducted in a controlled, experimental situation (a closed system, as Sayer, 1984, terms it). In positivist work within human geography the laws that are postulated operate in contexts where the impact of all potentially influential variables can be neither predicted nor evaluated; for this reason, there can be no absolute criteria for the verification or falsification of a hypothesis. Similarly in realist studies, the general tendencies that are the laws being studied are implemented in particular contingent conditions whose characteristics cannot be predicted and which, therefore, preclude any absolute testing for the proposed tendencies. In both cases theory has to be evaluated through trial and error as empirical material is addressed; this, they show, is the basis of Lakatos' (1978) concept of a 'scientific research programme'. Thus, as the example of Cox and McCarthy's work illustrates, the same empirical material can be used in the context of epistemologically very different research programmes. As Chouinard, Fincher and Webber (1984) state:

> The argument that proponents of rival traditions in human geography face similar methodological problems in research, and use similar methodological criteria in the evaluation of research design, indicates the need for more sophisticated assessments of the quality of research in human geography (p. 375).

Those assessments must be at the level of the explanatory framework. They assume, of course, that the concepts employed in the empirical research are substantively sound; if the definitions used to collect and collate data in one tradition do not conform to the theoretical categories of the other, then the same empirical material cannot be used in both.

For many researchers, then, there is a dialectic between their empirical research activity and their consideration of philosophy, with the former frequently preceding the latter. With some, ideological clarification has been achieved and empirical research protocols established. But for many, research practice involves debate (internal if not external) over how empirical findings are to be used, before, as and after they are produced. Their rigorous scientific descriptions are then available for use in a variety of ways, in the choice of how to use what has been learned empirically.

Conclusions

People make choices in contexts. Ideology is crucial to the making of those choices, and in human geography the basic set of beliefs that people have about societies underpins their choice, not so much of how to do empirical research as how to use the results obtained thereby – for most, those beliefs will be represented in their 'models of man'. Those ideologies are learned, and they structure individual interpretations of not only how to pursue their chosen science, but why. For some, the science is an end in itself, but to others it is a means to an end. The ends associated with the three approaches outlined here are very different (Johnston, 1986b): for positivists, the goal is social engineering, manipulating society towards certain goals and away from others; for humanistic scholars, it is increased self- and mutual awareness; and for structuralists (especially those linked to critical theory), it is emancipation, the removal of the false ideology that clouds interpretations of the mechanisms that drive society. The suggested integrations of those three, it has been argued here, are basically variants of the third approach.

Hence choice remains. It is not simply a choice between quantitative and qualitative research, for that can be made within each of the approaches (if a choice is necessary; it surely depends on the nature of the empirical research being undertaken). More importantly, it is a choice between determinism (whether structural or empirical), voluntarism or contextualism. And most importantly of all, it is an ideological, and hence a political, choice. In choosing to approach human geography in a particular way one is choosing – however implicitly – to promote a certain ideology of society.

Bibliography

Abler, R.F., Adams, J.S. and Gould, P.R. 1971: *Spatial organization*. Englewood Cliffs: Prentice-Hall.

Agnew, J.A. and Duncan, J.S. 1981: The transfer of ideas into Anglo-American human geography. *Progress in Human Geography* **5**, 42–57.

Althusser, L. 1969: *For Marx*. London: Penguin.

Althusser, L. and Balibar, E. 1970: *Reading Capital*. London: New Left Books.

Amedeo, D. and Golledge, R.G. 1975: *An introduction to scientific reasoning in geography*. New York: John Wiley.

Andreski, S. (ed.) 1974: *The essential Comte*. London: Croom Helm.

Appleton, J. 1975: *The experience of landscape*. Chichester: John Wiley.

Archer, J.C. and Taylor, P.J. 1981: *Section and party*. Chichester: John Wiley.

Ardrey, R. 1969 *The territorial imperative*. London: Fontana.

Asheim, B.T. 1979: Social geography – welfare state ideology or critical social science? *Geoforum* **10**, 5–18.

Ayer, A.J. 1964: *Language, truth and logic*. Second edition. London: Victor Gollancz.

——1968: *The origins of pragmatism*. London: Macmillan.

Baker, A.R.H. and Gregory, D. (eds.) 1984: *Explorations in historical geography: interpretative essays*. Cambridge: Cambridge University Press.

Ballabon, M.B. 1957: Putting the 'economic' into economic geography. *Economic Geography* **33**, 217–223.

Barnes, B. 1982: *T. S. Kuhn and social science*. London: Macmillan.

Barnes, J.A. 1979: *Who should know what? Social science, privacy and ethics*. London: Penguin.

Bassett, K and Short, J.R. 1980: *Housing and residential structure*. London: Routledge and Kegan Paul.

Bauman, Z. 1978: *Hermeneutics and social science*. London: Hutchinson.

Beavon, K.S.O. 1976: *Central place theory*. London: Longman.

Beck, R.N. 1969: *Perspectives in philosophy*. New York: Holt, Rinehart & Winston.

Bennett, R.J. 1979a: Space-time models and urban geographical research. In D.T. Herbert and R.J. Johnston(eds.) *Geography and the urban environment*. Volume 2. Chichester: John Wiley, 27–58.

——1979b: *Spatial time series*. London: Pion.

——1980: *The geography of public finance*. London: Methuen.

——1981a: Quantitative and theoretical geography in Western Europe. In R.J. Bennett (ed.) *European Progress in Spatial Analysis*. London: Pion, 1–34.

——1981b: A hierarchical control solution to allocation of the British Rate Support Grant. *Geographical Analysis* **13**, 300–314.

——1985: Quantification and relevance. In Johnston, R.J. (ed.) *The future of geogrpahy*. London: Methuen, 211–223.

——and Chorley, R.J. 1978: *Environmental systems: philosophy, analysis and control*. London: Methuen.

Berry, B.J.L. 1969: Book review. *Geographical Review* **59**, 450.

——1980: Creating future geographies. *Annals of the Association of American Geographers* 70, 449–458.

——and Horton, F.E. (eds.) 1970: *Geographic perspectives on urban systems*. Englewood Cliffs: Prentice-Hall.

——and Marble, D.F. 1960: Introduction. In Berry, B.J.L. and Marble, D.F. (eds.) *Spatial analysis*. Englewood Cliffs: Prentice-Hall, 1–9.

Bhaskar, R. 1975: *A realist theory of science*. Brighton: Harvester Press.

——1979: *The possibility of naturalism*. Brighton: Harvester press.

Billinge, M. 1977: In search of negativism: phenomenology and historical geography. *Journal of Historical Geography* 3, 55–67.

——1983: The Mandarin dialect: an essay on style in contemporary geographical writing. *Transactions Institute of British Geographers* **NS8**. 400–420.

——, Gregory, D. and Martin, R.L. (eds.) 1984: *Reflections on a revolution*. London: Macmillan.

Blakemore, M.J. 1981: From way-finding to map-making. *Progress in Human Geography* **5**, 1–24.

Blaut, J.M. 1961: Space and process. *The Professional Geographer* **13(4)**, 1–7.

——, McCleary, G. and Blaut, A.S. 1970: Environmental mapping in young children. *Environment and Behaviour* 2, 335–349.

Blaut, J.M. and Stea, D. 1971: Studies of geographic learning *Annals of the Association of American Geographers* **61**, 387–393.

Blouet, B.W. 1981: Preface in B.W. Blouet (ed.); *The origins of academic geography in the United States*. Hamden, Conn.: Archon Books.

Boden, M.A. 1979: *Piaget*. London: Fontana.

Bottomore, T. 1978: Marxism and sociology. In Bottomore, T. and Nisbet, R. (eds.) *A history of sociological analysis*. London: Heinemann, 118–148.

Braithwaite, R.B. 1953: *Scientific explanation*. Cambridge: Cambridge University Press.

Breitbart, M.M. 1981: Peter Kropotkin, the anarchist geographer In Stoddart, D.R. (ed.) *Geography, ideology and social concern*. Oxford: Basil Blackwell, 134–53.

Brewer, A. 1980: *Marxist theories of imperialism*. London: Routledge and Kegan Paul.

Brookfield, H.C. 1975: *Interdependent development*. London: Methuen.

Browett, J.G. 1984: On the necessity and inevitability of uneven spatial development. *International Journal of Urban and Regional Research* **8**, 155–176.

Brown, R.H. 1943: *Mirror for Americans: likeness of the Eastern Seaboard 1810*. New York: American Geographical Society.

Bunting, T.E. and Guelke, L. 1979: Behavioral and perception geography: a critical appraisal. *Annals of the Association of American Geographers* **69**, 448–462.

Burgess, E.W. and Bogue, D.J. 1967: Research in urban society: a long view. In Burgess, E.W. and Bogue, D.J. (eds.) *Urban sociology*. Chicago: Phoenix Books, 1–14.

Burnett, A.D. and Taylor, P.J., (eds.) 1981: *Political studies from spatial perspective*. Chichester: John Wiley.

Burton, I. 1963: The quantitative revolution and theoretical geography. *The Canadian Geographer* **7**, 151–162.

Butlin, R.A. 1978: The late middle ages c. 1350–1500. In Dodgshon, R.A. and Butlin, R.A., (eds.) *An historical geography of England and Wales*. London: Academic Press, 199–149.

Buttimer, A. 1979: Erewhon or nowhere land. In Gale, S. and Olsson, G. (eds.) *Philosophy in geography*. Dordrecht: D. Reidel, 9–37.

Buttimer, A. 1981: On people, paradigms and 'progress' in geography. In Stoddart, D.R. (ed.) *Geography, ideology and social concern*. Oxford: Basil Blackwell, 81–99.

——1983: *The practice of geography*. London: Longman.

Carlstein, T. 1980: *Time, resources, society and ecology*. Lund: Department of Geography, Royal University of Lund.

Caro, R.A. 1975: *The power broker: Robert Moses and the fall of New York*. New York: Vintage Books.

Castells, M. 1977: *The urban question*. London: Edward Arnold.

——1983: *The city and the grassroots*. London: Edward Arnold.

Chapman, G.P. 1977 *Human and environmental systems*. London: Academic Press.

Chase-Dunn, C. (ed.) 1982: *Socialist states in the world-system*. Beverly Hills: Sage.

Chisholm, M. 1967: General systems theory and geography. *Transactions, Institute of British Geographers* **42**, 45–52.

——1975 *Human geography: evolution or revolution?* London: Penguin.

——1979: *Rural settlement and land use*. London: Hutchinson.

Chorley, R.J. 1964: Geography and analogue theory. *Annals of the Association of American Geographers* **54**, 127–137.

—— 1973: Geography as human ecology. In R.J. Chorley (ed.): *Directions in geography*. London: Methuen, 155–170.

——and Haggett, P. (eds.) 1967: *Models in geography*. London: Methuen.

Chouinard, V., Fincher, R. and Webber, M. 1984: Empirical research in scientific human geography. *Progress in Human Geography* **8**, 347–380.

Christensen, K. 1982: Geography as a human science: a philosophic critique of the positivist-humanist split. In Gould, P. and Olsson, G. (eds.) *A search for common ground*. London: Pion, 37–57.

Clark, G.L. 1985: *Judges and the cities: interpreting local autonomy*. Chicago: University of Chicago Press.

Clark, G.L. and Dear, M. 1981 The state in capitalism and the capitalist state. In Dear, M.J. and Scott A.J. (eds.), *Urbanization and urban planning in capitalist society*. London: Methuen, 45–62.

——1984: *State apparatus: structures and language of legitimacy*. Boston: Allen and Unwin Inc.

Claval, P. 1983: *Models of man in geography*. Syracuse: Department of Geography, University of Syracuse, Discussion Paper 79.

Cliff, A.D. and Ord, J.K. 1980: *Spatial processes*. London: Pion.

Cliff, A.D. *et al* 1981: *Spatial diffusion*. Cambridge: Cambridge University Press.

Collingwood, R.G. 1946: *The idea of history*. Oxford: Oxford University press.

——1965: *Essays in the philosophy of history*. Austin: University of Texas Press.

Cooke, R.U. 1985a: Applied geomorphology. In Kent, A. (ed.) *Perspectives on a changing geography*. Sheffield: The Geographical Assocation, 36–47.

—— 1985b: *Geomorphological Hazards in Los Angeles*. London: George Allen and Unwin.

Cosgrove, D.E. (ed.) 1982: *Geography and the humanities*. Loughborough: Department of Geography, Loughborough University of Technology, Occasional Paper 5.

—— 1984: *Social formation and symbolic landscape*. London: Croom Helm.

Couclelis, H. 1982: Philosophy in the construction of geographyic reality. In Gould, P. and Olsson, G. (eds.) *A search for common ground*. London: Pion. 105–140.

—— 1983: Some second thoughts about theory in the social sciences. *Geographical Analysis* **15**, 28–33.

Couclelis, H. and Golledge, R.G. 1983: Analytic research, positivism, and behavioral geography. *Annals of the Association of American Geographers* **73**, 331–339.

Cox, K.R. 1976: American geography: social science emergent. *Social Science Quarterly* **57**, 182–207.

——1981: Bourgeois thought and the behavioral geography debate. In Cox, K.R. and Golledge, R.G. (eds.) *Behavioral problems in geography revisited*. London: Methuen, 256–280.

—— Residential mobility, neighbourhood activism, and neighbourhood problems. *Political Geography Quarterly* **2**, 99–118.

—— Neighborhood conflicts and urban social movements: questions of historicity, class and social change. *Urban Geography* **5**, 343–355.

——and Johnston, R.J. (eds.) 1982: *Conflict, politics and the urban scene*. London: Longman.

——and McCarthy, J.J. 1982 Neighbourhood activism as a politics of turf. In Cox, K.R. and Johnston, R.J (eds.), *Conflict, politics and the urban scene*. London: Longman, 196–218.

Cybriwsky, R. and Ley, D. 1974: Urban graffiti as territorial markers. *Annals of the Association of American Geographers* **64**, 491–505.

Daniels, S. 1985: Arguments for a humanistic geography. In Johnston, R.J. (ed.) *The future of geography*. London: Methuen, 143–158.

Dear, M.J. (1981) The state: a research agenda. *Environment and Planning A* **13**,

Dear, M.J. and Moos, A.I. 1986: Structuration theory in urban analysis: 2 Empirical application. *Environment and Planning A* **18**. 351–374.

Dearlove, J. 1979: *The reorganisation of British local government*. Cambridge: Cambridge University Press.

Downs, R.M. and Stea, D. 1973: Cognitive maps and spatial behavior: process and products. In R.M. Downs and D. Stea, (eds.) *Image and environment*. London: Edward Arnold, 8–26.

——1977: *Maps in minds*. New York: Harper and Row.

Duncan, J.S. 1981: From container of women to status symbol: the impact of social structure on the meaning of the house. In Duncan, J.S. (eds.) *Housing and identity*. London: Croom Helm, 36–59.

——1980: The superorganic in American cultural geography. *Annals of the Association of American Geographers* **70**, 181–198.

Duncan, S.S. 1979. Qualitative change in human geography – an introduction. *Geoforum* **10**, 1–5.

——1981: Housing policy, the methodology of levels, and urban research: the case of Castells. *International Journal of Urban and Regional Research* **5**, 231–254.

Dunford, M. 1980: *Historical materialism and geography*. Brighton: University of Sussex, Research Papers in Geography.

Dunford, M. and Perrons, D. 1983: *The arena of capital*. London: Macmillan.

Dunleavy, P. 1982: Perspectives on urban studies. In Blowers, A. *et al*. (eds) *Urban change and conflict: an interdisciplinary reader*. London: Harper and Row, 1–16.

Dunleavy, P. and Husbands, C.T. 1985: *British democracy at the crossroads*. London: George Allen and Unwin.

Ebdon, D.S. 1985: *Statistics in geography: a practical approach*. Oxford: Basil Blackwell.

Eliot Hurst, M.E. 1980: Geography, social science and society: towards a re-definition. *Australian Geographical Studies* **18**, 3–21.

—— 1985: Geography has neither existence nor future. In Johnston, R.J. (ed.) *The future of geography*. London: Methuen, 59–91.

Entrikin, J.N. 1976: Contemporary humanism in geography. *Annals of the Association of American Geographers* **66**, 615–632.

Evans, E.E. 1973: *The personality of Ireland: habitat, heritage and history*. Cambridge: Cambridge University Press.

Ewing, A.C. 1934: *Idealism: a critical survey*. London: Methuen.

Eyles, J. 1974: Social theory and social geography. In Board, C *et al*. (eds.) *Progress in geography* 6, London: Edward Arnold, 27–88.

—— 1981: Why geography cannot be Marxist: towards an understanding of lived experience. *Environment and Planning A* **13**, 1371–1388.

——and Lee, R. 1982: Human geography in explanation. *Transactions, Institute of British Geographers* **NS7**, 117–122.

Farber, M. 1943: *The foundation of phenomenology*. Cambridge, Mass.: Harvard University Press.

Fincher, R. 1983: The inconsistency of eclecticism. *Environment and Planning A* **15**, 607–622.

Forrest, R. *et al.* 1979: The inner city: in search of the problem. *Geoforum* **10**, 109–116.

Fothergill, S. and Gudgin, G. 1982: *Unequal growth: urban and regional employment change in the UK*. London: Heinemann.

Frazier, J.W. 1981: Pragmatism: geography and the real world. In Harvey, M.E. and Holly, B.P. (eds.) *Themes in geographic thought*. London: Croom Helm, 61–72.

Freeman, T.W. 1961 *A hundred years of geography*. London: G Duckworth.

——1980: *A history of modern British geography*. London: Longman.

Garfinkel, H. 1967: *Studies in ethnomethodology*. Englewood Cliffs: Prentice-Hall.

Gibson, E. 1978: Understanding the subjective meaning of places. In Ley, D. and Samuels, M.S. (eds.) *Humanistic geography*. London: Croom Helm, 138–154.

Giddens, A. 1974: Introduction. In Giddens, A. (ed.) *Positivism and sociology*. London: Heinemann, 1–22.

——1976: *New rules of sociological method*. London: Hutchinson.

——1979: *Central problems in social theory*. London: Macmillan.

——1981: *A contemporary critique of historical materialism*. London: Macmillan.

——1984: *The constitution of society*. Cambridge: Polity Press.

Glacken, C.J. 1967: *Traces on the Rhodian shore*. Berkeley: University of California Press.

Godelier, M. 1972: Structure and contradiction in *Capital*. In Blackburn, R. (ed.) *Ideology in social science*. London: Fontana, 334–368.

Gold, R.L. 1958: Roles in sociological field observations. *Social Forces* **36**, 217–223.

Golledge, R.G. 1980: A behavioral view of mobility and migration research. *The Professional Geographer* **32**, 14–21.

——1981: Misconceptions, misinterpretations, and misrepresentations of behavioral approaches in human geography. *Environment and Planning A* **13**, 1325–1344.

——1982: Fundamental conflicts and the search for geographical knowledge. In Gould, P. and Olsson, G. (eds.) *A search for common ground*. London: Pion, 11–23.

——1983: Models of man, points of view, and theory in social science. *Geographical Analysis* **15**, 57–60.

——and Amedeo, D. 1968: On laws in geography. *Annals of the Association of American Geographers* **58**, 760–774.

——and Rushton, G. 1984: A review of analytic behavioural research in geography. In Herbert, D.T. and Johnston R.J. (eds.) *Geography and the Urban Environment, Volume 5*, Chichester: John Wiley, 1–44.

Gould, P.R. 1973: On mental maps. In Downs R.M. an Stea D., (eds.) *Image and environment*. London: Edward Arnold, 182–220.

—— 1979: Geography 1957–1977: the Augean period. *Annals of the Association of American Geographers* **69**, 139–151.

——1982: Is it necessary to choose? Some technical, hermeneutic and emancipatory thoughts on inquiry. In Gould, P. and Olsson, G. (eds.) *A search for common ground*. London: Pion: 71–104.

——1985: *The geographer at work*. London: Routledge and Kegan Paul.

Gregory, D. 1978a: *Ideology, science, and human geography*. London: Hutchinson.

——1978b: The discourse of the past: phenomenology, structuralism and historical geography. *Journal of Historical Geography* **4**, 161–173.

——1978c: The process of industrial change 1730–1900. In Dodgshon, R.A. and Butlin, R.A. (eds.) *An historical geography of England and Wales.* London: Academic Press, 291–311.

——1980: The ideology of control: systems theory and geography. *Tijdschrift voor Economische en Sociale Geographie* **71**, 327–342.

——1981: Human agency and human geography. *Transactions, Institute of British Geographers* **NS6**, 1–18.

——1984: Book review. *Environment and Planning D: Society and Space 2*, 485–487.

Gregory, K.J. 1985: *The nature of physical geography.* London: Edward Arnold.

Gregson, N. 1986: On duality and dualism: the case of structuration and time geography. *Progress in Human Geography* **10**.

Grene, M. 1959: *Introduction to existentialism.* Chicago: University of Chicago Press.

Grigg, D.B. 1965: The logic of regional systems. *Annals of the Association of American Geographers* **55**, 465–491.

Guelke, L. 1974: An idealist alternative in human geography. *Annals of the Association of American Geographers* **64**, 193–202.

——1975: On rethinking historical geography. *Area* **7**, 135–138.

——1978: Geography and logical positivism. In Herbert, D.T. and Johnston, R.J. (eds.) *Geography and the urban environment* Volume 1. Chichester: John Wiley, 35–61.

——1976: The philosophy of idealism. *Annals of the Association of American Geographers* **66**, 168–169.

——1982: *Historical understanding in geography.* Cambridge: Cambridge University Press.

——1985: On the role of evidence in physical and human geography. *Geoforum* **16**, 131–137.

Habermas, J. 1972: *Knowledge and human interests.* London: Heinemann.

——1976: *Legitimation crisis.* London: Heinemann.

Hagerstrand, T. 1970: What about people in regional science? *Papers, Regional Science Association* **24**, 7–24.

Haggett, P. 1965: *Locational analysis in human geography.* London: Edward Arnold.

——1980: *Human geography: a modern synthesis.* Third Edition. New York: Harper and Row.

Hall, P. (ed.) 1981a: *The inner city.* London: Heinemann.

——1981b: Book review: the limitations of marxist urban studies. *New Society* **57** (982), 439–440.

Hanfling, O. 1981: *Logical positivism.* Oxford: Basil Blackwell.

Harris, C. 1971: Theory and synthesis in historical geography. *The Canadian Geographer* **15**, 147–172.

——1978: The historical mind and the practice of geography. In Ley, D. and Samuels, M.S. (eds.) *Humanistic geography.* London: Croom Helm, 123–137.

Harrison, R.T. and Livingstone, D.N. 1982: Understanding in geography: structuring the subjective. In Herbert, D.T. and Johnston, R.J. (eds.) *Geography and the urban environment* Volume 5. Chichester: John Wiley, 1–40.

Hart, J.F. 1982: The highest form of the geographer's art. *Annals of the Association of American Geographers* **72**, 1–29.

Hart, R.A. and Moore, G.T. 1973: The development of spatial cognition: a review. In Downs R.M. and Stea D. (eds.) *Image and environment.* London: Edward Arnold, 246–287.

Hartshorne, R. 1939: *The nature of geography.* Lancaster, Pa.: The Association of American Geographers.

——1984: in *The Geographical Journal* **150**, 129.

Harvey, D. 1969: *Explanation in geography.* London: Edward Arnold.

——1973 *Social justice and the city.* London: Edward Arnold.

——1974a: Population, resources and the ideology of science. *Economic Geography* **50** 256–277.

——1974b: What kind of geography for what kind of public policy? *Transactions, Institute of British Geographers* **63**, 18–24.

——1975: Class structure in a capitalist society and the theory of residential differentiation. In Peel, R., Chisholm, M. and Haggett, P. (eds.) *Processes in physical and human geography*. London: Heinemann, 354–72.

——1978: The urban process under capitalism. *International Journal of Urban and Regional Research* **2**, 101–132.

——1981 Marxist geography. In Johnston R. J., (ed.) *The dictionary of human geography*. Oxford: Basil Blackwell, 209–12.

——1982: *The limits to capital*. Oxford: Basil Blackwell.

——1984: On the history and present condition of geography: an historical materialist manifesto. *The Professional Geographer* **36**, 1–10.

——1985a: The geopolitics of capitalism. In Gregory, D. and Urry, J. (eds.) *Social relations and spatial structures*. London: Macmillan, 128–163.

——1985b: *The urbanization of capital*. Basil Blackwell: Oxford.

——1985c: *Consciousness and the urban experience*. Oxford: Basil Blackwell.

Hay, A.M. 1979: Positivism in human geography: response to critics. In Herbert D.T. and Johnston R.J. (eds.) *Geography and the urban environment* Volume 2. Chichester: John Wiley, 1–26.

——1985a: Scientific method in geography. In Johnston, R.J. (ed.) *The future of geography*. London: Methuen, 129–142.

——1985b: Statistical tests in the absence of samples: a note. *The Professional Geographer* **37**, 334–338.

Haynes, R.M. 1975: Dimensional analysis: some applications in human geography. *Geographical Analysis* **7**, 51–68.

——1978: A note on dimensions and relationships in human geography. *Geographical Analysis* **10**, 288–292.

Heathcote, R.L. 1965: *Back of Bourke*. Melbourne: Melbourne University Press.

Heilbroner, R.L. 1980: *Marxism: for and against*. New York: W. W. Norton.

Held, D. 1980: *Introduction to critical theory*. London: Hutchinson.

Herbert, D.T. 1978: Introduction: geographical perspectives and urban problems. In Herbert, D.T. and Smith, D.M. (eds.) *Social problems and the city: geographical perspectives*. Oxford: Oxford University Press, 1–9.

Hirst, P.Q. 1985: *Marxism and historical writing*. London: Routledge and Kegan Paul.

Hobsbawm, E.J. 1972: Karl Marx's contribution of historiography. In Blackburn, R. (ed.) *Ideology in social science*. London: Fontana, 265–283.

Holland, S. 1976: *Capital versus the regions*. London: Macmillan.

Hoskins, W.G. 1955: *The making of the English landscape*. London: Hodder and Stoughton.

Hudson, R. 1983: The question of theory in political geography: outlines for a critical theory approach. In Kliot, N. and Waterman, S. (eds.) *Pluralism and political geography*. London: Croom Helm, 29–35.

Huggett, R. 1980: *Systems analysis in geography*. Oxford: Oxford University Press.

Hugill, P.J. 1975: Social conduct on the golden mile. *Annals of the Association of American Geographers* **65**, 214–228.

Jackson, P. 1981: Phenomenology and social geography. *Area* **13**, 299–305.

——1983: Principles and problems of participant observation. *Geografiska Annaler* **65B**, 39–46.

——1985: Urban ethnography. *Progress in Human Geography* **9**, 157–176.

——and Smith, S.J. 1984: *Exploring social geography*. London: George Allen and Unwin.

James, P.E. and Martin, G.J. 1981: *All possible worlds: a history of geographical ideas.* New York: John Wiley.

Johnston, R.J. 1971: *Urban residential patterns.* London: Bell and Hyman.

——1978: *Multivariate statistical analysis in geography.* London: Longman.

——1979: *Geography and geographers: Anglo-American human geography since 1945.* London: Edward Arnold.

——1980a: *City and society.* London: Penguin.

——1980b: On the nature of explanation in human geography. *Transactions, Institute of British Geographers* NS5, 402–412.

——1980c: Political geography without politics *Progress in Human Geography* 4, 439–446.

——1981b Political geography. In Bennett R.J. and Wrigley N., (eds.) *Quantitative geography in Britain: retrospect and prospect.* London: Routledge and Kegan Paul, 374–381.

——1982a: *The American urban system.* New York: St. Martin's press.

——1982b *Geography and the state.* London: Macmillan.

——1983a: *Geography and geographers: Anglo-American human geography since 1945.* Second edition. London: Edward Arnold.

——1983b: Texts, actors and higher managers: judges, bureaucrats, and the political organisation of space *Political Geography Quarterly* 2, 3–20.

——1983c: Who needs theory? A response from the schizophrenic middle ground. In Waterman, S. and Kliot, N. (eds.) *Pluralism and political geography.* London: Croom Helm, 24–28.

——1983d: Resource analysis, resource management and the integration of human and physical geography. *Progress in Physical Geography* 6, 127–146.

——1984a: The region in twentieth-century British geography. *History of Geography Newsletter* 4, 26–35.

——1984b: *City and society: an outline for urban geography.* London: Hutchinson.

——1984c: *Residential segregation, the state and constitutional conflict in American urban areas.* London: Academic Press.

——1985a: Exploring the future of geography. In Johnston, R.J. (ed.) *The future of geography.* London: Methuen, 1–26.

——1985b: *The geography of English politics: the 1983 general election.* London: Croom Helm.

——1985c: To the ends of the earth. In Johnston, R.J. (ed.) *The future of geography.* London: Methuen, 326–338.

——1986a: Philosophy, ideology and geography. In Gregory, D. and Walford, R. (eds.) *New horizons in geography.* London: Macmillan.

——1986b: *On human geography.* Oxford: Basil Blackwell.

——1986c: Individual freedom in the world-economy. In Johnston, R.J. and Taylor P.J. (eds.) *A world in crisis? Geographical perspectives.* Oxford: Basil Blackwell, 173–195.

——1986d: Places matter. *Irish Geography* 18, 58–63.

——1986e: Theory and methodology in social geography. In Pacione, M. (ed.) *Progress in social geography.* London: Croom Helm.

——1986f: The state, the region and the division of labor. In Scott, A.J. and Storper, M.J. (eds.) *Production, work, territory.* Boston: George Allen and Unwin, 265–280.

——and Claval, P. (eds.) 1984: *Geography since the Second World War: an international survey.* London: Croom Helm.

——and Gregory S. 1984: The United Kingdom. In Johnston, R.J. and Claval, P. (eds.) *Geography since the second world war: an international survey.* London: Croom Helm, 107–131.

Jones, D. 1978: Implications of 'schooling' in economic anthropology for interpretations of the economic geography of non-industrial societies. In Berry, B.J.L. (ed.) *The nature of change in geographical ideas.* Northern Illinois University Press, de Kalb, 126–153.

Kaufmann, W. 1975: *Existentialism from Dostoevsky to Sartre*. New York: Meridian Books.

Keat, R. 1981: *The politics of social theory*. Oxford: Basil Blackwell.

——and Urry, J. 1975 *Social theory as science*. London: Routledge and Kegan Paul.

Keeble, D.E. 1967: Models of economic development. In Chorley, R.J. and Haggett, P. (eds.) *Models in geography*. London: Methuen.

——1976: *Industrial location and planning in the United Kingdom*. London: Methuen.

King, R.L. (ed.) 1985: *Geographical futures*. Sheffield: The Geographical Association.

Kirk, W. 1951: Historical geography and the concept of the behavioural environment. *Indian Geographical Journal* **25**, 152–160.

—— 1963 Problems of geography. *Geography* **48**, 357–371.

——1978 The road from Mandalay. *Transactions, Institute of British Geographers* **NS3**, 381–394.

Kolakowski, L. 1978: *Main currents of Marxism*. Three volumes. Oxford: Clarendon Press.

Kraft, V. 1953 *The Vienna circle: the origin of neo-positivism*. New York: Philosophical Library.

Kuhn, T.S. 1962: *The structure of scientific revolutions*. Chicago: University of Chicago Press.

Kurzweil, E. 1980: *The age of structuralism*. New York: Columbia University Press.

van der Laan, L. and Piersma, A. 1982: The image of man: paradigmatic cornerstone in human geography. *Annals of the Association of American Geographers* **72**, 411–426.

Lacey, A.R. 1976: *A dictionary of philosophy*. London: Routledge and Kegan Paul.

Lakatos, I. 1978: Falsification and the methodology of scientific research programmes. In Worrall, J. and Currie, G. (eds.) *The methodology of scientific research programmes, philosophical papers, volume 1*. Cambridge: Cambridge University Press, 401–419.

Larrain, J. 1979: *The concept of ideology*. London: Hutchinson.

Leach, E.R. 1974 *Lévi-Strauss*. London: Fontana.

——1981: British social anthropology and Lévi-Straussian structuralism. In Blau, P.M. and Merton, R.K. (eds.) *Continuities in structural enquiry*. Beverly Hills: Sage Publications, 27–50.

Leeds, A. 1984: Cities and countryside in anthropology. In Rodwin, L. and Hollister, R.M. (eds.) *Cities of the mind*. New York: Plenum Press, 291–312.

Leonard, S. 1982: Urban managerialism. *Progress in Human Geography* **6**, 190–215.

Lewis, G.M. 1981: Amerindian antecedents of American academic geography. In Blouet, B.W. (ed.): *The origins of academic geography in the United States.* Hamden, Conn.: Archon Books, 19–36.

Lewis, J. and Melville, B. 1978: The politics of epistemology in regional science. *London Papers in Regional Science* **8**. London: Pion, 82–100.

Lewis, O. 1957: *La vida*. London: Panther Books.

Lewis, P.F. 1979 Axioms for reading the landscape. In Meinig, D.W. (ed.) *The interpretation of ordinary landscapes*. New York: Oxford University Press, 11–32.

Lewis, P.W. 1965: Three related problems in the formulation of laws in geography. *The Professional Geographer* **17(5)**, 24–27.

Ley, D. 1974: *The black inner city as frontier outpost*. Washington DC: Association of American Geographers.

——1977: Social geography and the taken-for-granted world. *Transactions, Institute of British Geographers* **NS2**, 498–512.

——1978: Social geography and social action. In Ley, D. and Samuels, M.S. (eds.): *Humanistic geography*. London: Croom Helm, 41–57.

——1981: Behavioral geography and the philosophies of meaning. In Cox, K.R. and Golledge, R.G. (eds.) *Behavioral problems in geography revisited*. London: Methuen, 209–30.

——1983: *A social geography of the city*. New York: Harper and Row.

Lipsey, D. 1979: Book review. *New Society* **50(890)**, 25 October, 217–218.

Livingstone, D.N. and Harrison, R.T. 1981: Immanuel Kant, subjectivism, and human geography: a preliminary investigation. *Transactions, Institute of British Geographers* **NS6**, 359–374.

Lloyd, P.E. 1979: The components of industrial change for Merseyside Inner Area: 1966–75. *Urban Studies* **16**, 45–60.

——and Dicken, P. 1978: *Location in space*. London: Harper and Row.

Lowenthal, D. 1961: Geography, experience and imagination: towards a geographical epistemology. *Annals of the Association of American Geographers* **51**, 241–260.

——1975a: Past time, present place: landscape and memory. *Geographical Review* **65**, 1–36.

——1975b The place of the past in the American landscape. In Lowenthal, D. and Bowden, M.J. (eds.) *Geographies of the mind*. New York: Oxford University Press, 89–118.

——1985: *The past is a foreign country*. Cambridge: Cambridge University Press.

Lowenthal, D. and Prince, H.C. 1964: The English landscape. *Geographical Review* **54**, 309–346.

Lynch, K. 1960: *The image of the city*. Cambridge, Mass.: MIT Press.

Lyons, J. 1977: *Chomsky*. London: Fontana.

McDowell, L. and Massey, D. 1984: A woman's place? In Massey, D. and Allen, J. (eds.) *Geography matters!* Cambridge: Cambridge University Press, 128–147.

Macquarrie, J. 1972: *Existentialism*. London: Hutchinson.

Magee, B. 1973: *Popper*. London: Fontana.

Mann, M. 1984: The autonomous power of the state: its origins, mechanisms and results. *European Journal of Sociology* **25**, 185–213.

Marshall, J.U. 1985: Geography as a scientific enterprise. In Johnston, R.J. (ed.) *The future of geography*. London: Methuen, 113–128.

Martensson, S. 1979: *On the formation of biographies*. Lund: C.W.K. Gleerup.

Martin, R.L. and Oeppen, J.E. 1975: The identification of regional forecasting models using space-time correlation functions. *Transactions, Institute of British Geographers* **66**, 95–118.

Marx, K. 1971: Existence and consciousness. In Thompson, K. and Tunstall, J. (eds.) *Sociological perspectives*. London: Penguin.

——1976: *Capital*. London: Penguin.

Massey, D. 1979: A critical evaluation of industrial-location theory. In Hamilton, F.E.I. and Linge, G.J.R. (eds.) *Spatial analysis, industry and the industrial environment*. Chichester: John Wiley, 57–72.

——1984: *Spatial divisions of labour: social structures and the geography of production*. London: Macmillan.

——and Allen, J. (eds.) 1984: *Geography matters!* Cambridge: Cambridge University Press.

——and Meegan, R.A. 1979: The geography of industrial reorganisation. *Progress in Planning* **10**, 155–237.

Mead, G.H. 1934: *Mind, self and society*. (edited by C. Morriss). Chicago: University of Chicago Press.

Meinig, D.W. 1979: Reading the landscape: an appreciation of W.G. Hoskins and J.B. Jackson. In Meinig, D.W. (ed.) *The interpretation of ordinary landscapes*. New York: Oxford University Press, 195–244.

——1983: Geography as an art. *Transactions, Institute of British Geographers* **NS8**, 314–328.

Mepham, J. 1973: The structuralist sciences and philosophy. In Robey, D. (ed.) *Structuralism: an introduction*. Oxford: Oxford University Press, 104–137.

Mercer, D.C. 1978: Book review. *Progress in Human Geography* **2**, 537–542.

——and Powell, J.M. 1972: *Phenomenology and related non-positivistic viewpoints in the social sciences*. Clayton, Victoria: Monash Publications in Geography 1.

Mikesell, M.W. 1978: Tradition and innovation in cultural geography. *Annals of the Association of American Geographers* **68**, 1–16.

Mitchell, B. and Draper, D. 1982: *Relevance and ethics in geography*. London: Longman.

Moos, A.I. and Dear, M.J. 1986: Structuration theory in urban analysis: 1 theoretical exegesis. *Environment and Planning A* **18**, 231–52.

Morris, D. 1967: *The naked ape*. London: Jonathan Cape.

Muir, R. 1978: Radical geography or a new orthodoxy? *Area* **10**, 322–327.

——1979: Radical geography and Marxism. *Area* **11**, 126–127.

Mulkay, M.J. 1975: Three models of scientific development: *Sociological Review* **23**, 509–526.

Nell, E. 1972: Economics: the revival of political economy. In Blackburn, R. (ed.) *Ideology in social science*. London: Fontana, 76–95.

Newman, J.L. 1973: The use of the term 'hypothesis' in geography. *Annals of the Association of American Geographers* **63**, 22–27.

Nystuen, J.D. 1963; Identification of some fundamental spatial concepts. *Papers of the Michigan Academy of Science, Arts and Letters* **48**, 373–384.

Olafson, F.A. 1967: *Principles and persons*. Baltimore: The Johns Hopkins Press.

O'Loughlin, J. 1986: World power competition and local conflicts in the Third World. In Johnston, R.J. and Taylor, P.J. (eds.) *A world in crisis? Geographical perspectives*. Oxford: Basil Blackwell, 231–268.

Olsson, G. 1975: *Bird in egg*. Ann Arbor: Department of Geography, University of Michigan; London: Pion.

——1978: Of ambiguity or far cries from a memorializing mamafesta. In Ley, D. and Samuels, M.S. (eds.): *Humanistic geography*. London: Croom Helm, 109–120.

——1979 Social science and human action or on hitting your head against the ceiling of language. In Gale, S. and Olsson, G. (eds.) *Philosophy in geography*. Dordrecht: Reidel, 287–308.

——1982: -/-. In Gould, P. and Olsson, G. (eds.) *A search for common ground*. London: Pion, 223–231.

Openshaw, S. and Taylor, P.J. 1980: A million or so correlation coefficients: three experiments on the modifiable areal unit problem. In Wrigley, N. (ed.) *Statistical applications in the spatial sciences*. London: Pion, 127–144.

——1977: Environmental ideologies. *Environment and Planning A* **9**, 3–14.

Outhwaite, W. 1975: *Understanding of social life: the method called verstehen*. London: George Allen and Unwin.

Pahl, R.E. 1979: Socio-political factors in resource allocation. In Herbert, D.T. and Smith, D.M. (eds.) *Social problems and the city: geographical perspectives*. Oxford: Oxford University Press, 33–46.

Paterson, J.H. 1974: Writing regional geography. In Board, C. *et al.* (eds.) *Progress in Geography 6*. London: Edward Arnold, 1–26.

Peet, J.R. 1975; Inequality and poverty: a Marxist-geographic theory. *Annals of the Association of American Geographers* **65**, 564–571.

——1977: The development of radical geography in the United States. *Progress in Human Geography* **1**, 64–87.

Piaget, J. 1971: *Structuralism*. London: Routledge and Kegan Paul.

——and Lyons, J.V. 1981: Marxism: dialectical materialism, social formation and the geographical relations. In Harvey, M.E. and Holly, B.P. (eds.) *Themes in geographic thought*. London: Croom Helm, 187–205.

Pickles, J. 1985: *Phenomenology, science and geography: spatiality and the human sciences*. Cambridge: Cambridge University Press.

Penning-Rowsell, E.C. 1981: Fluctuating fortunes in gauging landscape value. *Progress in Human Geography* **5**, 25–41.

Platt, J. 1981: The social construction of positivism and its significance in British sociology, 1950–80. In Abrams, P. *et al.* (eds.) *Practice and progress: British sociology 1950–1980*. London: George Allen and Unwin, 73–87.

Pocock, D.C.D. 1981a: Place and the novelist. *Transactions, Institute of British Geographers* **NS6**, 337–347.

——1981b: Introduction: imaginative literature and the geographer. In Pocock D.C.D. (ed.) *Humanistic geography and literature*. London: Croom Helm, 9–19.

Pooler, J.A. 1977: The origins of the spatial tradition in geography: an interpretation. *Ontario Geography* **11**, 56–83.

Popper, K.R. 1945 *The open society and its enemies*. London: Routledge and Kegan Paul.

——1972: *Conjectures and refutations*. Fourth edition. London: Routledge and Kegan Paul.

——1976: *Unended quest*. London: Fontana.

Powell, J.M. 1970: *The public lands of Australia Felix*. Melbourne: Oxford University Press.

——1971: Utopia, millenium and the cooperative ideal. *The Australian Geographer* **11**, 606–618.

——1977: *Mirrors of the new world*. Folkestone: Dawson.

——1980: The haunting of Saloman's house: geography and the limits of science. *The Australian Geographer* **14**, 327–341.

Pred. A.R. 1967: *Behavior and location: foundations for a geographic and dynamic location theory*. Lund: C.W.K. Gleerup.

——1977a: *City-systems in advanced economies*. London: Hutchinson.

——1977b: The choreography of existence: comments on Hagerstrand's time-geography and its usefulness. *Economic Geography* **53**, 207–221.

——1979: The academic past through a time-geographic looking glass. *Annals of the Association of American Geographers* **69**, 175–180.

——1981a: Social reproduction and the time-geography of everyday life. *Geografiska Annaler* **63B**, 5–22.

——1981b: Production, family, and free-time projects: a time-geographic perspective on the individual and societal change in nineteenth century US cities. *Journal of Historical Geography* **7**, 3–36.

——1984a: From here and now to there and then: some notes on diffusions, defusions and disillusions. In Billinge, M., Gregory, D. and Martin, R.L. (eds.) *Reflections of a revolution: geography as spatial science*. London: Macmillan, 86–103.

——1984b: Place as historically contingent process: structuration and the time-geography of becoming places. *Annals of the Association of American Geographers* **74**, 279–297.

——1984c: Structuration, biography formation, and knowledge: observations on port growth during the late mercantile period. *Environment and Planning D: Society and Space* **2**, 251– 276.

Prince, H.C. 1971: Real, imagined and abstract worlds of the past. In Board, C. *et al*. (eds.) *Progress in Geography 3*. London: Edward Arnold, 1–86.

Quaini, M. 1982: *Geography and Marxism*. Oxford: Basil Blackwell.

Rees, J.A. 1985: *Natural resources: allocation, economics and public policy*. London: Methuen.

Relph, E. 1970: An inquiry into the relations between phenomenology and geography. *The Canadian Geographer* **14**, 193–201.

——1976: *Place and placelessness*. London: Pion.

——1981a: *Rational landscapes and humanistic geography*. London: Croom Helm.

——1981b Phenomenology. In Harvey, M.E. and Holly, B.P. (eds.) *Themes in geographic thought*. London: Croom Helm, 99–114.

Rose, C. 1980: Human geography as text interpretation. In Buttimer, A. and Seamon, D. (eds.) *The human experience of space and place*. London: Croom Helm, 123–134.

——1981: Wilhelm Dilthey's philosophy of historical understanding. In Stoddart, D.R. (ed.): *Geography, ideology and social concern*. Oxford: Basil Blackwell, 99–133.

Rossi, I. 1981: Transformational structuralism: Lévi-Strauss's definition of social structure. In Blau, P.M. and Merton R.K. (eds.) *Continuities in structural inquiry*. Beverly Hills: Sage Publications, 51–80.

Rowles, G. 1978: Reflections on experiential field work. In Ley, D. and Samuels, M.S. (eds.) *Humanistic geography*. London: Croom Helm, 173–193.

Rushton, G. 1969: Analysis of spatial behavior by revealed space preferences. *Annals of the Association of American Geographers* **59**, 391–340.

Sack, R.D 1974: The spatial separatist theme in geography. *Economic Geography* **50**, 1–19.

——1980a: Conceptions of geographic space. *Progress in Human Geography* **4**, 313–345.

——1980b: *Conceptions of space in social thought*. London: Macmillan.

——1983: Human territoriality: a theory. *Annals of the Association of American Geographers* **73**, 55–74.

Samuels, M.S. 1978a: Existentialism and human geography. In Ley, D. and Samuels, M.S. (eds.) *Humanistic geography*. London: Croom Helm, 22–40.

——1978b: Individual and landscape: thoughts on China and the Tao of Mao. In Ley, D. and Samuels, M.S. (eds.) *Humanistic geography*. London: Croom Helm, 283–296.

——1979: The biography of landscape. In Meinig, D.W. (ed.) *The interpretation of ordinary landscapes*. New York: Oxford University Press, 51–80.

——1981: An existential geography. In Harvey, M.E. and Holly, B.P. (eds.) *Themes in geographic thought*. London: Croom Helm, 115–133.

Santos, M. 1975: *The shared space*. London: Methuen.

Saunders, P. 1981: *Social theory and the urban question*. London: Hutchinson.

Saussure, de. F. 1966: *Course in general linguistics*. New York: McGraw Hill.

Sayer, A. 1979a: Epistemology and conceptions of people and nature in geography. *Geoforum* **10**, 19–44.

——1979b: Understanding urban models versus understanding cities. *Environment and Planning A* **11**, 853–862.

——1982a: Explanation in economic geography: abstraction versus generalization. *Progress in Human Geography* **6**, 68–88.

——1982b: Explaining manufacturing shift: a reply to Keeble. *Environment and Planning A* **14**, 119–125.

——1984: *Method in social science: a realist approach*. London: Hutchinson.

——1985: Realism and geography. In Johnston, R.J. (ed.) *The future of geography*. London: Methuen, 159–173.

Sayer, D. 1979: *Marx's method*. Brighton: Harvester Press.

Scarbrough, E. 1984: *Political ideology and voting*. Oxford: Clarendon Press.

Scargill, D.I. 1985: Space, place and region: towards a transformed regional geography. *Geography* **70**, 138–141.

Scheibling, J. 1977: Debates et combats sur la crise de la geographie. *La Pensée* **194**, 41–56.

Schutz, A. 1964: *Collected papers II: studies in social theory*. The Hague: Martinus Nijhoff.

——A. 1971: *Collected Papers I: the problem of social reality*. The Hague: Martinus Nijhoff.

——A. 1972: *The phenomenology of the social world*. Translated by G. Walsh and F. Lehnert. London: Heinemann. First German edition 1932.

Seamon, D. 1979: *A geography of the lifeworld*. London: Croom Helm.

Sensat, J. 1979: *Habermas and Marxism*. Beverly Hills: Sage Publications.

Shaw, W.H. 1978: *Marx's theory of history*. London: Hutchinson.

Short, J.R. 1984: *The urban arena*. London: Macmillan.

Simmons, I.G. and Cox, N.J. 1985: Holistic and reductionist approaches to geography. In Johnston, R.J. (ed.) *The future of geography*. London: Methuen, 43–58.

Sklair, L. 1981: Sociologies and Marxisms: the odd couples. In Abrams, P. *et al.* (eds.) *Practice and progress: British sociology 1950–1980*. London: George Allen and Unwin, 151–171.

Slater, D. 1973: The poverty of modern geographical enquiry. *Pacific Viewpoint* **16**, 159–176.

Smith, D.M. 1977: *Human geography: a welfare approach*. London: Edward Arnold.

—— 1979: Modelling industrial location. In Hamilton, F.E.I. and Linge, G.J.R. (eds.) *Spatial analysis, industry and the industrial environment.* Chichester: John Wiley, 37–55.

——1981: Marxian economics. In Johnston, R.J. (ed.) *The Dictionary of Human Geography.* Oxford: Basil Blackwell, 203–9.

——1981b: *Industrial location: an economic geographical analysis.* New York: John Wiley.

Smith, Neil. 1979: Geography, science and post-positivist modes of explanation. *Progress in Human Geography* 3, 356–383.

—— 1984: *Uneven development.* Oxford: Basil Blackwell.

Smith, N. and Wilson, D. 1979a: *Modern linguistics: the results of Chomsky's revolution.* London: Penguin.

Smith, S.J. 1981: Humanistic method in contemporary social geography. *Area* 13, 293–298.

——1984: Practicing humanistic geography. *Annals of the Association of American Geographers* 74, 353–374.

Smith, T.R. 1983: More thoughts on theory in the social sciences. *Geographical Analysis* 15, 40–42.

Soja, E.W. 1980: The socio-spatial dialectic. *Annals of the Association of American Geographers* 70, 207–225.

——1985: The spatiality of social life: towards a transformative retheorisation. In Gregory, D. and Urry, J. (eds.) *Social relations and spatial structures.* London: Macmillan, 90–127.

——and Hadjimichalis, C. 1979: Between geographical materialism and spatial fetishism: some observations on the development of Marxist spatial analysis. *Antipode* 11(3), 3–11.

Spiegelberg, H. 1975: *Doing phenomenology.* The Hague: Martinus Nijhoff.

——1976 *The phenomenological movement: a historical introduction.* Second edition; two volumes. The Hague: Martinus Nijhoff.

Stoddart, D.R. 1966: Darwin's impact on geography. *Annals of the Association of American Geographers* 56, 683–98.

Storper, M., Walker, R.A., Widess, E. (1981): Performance regulation and industrial location: a case study. *Environment and Planning A* 13, 321–338.

Taylor, P.J. 1976: An interpretation of the quantification debate in British geography. *Transactions, Institute of British Geographers* NS1, 129–142.

——1981: Factor analysis in geographical research. In Bennett, R.J. (ed.) *European Progress in Spatial Analysis.* London: Pion, 251–267.

——1982: A materialist framework for political geography. *Transactions, Institute of British Geographers* NS7, 15–34.

——1983: The question of theory in political geography. In Waterman, S. and Kliot, N. (eds.) *Pluralism and political geography.* London: Croom Helm.

——1985a: *Political geography: world-economy, nation-state and locality.* London: Longman.

——1985b: The value of a geographical perspective. In Johnston, R.J. (ed.) *The future of geography.* London: Methuen, 92–109.

——1986a: The world-systems project. In Johnston, R.J. and Taylor, P.J. (eds.) *A world in crisis? Geographical perspectives.* Oxford: Basil Blackwell, 269–289.

——1986b: Chaotic conceptions, antinomies, dilemmas and dialectics: who's afraid of the capitalist world-economy? *Political Geography Quarterly* 5.

——1986c: The myth of developmentalism. In Gregory, D. and Walford, R. (eds.) *New horizons in geography.* London: Macmillan.

——and Johnston, R.J. 1979: *Geography of elections.* London: Penguin.

——and Johnston, R.J. 1984: The geography of the British state. In Short, J.R. and Kirby, A.M. (eds.) *The Human geography of contemporary Britain.* London: Macmillan, 23–39.

Thayer, H.S. 1973: *Meaning and action: a study of American pragmatism*. Indianapolis: Bobbs-Merrill.

Thomas, D. 1979 *Naturalism and social science*. Cambridge: Cambridge University Press.

Thrift, N.J. 1979 Unemployment in the inner city: urban problem or structural imperative? In Herbert, D.T. and Johnston, R.J. (eds.) *Geography and the urban environment* Volume 2. Chichester: John Wiley, 125–226.

——1983: On the determination of social action in space and time. *Environment and Planning D: Society and Space* 1, 23–58.

——1986: The geography of international economic disorder. In Johnston, R.J. and Taylor, P.J. (eds.) *A world in crisis? Geographical perspectives*. Oxford: Basil Blackwell, 12–67.

Timms, D.W.G. 1971: *The urban mosaic*. Cambridge: Cambridge University Press.

Tocalis, T.R. 1978: Changing theoretical foundations of the gravity concept of human interaction. In Berry, B.J.L. (ed.) *The nature of change in geographical ideas*. de Kalb: Northern Illinois University Press, 65–124.

Tuan, Y-F 1974a: Space and place: humanistic perspectives. In C. Board *et al.* (eds.) *Progress in Geography 6*. London: Edward Arnold, 211–252.

——1974b: *Topophilia*. Englewood Cliffs: Prentice-Hall.

——1976: Humanistic geography. *Annals of the Association of American Geographers* 66, 266–276.

——1977: *Space and place*. London: Edward Arnold.

——1978: Literature and geography: implications for geographical research. In Ley, D. and Samuels, M.S. (eds.) *Humanistic geography*. London: Croom Helm, 194–206.

——1979: *Landscapes of fear*. Oxford: Basil Blackwell.

—— 1983: Geographical theory: queries from a cultural geographer. *Geographical Analysis* 15, 69–72.

Urry, J. 1981: Localities, regions and social class. *International Journal of Urban and Regional Research* 5, 455–474.

Walker, R.A. 1978: The transformation of urban structure in the nineteenth century and the beginnings of suburbanization. In Cox, K.R. (ed.) *Urbanization and conflict in market societies*. Chicago: Maaroufa Press, 165–212.

—— 1981a: A theory of suburbanization: capitalism and the construction of space in the United States. In Dear, M.J. and Scott, A.J. (eds.) *Urbanization and urban planning in capitalist society*. London: Methuen, 383–430.

——1981b: Left-wing libertarianism, an academic disorder: a response to David Sibley. *The Professional Geographer* 33 5–9.

Wallace, I. 1978: Towards a humanized conception of economic geography. In Ley. D. and Samuels, M.S. (eds.) *Humanistic geography*. London: Croom Helm, 91–108.

Wallerstein, I. 1974: *The modern world-system: capitalist agriculture and the origins of the capitalist world-economy in the sixteenth century*. New York: Academic Press.

——1980: *The modern world-system Volume II: mercantilism and the consolidation of the European world-economy 1600–1750*. New York: Academic Press.

——1983: *Historical capitalism*. London: Verso.

——1984: *The politics of the world-economy*. Cambridge: Cambridge University Press.

Watson, J.W. 1983: The soul of geography. *Transactions, Institute of British Geographers* NS8, 385–299.

Wilson, A.G. 1970: *Entropy in urban and regional modelling*. London: Pion.

——1980: *Geography and the environment: systems analytic methods*. Chichester: John Wiley.

——1981: *Catastrophe theory and bifurcation*. London: Croom Helm.

Wolff, K.H. 1979: Phenomenology and sociology. In Bottomore T. and Nisbet R. (eds.) *A theory of sociological analysis*. London: Heinemann, 498–556.

Wooldridge, S.W. 1936: The Anglo-Saxon settlement. In Darby, H.C. (ed.) *An historical geography of England before 1500*. Cambridge: Cambridge University Press, 88–132.

Wright, J.K. 1947: *Terrae incognitae:* the place of imagination in geography. *Geographical Review* **37**, 1–15.

Zorbaugh, H.W. 1926: The natural areas of the city. *Publications of the American Sociological Society* **20**, 188–197.

General index

Author index